The Essential
Herman Kahn

The Essential Herman Kahn

In Defense of Thinking

Edited by Paul Dragos Aligica and
Kenneth R. Weinstein

LEXINGTON BOOKS

A division of
ROWMAN & LITTLEFIELD PUBLISHERS, INC.
Lanham • Boulder • New York • Toronto • Plymouth, UK

LEXINGTON BOOKS

A division of Rowman & Littlefield Publishers, Inc.
A wholly owned subsidiary of The Rowman & Littlefield Publishing Group, Inc.
4501 Forbes Boulevard, Suite 200
Lanham, MD 20706

Estover Road
Plymouth PL6 7PY
United Kingdom

British Library Cataloguing in Publication Information Available

Library of Congress Cataloging-in-Publication Data

Kahn, Herman, 1922–1983
 [Selections. 2009]
 The essential Herman Kahn : in defense of thinking / edited by Paul Dragos
Aligica and Kenneth R. Weinstein.
     p. cm.
 Includes bibliographical references and index.
 ISBN 978-0-7391-2828-2 (cloth : alk. paper) — ISBN 978-0-7391-2829-9 (pbk. :
alk. paper) — ISBN 978-0-7391-3514-3 (electronic)
 1. Forecasting—History—20th century—Sources. 2. Futurologists—United
States—History—20th century—Sources. 3. Futurologists—United States—
Biography. 4. Kahn, Herman, 1922–1983—Influence. I. Aligica, Paul Dragos. II.
Weinstein, Kenneth R., 1961– III. Title.
 CB158.K34 2009
 303.49—dc22   2008055654

Contents

Acknowledgments

The copyrights of Herman Kahn's most significant works are held by Hudson Institute. The selection of texts presented in this book is based on these works. We would like to thank Hudson Institute, its Board of Trustees, and especially Deborah Kahn Cunningham for the copyright permissions.

In preparing this book we benefited from the help of Claire Morgan, Evan Minsberg, Robert Zarate, Olga Nicoara, and Costel Stavarache. We would like to convey our appreciation for their efforts.

Finally, we offer our thanks to the Mercatus Center at George Mason University and Hudson Institute. We have benefited immensely from the opportunity of being associated with these two great institutions and we would like to express our deep gratitude to them.

Introduction

Paul Dragos Aligica and Kenneth R. Weinstein

By the time of his untimely death in 1983, Herman Kahn was recognized by both friends and intellectual adversaries as "one of the world's most creative and best minds." He was one of the preeminent and best known futures studies scholars, a founding father of the field, with extensive and vital contributions to the debates on the nature of global economic development and its impact on human societies and their environment, as well as a key figure in the field of strategic studies, an area where he was also considered a founder and a leader. His work was followed all over the world and the directions he traced in the public debate on very sensitive issues of crucial public concern have continued to be unaltered today, more than twenty years after his unexpected death. Yet, in spite of the incessant influence of his arguments and ideas, today his intellectual legacy is still to be accounted for and the breath and depth of his contributions are still to be reviewed and analyzed in a systematic way.

Given that Kahn was a prolific author and that his line of reasoning touched on so many issues and topics, capturing the essence, unity, and coherence of his argument hasn't been very easy. This difficulty has been compounded by two factors: First, by the prolixity and complexity of some of his writings that made the study and systematization of his work difficult. Second, by the reality that the ideas advanced by Kahn had a very profound and subtle impact on the public discourse. The measure of this impact is given by the fact that an important part of the ideas he promoted meanwhile have become part of the public discourse in such a profound manner that now we tend to take them for granted. All of the above explain why there are very few, if any, books summarizing Kahn's essential

1

contributions and why his work, scattered into so many publications, is not as well known as it should be.

This volume is an attempt to cope with this predicament and offer the public for the first time an anthology consisting of the essence of Kahn's work. The two decades that have passed since his death allow us today to approach his intellectual legacy undisturbed by the "sound and fury" of the many public debates and controversies he participated in and to focus on some of the deepest and most enduring dimensions of his contributions. The book will try to bring together out of the several thousands pages published by Kahn during his life, the "essential Kahn," the most relevant, consequential and interesting themes, ideas, and arguments of his work. Thus the anthology will met the needs of those interested in Kahn's ideas but who do not have the time and energy to access his (mostly out of print) books, to make their way through the ample number of pages, and to sort out the essential from the accidental, the perennial from the contextual.

A careful overview of Kahn's work reveals that a consistent internal logic is running through it, connecting all its different parts. However, his negligent way of presenting his ideas left that overall consistency hidden and never explicitly articulated. It is always for the student to reconstruct the logic bringing together the elements of the system. And given the diversity of themes covered by Kahn and the variety of approaches he employed, that task is always daunting. That lack of systematization and order was thus probably the crucial shortcoming affecting in the long run Kahn's impressive intellectual legacy. In this respect, this anthology should be seen as a first step in the effort of intellectual reconstruction and revitalization of that legacy.

In terms of substance, the issues that Kahn took as focal points for his work (the geostrategy of war and peace; the relationship between culture and economic development; the practical, epistemic, and methodological problems of dealing with the future and the necessity of broad and future-oriented studies; the tension between the academic approach and the decision-makers' approach; the ideological dimensions of cultural change in affluent societies; the morality and feasibility of global economic development—to name just a few of them) continue to be as relevant today as thirty years ago. This book tries to put together a sample covering as many such topics as possible. At the same time, it tries to systematize this sample into thematic clusters, organized in a manner that sets in the clearest possible light the internal logic of Kahn's thought. That being said, we should also note that our effort has deliberately avoided any attempt to impose our own interpretation of this logic. Given the challenging nature of many of Kahn's arguments, we consider that it is more sensible and constructive to let the readers use their own interpretive frameworks when they assess the nature and implications of these arguments.

With these ends in view, the anthology is organized into four sections, each concentrating on one of the main dimensions of Kahn's work. The first section introduces the topic that has made Kahn famous: grand strategy and thermonuclear war. The selection focuses on his analysis of key strategic notions such as "deterrence" and "escalation," his assessment of the "revolution in warfare" brought on by the atomic bomb, the major pitfalls in the debates regarding thermonuclear strategies, and the moral and political dimensions of these debates. In other words, the section includes the arguments that caused the uproar that reportedly led film director Stanley Kubrick to pattern the main character of the classic film *Dr. Strangelove* after Kahn, and to the remarkable celebrity Kahn enjoyed thereafter.

The second section brings together Kahn's analyses of the problem of economic growth and cultural change, seen from a "long view" perspective. After making his seminal contributions to the debates regarding thermonuclear war, Kahn turned his attentions to economics, politics, and their cultural underpinnings as he began devoting more and more of his time to topics related to economic development, technology, and their impact on human nature and the environment. He very soon became a key contender in the disputes regarding the "doomsday," "limits to growth" theses advanced by the Club of Rome and its followers. In his spirited and optimistic arguments he made a strong case for the feasibility, desirability, and morality of global economic growth, arguing that even given all the likely human, environmental, and material costs and risks, "the case is close to if not fully overwhelming." This section of our anthology brings together some of the most interesting and powerful arguments made by Kahn in this respect as well as his fascinating analysis of the relationship between on the one hand, economic growth and affluence and on the other, cultural and ideological change.

Due to his work on geostrategic issues and the "limits to growth" theses, a work heavily involving predictions and scenarios, Kahn was very soon recognized as one of the intellectual leaders of the emerging field of "futures studies" or "futurology." The third section of the book reunites the main texts defining Kahn's perspective on the methodological and epistemological problems of dealing with the future. The section covers issues such as: the methodological framework for building alternative futures; the objectives of future-oriented policy research; the agnostic use of information and concepts; scenarios and scenario building; the uses of the method of classes of variables in predictions; and the problem of technological innovation and impact assessment. In reading this section, one should keep in mind that for Kahn the research process is always action-oriented and thus future-oriented. Consequently, the ultimate test of any intellectual endeavor has to be its relevance for policy and social action.

Kahn was a strong believer in the role of ideas on social change. The ultimate end of his efforts was always to have an impact on the public debates shaping the future. The last section of the book groups together under the label "Observations, Recommendations, and Parting Polemics" a miscellany of his most eloquent and representative pages in this respect. In them his normative stances are explicitly stated, his critical position regarding the "Western cultural trends" made crystal-clear, his views on the "the tasks ahead" outlined, and his vision about futurology as an ideological force and a cultural bulwark for economic development, explicitly discussed as a "growth-oriented ideology based on futurology."

In order to get a better understanding of the way Kahn viewed his work, it is important to note that he always considered that the "broad," future-oriented studies he was envisioning were possible only as a collective effort. Hence, the profoundly collaborative nature of his intellectual endeavors. Kahn's vision of interdisciplinary collaboration went beyond the idea of putting together in an orderly way different pieces of analysis and conclusions coming from different disciplines. He thought that although it is impossible to have a complete specialized interdisciplinary personal knowledge of an issue, it is always possible to assemble teams of experts and combine their knowledge in a useful manner. Or, at least, it is possible to engage in as many bilateral intellectual partnerships and as many dialogues as possible. That is the reason why Kahn's work has such a collaborative bent and why many of the arguments and ideas included in the present selection were coauthored or presented as a "Hudson Institute product."

Herman Kahn's work was bounded by a spectacular series of paradoxes: thinking the unthinkable, disciplining the interdisciplinary, institutionalizing the imaginative, anchoring in facts the counterfactual, predicting the unpredictable. Seen from the perspective of the beginning of the third millennium, Herman Kahn's methodological and substantive contributions to the development of a modern way of approaching the future and the large scale and multifaceted problems confronting humanity in his age, gain a new and clearer perspective. By the time he was making these contributions his voice and name were overwhelmingly associated with his influential participation in various controversial public debates such as the nuclear strategy of the United States or the "limits to growth" dispute. Now, that those controversies have moved to new dimensions, and new protagonists are occupying the forefront of the public debate, the new circumstances allow us to go beyond the controversial and contextual and to fully appreciate in an detached and unbiased way the foundational contributions brought by Herman Kahn not only to the intellectual development of strategic studies, futurology, and policy sciences but also to the materialization of the major themes defining the contemporary public discourse. Our hope is that this anthology will amount to a constructive contribution in this respect.

I

THINKING ABOUT THE UNTHINKABLE: SCENARIOS, GRAND STRATEGY, AND THERMONUCLEAR WAR

1

⸻

In Defense of Thinking

Seventy-five years ago white slavery was rampant in England. Each year thousands of young girls were forced into brothels and kept there against their will. While some of the victims had been sold by their families, a large proportion were seized and held by force or fraud. The victims were not from the lower classes only; no level of English society was immune to having its daughters seized. Because this practice continued in England for years after it had been largely wiped out on the Continent, thousands of English girls were shipped across the Channel to supply the brothels of Europe. One reason why this lasted as long as it did was that it could not be talked about openly in Victorian England; moral standards as subjects of discussion made it difficult to arouse the community to necessary action. Moreover, the extreme innocence considered appropriate for English girls made them easy victims, helpless to cope with the situations in which they were trapped. Victorian standards, besides perpetuating the white slave trade, intensified the damage to those involved.

Social inhibitions which reinforce natural tendencies to avoid thinking about unpleasant subjects are hardly uncommon. The psychological factors involved in ostrich-like behavior have parallels in communities and nations. Nevertheless, during the sixty years of the twentieth century many problems have come increasingly into the realm of acceptable

[*Thinking about the Unthinkable* (New York: Horizon Press, 1962).]

public discussion. Among various unmentionable diseases, tuberculosis has lost almost all taint of impropriety; and venereal disease statistics can now be reported by the press. Mental illness is more and more regarded as unfortunate instead of shameful. The word "cancer" has lost its stigma, although the horror of the disease has been only partially abated by medical progress.

Despite the progress in removing barriers in the way of discussing diseases formerly considered shameful, there are doubtless thousands going without vital medical treatment today because of their inhibitions against learning, thinking, or talking about certain diseases. Some will not get treatment because they do not know enough to recognize the symptoms, some because they are consciously ashamed to reveal illness, and some because they refuse to think about their condition—it seems too horrible to think about.

It may now be possible to condemn unequivocally the extremes of Victorian prudery, but less doctrinaire forms of ostrichism must be considered with more care; they are, after all, often based on healthy instincts. Everyone is going to die, but surely it is a good thing that few of us spend much time dwelling on that fact. Life would be nearly impossible if we did. If thinking about something bad will not improve it, it is often better not to think about it. Perhaps some evils can be avoided or reduced if people do not think or talk about them. But when our reluctance to consider danger brings danger nearer, repression has gone too far.

In 1960 I published a book[1] that attempted to direct attention to the possibility of a thermonuclear war, to ways of reducing the likelihood of such a war, and to methods for coping with the consequences should war occur despite our efforts to avoid it. The book was greeted by a large range of responses—some of them sharply critical. Some of this criticism was substantive, touching on greater or smaller questions of strategy, policy, or research techniques. But much of the criticism was not concerned with the correctness or incorrectness of the views I expressed. It was concerned with whether any book should have been written on this subject at all. It is characteristic of our times that many intelligent and sincere people are willing to argue that it is immoral to think and even more immoral to write in detail about having to fight a thermonuclear war.

By and large this criticism was not personal; it simply reflected the fact that we Americans and many people throughout the world are not prepared to face reality, that we transfer our horror of thermonuclear war to reports about the realities of thermonuclear war. In a sense we are acting like those ancient kings who punished messengers who brought them bad news. This did not change the news; it simply slowed up its delivery. On occasion it meant that the kings were ill informed and, lacking truth, made serious errors in judgment and strategy.

In our times, thermonuclear war may seem unthinkable, immoral, insane, hideous, or highly unlikely, but it is not impossible. To act intelligently we must learn as much as we can about the risks. We may thereby be better able to avoid nuclear war. We may even be able to avoid the crises that bring us to the brink of war. But despite our efforts we may some day come face to face with a blunt choice between surrender or war. We may even have war thrust upon us without being given any kind of a choice. We must appreciate these possibilities. We cannot wish them away. Nor should we overestimate and assume the worst is inevitable. This leads only to defeatism, inadequate preparations (because they seem useless), and pressures toward either preventive war or undue accommodation.

Many terrible questions are raised when one considers objectively and realistically the problems created by the Cold War and the armaments race. For some years I have spent my time on exactly these questions—both in thinking about ways to prevent war, and in thinking about how to fight, survive, and terminate a war, should it occur. My colleagues and I have sought answers to such questions as these: How likely is accidental war? How can one make it less likely? How dangerous is the arms race today? What will it be like in the future? What would conditions be if a nuclear attack leveled fifty of America's largest cities? Would the survivors envy the dead? How many million American lives would an American President risk by standing firm in differing types of crises? By starting a nuclear war? By continuing a nuclear war with the hope of avoiding surrender? How many European and Soviet and other lives would he risk?

These questions can be put in a more concrete and hence more upsetting form. Consider, for example, the debate about the defense of Europe. We have increased our nonnuclear forces to meet without initial use of nuclear weapons a possible Soviet conventional attack in Europe. But our present doctrine also seems to indicate that if the strengthened forces prove inadequate to repel the attack, we will initiate the use of nuclear weapons.

The questions now become more unpleasant since we must acknowledge the likelihood that this use of nuclear weapons might not be limited. Whether we intend it or not, we may have obligated ourselves to go to an all-out central war. Attempts at restraint may turn out to be unreliable; passion, irrationality, and technical difficulties of control and discrimination might cause escalation into all-out war. In this context we must ask ourselves several questions. First, would we in fact initiate an all-out war if the Soviets attacked Europe? Would we even risk one by initiating a lesser response which could easily escalate into all-out war? What would be the European attitude toward fighting a "limited" nuclear (or even a large conventional) war on their territory?

In seeking the answers to these questions, the President must estimate the cohesion of the Alliance, and weigh the possibility of tens of millions, possibly hundreds of millions, of American and European casualties—not to speak of Russians and others. He must ask himself whether he is willing to sacrifice, or so much as risk, New York in order to defend Paris or London or revenge their destruction. If he concludes that he is not—and there are many who think that he would not willingly make the trade—then he must ask himself whether he wishes to change either his commitments or his preparations.

He may conclude that even if he is not willing to initiate a war or a limited reprisal that could easily develop into war, he must maintain a pretense of being willing. Perhaps the facade will work. After all, even if he is not willing to go to an all-out war, the Soviets cannot rely on this. The uncertainty regarding his response may deter them from testing his resolve.

The President may be unwilling to go to all-out war, and also unwilling to rely on the deterrent effect of Russian uncertainty about our response acting as a deterrent. In that case he has to have realistic contingency plans for lesser responses than all-out war, to be used in the event the Soviets are not deterred. He must then ask himself: Should he disclose these contingency plans to the Soviets so as to make credible the action we will take to make their aggression unprofitable? Should he keep these plans secret so that the Soviets will not be encouraged to expect a less than all-out response? How will our allies react to either policy? Will their attitude change in an intense crisis? Would we prefer an ally to be involved in a disastrous local war rather than see its resources added to the Communist bloc?

Perhaps, in addition to having a "wider choice than humiliation or holocaust," the President may wish to prepare for the possibility of holocaust, and for the problems involved in lessening the damage. Even if we are not willing to fight an all-out thermonuclear war, it may still be forced on us, or occur inadvertently.

Consider as well the problem of deterring the Soviets from striking the United States either because they may be planning an aggression or because there is some crisis in which U.S. policy (perhaps the mere existence of the United States) may threaten their ability to surmount the crisis. In desperation they may feel that striking the United States would be less risky than not striking. How risky must we make such an action? What kind of punishment would deter the Soviets even if they were desperate? The threat of 100 million dead Russians? Ten million? The destruction of Moscow and Leningrad? With their citizens? Without their citizens, i.e., evacuated? How certain must this threat be? Just how stable, then, is our present "balance of terror"? How is it most likely to break down? If it does break down what will be the consequence?

Consider another unpleasant question. When the movie *On the Beach* depicted a war in the early sixties, the result of which was the total annihilation of all humanity by radioactivity, almost all the reviewers and many scientists indicated that it was a realistic estimate of the results of a nuclear war. Are we really risking an end to all human life with our current system? If true, are we willing to risk it? Do we then prefer some degree of unilateral disarmament? If we do, will we be relying on the Russians to protect us from the Chinese? Will the world be more or less stable? Should we attempt to disarm unilaterally? If the answers to these last questions depend on the degree of damage that is envisaged, are we willing to argue that it is all right to risk a half billion or a billion people but not three billion?

There seem to be three basic objections to asking these types of questions:

1. No one should attempt to think about these problems in a detailed and rational way.
2. What thinking there is on these problems, should be done in secret by the military exclusively, or at least by the government.
3. Even if some of this thinking must be done outside the government the results of any such thought should not be made available to the public.

1. NO ONE SHOULD ATTEMPT TO THINK ABOUT THESE PROBLEMS IN A DETAILED AND RATIONAL WAY.

The arguments against hard thinking by anyone at all about the realities of thermonuclear war break down into a number of categories: First, it is argued that thinking about the indescribable horror of nuclear war breeds callousness and indifference to the future of civilization in our planners and decision-makers. It is true that detailed and dispassionate discussion of such questions is likely to look incredibly hard-hearted. It should also be clear, at least to thoughtful readers, that such questions must be considered. The reality may be so unpleasant that decision-makers would prefer not to face it; but to a great extent this reality has been forced on them, or has come uninvited. Thanks to our ever increasing technology we are living in a terrible and dangerous world; but, unlike the lady in the cartoon we cannot say, "Stop the world, I want to get off." We cannot get off. Even the most utopian of today's visionaries will have to concede that the mere existence of modern technology involves a risk to civilization that would have been unthinkable twenty-five years ago. While we are going to make major attempts to change the nature of this reality, accepting great risks if necessary, most of us are unwilling to choose either a pronounced degree of unilateral disarmament or a preventive war designed to "settle" our problems one way or another. We therefore must face the facts that thermonuclear bombs now exist in the hands of at least four powers; that at least one of these powers has announced it is interested in the destruction of our society, albeit by peaceful means if possible; that the number of thermonuclear powers may grow; that the power most likely to obtain these weapons next, China, stands on the thesis that war with us is inevitable; and, finally, that the possibilities of an immediate solution by negotiation are indeed slim. Unless we are willing to abdicate our responsibilities we are pledged to the maintenance of terrifying weapon systems with known and unknown, calculable and incalculable risks, unless and until better arrangements can be made.

If we are to have an expensive and lethal defense establishment, we must weigh all the risks and benefits. We must at least ask ourselves what are the likely and unlikely results of an inadvertent war, the possibilities of accident, irresponsibility, or unauthorized behavior on the other side as well as on our own.

A variation of the objection to careful consideration of these problems focuses on the personality of the thinker. This argument goes: Better no thought than evil thought; and since only evil and callous people can think about this, better no thought. Alternatively, the thinker's motives are analyzed: This man studies war; he must like war—much like the suspicion that a surgeon is a repressed sadist. Even if the charge were true, which in general it is not, it is not relevant. Like the repressed sadist who can perform a socially useful function by sublimating his urges into surgery, the man who loves war or violence may be able to successfully sublimate his desires into a careful and valuable study of war. It does indeed take an iron will or an unpleasant degree of detachment to go about this task. Ideally it should be possible for the analyst to have a disciplined empathy. In fact, the mind recoils from simultaneously probing deeply and creatively into these problems and being conscious at all times of the human tragedy involved.

This is not new. We do not continually remind the surgeon while he is operating of the humanity of his patient. We do not flash pictures of his patient's wife or children in front of him. We want him to be careful, and we want him to be aware of the importance and frailty of the patient; we do not want him to be distracted or fearful. We do not expect illustrations in a book on surgery to be captioned: "A particularly deplorable tumor," or "Good health is preferable to this kind of cancer." Excessive comments such as, "And now there's a lot of blood," or "This particular cut really hurts," are out of place although these are important things for a surgeon to know. To mention such things may be important. To dwell on them is morbid, and gets in the way of the information. The same tolerance needs be extended to thought on national security.

Some feel that we should consider these problems but view them with such awe and horror that we should not discuss them in normal, neutral, professional everyday language. I tend to disagree; at least so far as technical discussions and research are concerned. One does not do research in a cathedral. Awe is fine for those who come to worship or admire, but for those who come to analyze, to tamper, to change, to criticize, a factual and dispassionate, and sometimes even colorful, approach is to be preferred. And if the use of everyday language jars, that is all the more reason for using it. Why would one expect a realistic discussion of thermonuclear war not to be disturbing?

The very complexity of the questions raised is another reason why many object to their consideration. There is no doubt that if we reject hard thinking about alternatives in favor of uncritical acceptance of an extreme position we make the argument simpler—and most of us prefer simple arguments. Consider, for example, the following statement by C. P. Snow.

> We are faced with an either-or, and we haven't much time. The either is acceptance of a restriction of nuclear armaments. This is going to begin, just as a token, with an agreement on the stopping of nuclear tests. The United States is not going to get the 99.9 percent "security" that it has been asking for. This is unobtainable, though there are other bargains that the United States could probably secure. I am not going to conceal from you that this course involves certain risks. They are quite obvious, and no honest man is going to blink them. That is the either. The or is not a risk but a certainty. It is this. There is no agreement on tests. The nuclear arms race between the United States and the U.S.S.R. not only continues but accelerates. Other countries join in. Within, at the most, six years, China and several other states will have a stock of nuclear bombs. Within, at the most, ten years, some of those bombs are going off. I am saying this as responsibly as I can. That is the certainty. On the one side, therefore, we have a finite risk. On the other side we have a certainty of disaster. Between a risk and a certainty, a sane man does not hesitate. ("The Moral Un-neutrality of Science," *Science*, January 27, 1961)

The speech from which the above excerpt was taken attracted much favorable comment.

In spite of the wide acclaim, and the scientific and literary distinction of the author, the statement is neither accurate nor responsible. The United States is not asking for 99.9 percent security via the arms control route. In fact, we seem to be willing to accept agreements of a much lower reliability than almost anybody—even passionate arms controllers—would have been willing to accept a few years ago when they did not know how difficult it is to get reliably enforceable agreements. Much more important, the "or" described by C. P. Snow is not a certainty. Unless he has information denied to the rest of us, he cannot know that within ten years some of these bombs are going off. Even more important, he cannot know that some of these bombs going off will result in a certainty of disaster.

The reader may feel, possibly correctly, that I may have been unfair to C. P. Snow by taking his remarks too literally. Let me concede the possibility. What is startling is not so much that Sir Charles made the remarks, but that there was so little criticism of them. Imagine the uproar that would have occurred if an equally distinguished man had said that, "There is no probability at all of war in the next ten years." If the actual probability had been one-half, each remark might be equally off, at least in the arithmetical sense, but only the first would be regarded as an acceptable position by most people. It should be noted that either remark can be dangerous: The first by increasing the pressure for undue accommodation or preventive war; the second by decreasing the pressure for a reasonable compromise, and safety precautions.

I believe that the reason for the widespread acceptance of the attitude expressed by Sir Charles lies in his last sentence. It would be very simple indeed if all we had to do was to choose between a certainty and a risk of disaster. Responsible decision-makers would not need to hesitate. Unfortunately for their peace of mind, however, it is by no means clear on which side the certainties and risks lie. It may even be true that there is a certainty of disaster no matter what we do. It is even conceivable that this certainty can be demonstrated; that some detached and infinitely wise observer can prove that it is impossible for us poor creatures on earth to get out of the difficulties we are in. He may even be able to show that, having weapons of mass destruction, we must sooner or later use them, and maybe more than once, until only the peace of utter destruction puts an end to the repetition.

On the other hand, there may be different paths to safety, each involving degrees of risk and varying outcomes. I believe there are. But I recognize that balancing the risks is difficult. It cannot be done rigorously, though analysis should help. In the end, the best of policies must involve judicious guesses, informed acts of faith, and careful steps in the dark. It is well to recognize these for what they are, to be conscious that some new and seemingly appealing path that avoids the familiar horrors may be riskier than the present perilous one.

The automatic balance of terror is not only a falsely simple view of the world, it is in some ways a comforting view. To see why this is so, consider Richard Nixon's remark to Khrushchev, "We must live together or die together." That is indeed a comforting remark because it indicates an easy choice between national sanity and insanity. Nixon could have said, "We must live together or one of us will die." This is not a comforting remark. It not only has a threatening sound, it indicates that carelessness can be dangerous and that survival is not necessarily dependent on one's own acts.

Both remarks are inaccurate, of course, but if I had to choose, I would say that the second is probably more accurate than the first for the time being. If one wishes to be accurate in these matters, he must be lengthy and complex. He can start by saying that we must live together or one of us will be hurt to a great degree and the other to a lesser degree, the exact amounts depending on such "technical details" as how the war starts, how it is fought, and how it is terminated.

The mutual annihilation view is also comforting to many idealistic individuals, particularly those who intrinsically abhor any use of force. The bizarreness of a war in which both sides expect to be annihilated confirms their intuition that this whole business of military preparations is silly: A stupid and dangerous game which we ought to discourage nations—our own country, at least—from playing. Those who believe this can afford to scoff at attempts to reduce casualties from, say, 100 million to 50 million Americans; the situation is hopeless anyway; the only respectable cause is the total elimination of war.

To summarize: Many people believe that the current system must inevitably end in total annihilation. They reject, sometimes very emotionally, any attempts to analyze this notion. Either they are afraid of where the thinking will lead them or they are afraid of thinking at all. They want to make the choice one between a risk and the certainty of disaster, between sanity and insanity, between good and evil; therefore, as moral and sane men they need no longer hesitate. I hold that an intelligent and responsible person cannot pose the problem so simply.

Interestingly enough, my view is somewhat comforting too. If C. P. Snow is right and if Bertrand Russell is also right in proclaiming that our irrational desire to maintain an obsolete system jeopardizes the future of the human race, one can make a very persuasive case for almost any kind of arms control, including unilateral disarmament and preventive war (to achieve forcible arms control), as being better than the current system. Disagreeing with both these gentlemen, I can counsel strongly against both. However one reason why many do not wish to consider these questions objectively is the fear that a case will be made for one of these extreme views.

Often the reluctance to think about these problems is not caused by the advocacy of any particular Weltanschauung. Rather it is based on nothing sounder than a supernatural fear of the magical power of words (to talk about cancer is to bring on cancer) or of actions (to build shelters is to create the need for their use). Many have this primitive belief that speaking of evil or preparing for evil creates evil. Some years ago there was a great outcry at the news that a study had been made of the possible conditions under which the United States might surrender during a war. Legislation was passed preventing appropriations for studies of this subject. One might ask whether failure to think about all the ways in which a war might end makes it more likely for us to win a war, or whether it merely prevents thinking about possible Soviet strategies designed to bring about our surrender. Or does it even prevent thinking about the possibility of achieving a peace treaty under relatively advantageous terms while sparing unnecessary slaughter?

An objection is frequently made on a more sophisticated level. An example is the so-called self-fulfilling prophecy: If you are hostile and suspicious toward someone, you will often act so. Even if he was innocent before, he will notice your attitude, which arouses hostility and suspicion in him. With your suspicions now confirmed you become more hostile, thus intensifying his suspicions. The mutual counteractions lead either to immediate violence or to a level of tension at which the possibility of violence is ever present.

The self-fulfilling prophecy sometimes occurs both between individuals and between nations, but realizing this does not settle the question. In 1959 and 1960, I gave a series of lectures. At almost every one of them, someone urged that mutual trust could act as self-fulfilling prophecy. Just before the first time it was brought up, I had been through a relevant experience. I described it then and have used it several times since to illustrate that prophecies can be self-defeating as well as self-fulfilling.

A person I know is an embezzler who has served time in jail twice. At the time I was first asked the question about self-fulfilling prophecies he was under indictment for the third time, and out on bail. After he had been indicted I asked him, "Why did you do it? You have already been caught twice. Why do you keep repeating this behavior? It's not only immoral, it obviously isn't successful. Why do you do it?" He looked me right in the eye and said, "I can't help it. People trust me."

He put the blame where he thought it belonged, on the excessive trust of others. He is an outgoing fellow; he does not have much character and he just cannot control himself when he is excessively tempted. His story is an example of a "self-defeating prophecy." His victims trusted him and did not guard against him; so they were victimized. If one worries about having funds embezzled one may take precautions that defeat an attempt at embezzlement. Self-defeating prophecies probably play a bigger role in human affairs than self-fulfilling prophecies. Similarly, if one prepares for war, one may possibly deter war. This can happen. Indeed it has often happened in the past.[2]

For this reason we simply cannot reject programs solely because they reflect some hostility and suspicion of the Soviet Union. Hostility and suspicion are justified. These occur even in ordinary private and commercial life; people have contracts, courts, and police. There are even better reasons to reject a totally trusting international policy toward the Soviet Union. Our suspicions were not created by our own imaginations working overtime. Indeed, some suspicion would exist even in an atmosphere of cordiality and entente. A policy that cannot coexist with a degree of suspicion is not a viable policy in today's world, or indeed any world. The last objection to detailed thought on thermonuclear war rests on the view that the subject is not only unpleasant but difficult.

Many people feel that it is useless to apply rationality and calculation in any area dominated by irrational decision-makers. This is almost comparable to feeling that it would be impossible to design a safety system for an insane asylum by rational methods, since, after all, the inmates are irrational. Of course, no governor or superintendent would consider firing the trained engineer, and turning the design over to one of the lunatics. The engineer is expected to take the irrationality of the inmates into account by a rational approach. Rational discussions of war and peace can explicitly include the possibility of irrational behavior.

Of course, analysts may be misled by oversimplified models or misleading assumptions, and their competence readily attacked. However, except for irrelevant references to game theory and computers, such attacks are rare, and are usually so half-hearted that it is clear that their main motivation is not to expose incompetence. Given the difficulty of the problems, one would expect the critics to work more effectively on the obvious methodological problems and other weaknesses of present-day analysts.

These weaknesses may make it impossible for the best-trained analyst to arrive at any better policy suggestions than relatively informed intuitions, no matter how objectively and carefully he works. In fact, the net effect of his research might be to make the analyst's recommendations persuasive rather than correct. Moreover, in his objective discussion of the case, he might weaken moral barriers, customs, and sanctions which might better be left strong. It is also conceivable that by raising these issues, he might automatically create a controversy which would impede the development of ideas or programs deriving from trial and error or originating in a spirit of compromise. Last, and possibly most important, by making recommendations which help make the current system acceptable, he may prevent the "patient" from going to the doctor and accepting the drastic surgery which is really necessary to cure his ills. There may be a great deal of wisdom in the ancient proverb that "the good is the enemy of the best."

For all of the above and other reasons it is possible that the most objective and careful discussions may still influence events in a wrong direction. Indeed, the final outcome of decisions that are well meaning, informed, and intelligent can be disastrous. However, few would argue that this is a good reason to be malevolent, uninformed, or stupid. Those of us who have not received any divine revelation as to the correct course must do the best we can with the knowledge and intellectual tools we have available. I for one do not believe that it makes sense to depend any more than can be helped on blind luck or faith—even though I concede we will need both if we are to negotiate safely the treacherous terrain before us.

2. WHAT THINKING THERE IS ON THESE PROBLEMS, SHOULD BE DONE IN SECRET BY THE MILITARY EXCLUSIVELY, OR AT LEAST BY THE GOVERNMENT.

The second class of objections seems to be that the study of warfare should be left to professional military officers. In fact, one reviewer of *OTW* said:

> I can understand and respect career military officers who have chosen the "honorable profession of arms" as a way of life, often at a sacrifice in comfort and emoluments and who are subsequently assigned the duty of formulating war plans to meet all eventualities. But Mr. Kahn is a physicist, a scholar and a civilian. To be blunt, his book makes me ashamed that we are fellow countrymen.

Clemenceau once said, "War is too important to be left to the generals." A colleague of mine, Albert Wohlstetter, has paraphrased the remark to the even more appropriate, "Peace is too important to be left to the generals."

If we treat all questions of the deterrence and fighting of war as a subject to be entrusted solely to those in uniform we should not be surprised if we get narrow policies. The deterring or fighting of a thermonuclear war certainly needs specialists in and out of uniform; but it involves all of us and every aspect of our society.

Many liberals feel more confident knowing that civilians not directly in the governmental apparatus can influence military policy by the thought they give to its problems. But others do not; in fact, the research corporation working under contract with the United States government has become a whipping-boy for certain sectors of the liberal press. There are many and good reasons, however, why these organizations exist, and will in all probability grow in the future.

The principal advantages of the private consultant are two-fold: a lack of compulsion to deal with "first things first," and an independent point of view. As to the first of these, most people do not appreciate just how ill-equipped our government is to perform long-range planning. The most able officials are constantly involved in the meeting of day-to-day crises, Congressional investigations, budgetary problems, and administrative detail, with little time to devote to the long-range problems in which the civilian nongovernment research corporation specializes. Rarely, if ever, can a government agency allow one man to be free from what Professor Samuel Sharp calls the "tyranny of the in-and-out box" for more than just a few months. Moreover, it is especially unlikely that a man can be spared to work on a long-range problem that in all probability will never arise. However, we know that just this sort of problem can be vitally important.

The independence is equally important. Unless the researcher is allowed to make mistakes—indeed to be "irresponsible"—it is unlikely that he will consider carefully enough the full range of alternatives or make the kind of constructive advance in thinking that is, in effect, a devastating criticism of current thinking. We must even allow researchers to be wrongheaded and stubborn, since it is rare that new controversial ideas in the policy field are created fully documented, or that the documentation can be obtained without additional research or work that will only be done if the undocumented, unpopular idea is vigorously supported or pressed even in the absence of the necessary research. In effect, one of the main purposes of the independent research institution is to be a sort of loyal opposition which is privy to most of an agency's "secrets," and yet can be disowned by the agency.

There are other less important but still, by themselves, sufficient reasons for the existence of the independent research institute. They tend to be somewhat competitive and thus provide a freer market for ideas and skilled professional review and criticisms. It is difficult for "outsiders" to do this partly because of security reasons but mainly because technology is growing at an increasingly rapid rate. Paradoxical as it sounds, reality has left experience far behind, and central as "common sense" is, it is not enough. Even the simple study of weapons effects has grown so complicated that many scientists have spent almost a lifetime working on them alone. A detailed analysis of a military-political problem may occasionally involve computer studies or even fairly sophisticated problems in mathematics; it may involve economic analyses both of the input-output type and the more conventional kinds; it will unquestionably draw on engineering and physics, and, most important, it will require, in the words of William Lee Miller, "profound historical imagination, a playing on the possibilities in every direction, and an acute moral sense."[3] As in many other fields, life has become so complex that the individual must be supplemented and aided by the team. The question then arises as to why these groups cannot be employed solely and directly by the government. Some of them can be, and in fact are. However, on many problems independent research workers bring to their groups specialties and skills in short supply. Such institutions often provide a more efficient way to utilize scarce human resources.

Inevitably the fact that most people studying national defense are paid by some agency of the government gives rise to the allegation of subservience rather than independence, that their studies are bought. Alternatively, it is argued that the corruption is more subtle than purely monetary influence; the analyst is attracted by the excitement of knowing about or influencing national policy, or he is bought by being given access to information, to laboratories, etc. According to this view, the government gets the analyst, one way or another, to cooperate in producing distorted work.

There may be some germ of truth in such accusations, but by and large ad hominem charges are irrelevant. Any serious analysis should be studied, discussed, and answered on its own merits. The analyst's motivation may have some place in the discussion, but surely it is a minor one if the analysis is serious. I am reminded of a remark by Leo Szilard on the difference between politicians and scientists. He made the point that politicians always ask, "Why did he say it?" whereas scientists ask, "Is it true?"[4] Of course, a man's motives are important. But in a discussion of national security they are probably less important than, "Is he right?" Part of our national maturity must be the ability to discuss issues on their merits, whether they are brought up by generals, politicians, researchers, academicians, right-wingers, left-wingers, Russians, neutralists, or others.

It is undeniably true that research organizations vary in their independence and individuals in the most independent research organizations do sometimes seem to act more as advocates than as impartial scientists. Man is incurably partisan, but so long as the primary loyalty of the private research organization is clearly to intellectual integrity, the harm done by partisan individual researchers is small. Indeed their partisanship can have value. It increases the probability that a thorough study and a vigorous case will be made for the various partisan causes. Moreover, the demand for competent researchers is today so large that few of them could feel any economic pressure to slant their work. Finally, even if their freedom is not always complete, it is very large compared to that of a conscientious government official who is "locked in" by the commitments of his superiors. The government official is often torn by conflicting departmental and national loyalties as well as restricted by official channels. The private organization, where those who negotiate contracts are often divorced from those who perform the study, has many fewer such problems.

Critics frequently refer to the icy rationality of the Hudson Institute, the RAND Corporation, and other such organizations. I'm always tempted to ask in reply, "Would you prefer a warm, human error? Do you feel better with a nice emotional mistake?" We cannot expect good discussion of security problems if we are going to label every attempt at detachment as callous, every attempt at objectivity as immoral. Such attitudes not only block discussion of the immediate issues, they lead to a disunity and fragmentation of the intellectual community that can be disastrous to the democratic dialogue between specialist and layman. The former tends to withdraw to secret and private discussions; the latter becomes more and more innocent, or naive, and more likely to be outraged if he is ever exposed to a professional discussion.

3. EVEN IF SOME OF THIS THINKING MUST BE DONE OUTSIDE THE GOVERNMENT THE RESULTS OF ANY SUCH THOUGHT SHOULD NOT BE MADE AVAILABLE TO THE PUBLIC.

Finally, there is the objection that thermonuclear war should not, at least in detail, be discussed publicly. Even some who admit the usefulness of asking unpleasant questions have advocated raising them only in secret. One objector pointed out to me that if a parent in a burning building is faced with the problem of having to save one of two children, but not both, he will make a decision on the spur of the moment; it wouldn't have made any difference if the parent had agonized over the problem ahead of time, and it would have been particularly bad to agonize in the presence of the children. This may be true, but other considerations dominate our nation's choices; our capabilities for action and the risks we are assuming for ourselves and thrusting on others will be strongly influenced by our preparations both intellectual and physical. Other reasons for this objection to public discussion range all the way from concern about telling the Soviets too much, and a fear of weakening the resolve of our own people, through a feeling that public discussion of death and destruction is distastefully comparable to a drugstore display of the tools, methods, and products of the mortician. Perhaps some or all of these objections to public discussion are well taken. I do not know for sure, but I think they are wrong.

They are wrong if we expect our people to participate rationally in the decision-making process in matters that are vital to their existence as individuals and as a nation. As one author has put it: "In a democracy, when experts disagree, laymen must resolve the disagreement." One issue is whether it is better that the lay public, which will directly or indirectly decide policy, be more or less informed. A second issue is whether the discussion itself may not be significantly improved by eliciting ideas from people outside of official policy-making channels.

There are in any case at least two significant obstacles to full public debate of national security matters. The first, of course, is the constantly increasing problem of communication between the technologist and the layman, because of the specialization (one might almost say fragmentation) of knowledge. The other lies in the serious and paramount need to maintain security. Technical details of weapons' capabilities and weaknesses must remain classified to some degree. Nonetheless, technical details may be of vital importance in resolving much broader problems.[5] Moreover, those who feel that in some areas "security" has been unnecessarily extended must concede that in certain areas it has its place. To that extent the functioning of the democratic processes must be compromised with the requirements of the Cold War and modern technology. Certainly the wisdom of the Turkish Radar or the U-2 overflights were not amenable to the usual democratic processes of discussion. Fortunately, nonclassified sources often give reasonable approximations to the classified data. I would say that many of the agonizing problems facing us today can be debated and understood just about as easily without classified material as with—provided one carefully considers the facts that are available.

It is quite clear that technical details are not the only important operative facts. Human and moral factors must always be considered. They must never be missing from policies and from public discussion. But emotionalism and sentimentality, as opposed to morality and concern, only confuse debates. Nor can experts be expected to repeat, "If, heaven forbid," before every sentence. Responsible decision-makers and researchers cannot afford the luxury of denying the existence of agonizing questions. The public, whose lives and freedom are at stake, expects them to face such questions squarely and, where necessary, the expert should expect little less of the public.

NOTES

1. *On Thermonuclear War* (Princeton, N.J.: Princeton University Press), hereafter referred to as *OTW*.

2. For example, it is fair to say that from 1871 until its failure in 1914 through a series of coincidences, deterrence kept the peace. During this period the major nations of Europe remained at peace despite the fact that large segments of each nation desired war on numerous occasions, that there were bitter national antagonisms, and the consequences of war were not only nowhere near as serious as today, but were regarded as far less serious than they actually were. Both Soviet and U.S. behavior today over such controversies as Berlin indicate prudent behavior as a result of fear of war. Indeed the Soviet doctrine of coexistence sprang directly from an appreciation of the power of modern nuclear weapons. None of the above implies that deterrence is bound to work indefinitely (indeed the first example indicates how it might fail); only that it is possible to worsen our current situation by unwisely weakening deterrence.

3. From a review of *OTW* in *Worldview*, Apr. 11, 1961. The review goes on to state, "Mr. Kahn, consequently, is surely right when he says that we need the thought of persons outside military strategy and mathematical calculation to deal with world politics in our strange era. And this, precisely, is what is lacking in *On Thermonuclear War*." I would not disagree too much with any part of this comment. Although it is important to keep strategists in their place, it is also important to realize that they have their place. Technical studies should not be allowed to dominate our thinking but should be taken into account. Nor should these technical treatments of thermonuclear war be considered unacceptable unless they include extensive accounts of such related problems as foreign policy, limited war, arms control, or the moral and theological problems of war and peace. I certainly agree that every one of these related problems is of vital concern and the specialist on thermonuclear war must consider them either explicitly or implicitly. But the importance of related topics hardly diminishes the need for specialized studies of thermonuclear war—in itself a subject too vast to be completely grasped. It is certainly the case that technical and specialized studies on foreign policy, limited war, or arms control that do not include an extensive account of thermonuclear war seldom meet objection on this score.

4. Szilard is probably being too respectful of his scientific colleagues who also seem to indulge in ad hominem arguments—especially when they are out of their technical specialty.

5. For instance, who can presume to say whether military advantages of atomic weapons testing outweigh the obvious political and physical disadvantages unless he knows what the military advantages are?

2

—∽∾∽—

Twelve Nonissues and Twelve Almost Nonissues

The debate over nuclear war and national security policy is often more confused and confusing than informative and productive. In order to make it as useful and accurate as possible, it is important to separate issues that are relevant to government policy from issues that may be valid from some perspectives but are not serious policy options. Misconceptions and illusions do not contribute to the formulation of substantive recommendations and programs.

TWELVE NONISSUES

The following twelve assertions, however common and sincerely held, in terms of policy-making are basically irrelevant, impractical, inaccurate, or foolish and should be eliminated from the debate at the outset.

1. *We must halt the nuclear "arms race" in order to achieve the redemption of mankind.* This concept has recently been popularized in a book by Jonathan Schell:

> . . . today the only way to achieve genuine national defense for any nation is for all nations to give up violence together . . . if we had begun with Gandhi's law of love we would have arrived at exactly the same arrangement E. M. Forster told us, "Only connect!" Let us connect. Auden told us, "We must

---

[*Thinking about the Unthinkable in the 1980s* (New York: Simon & Schuster, 1984).]

love one another or die." Let us love one another Christ said, "I come not to judge the world but to save the world." Let us, also, not judge the world but save the world. (*The Fate of the Earth* [New York: Alfred A. Knopf. Inc., 1982], pp. 224 and 230)

This concept has also been suggested in "A Pastoral Letter on War and Peace" by the National Conference of Catholic Bishops ("The Challenge of Peace: God's Promise and Our Response," reprinted in *Origins*, May 19, 1983). Redemption may be an appropriate and correct concern for a church, but it has nothing to do with any policies that the government can—or should—carry out. If there is a "redemption of mankind," it will not occur as a result of a great debate on national security policy or defense. It is, then, the "nonissue" of least relevance to government policy on nuclear war.

2. *The control of nuclear weapons should be pursued through the creation of an effective world parliamentary government and/or total worldwide disarmament.* A world government of sorts already exists: the UN Security Council. It is definitive on almost any issue on which a majority, including the five great powers (the United States, Soviet Union, China, Great Britain, and France), can agree. History, however, has proven its basic ineffectiveness.

The effort of trying to establish a more effective world government would itself involve major problems. In fact, it is very doubtful if the creation of the Security Council, or a successor body, could be negotiated today. The small nations intentionally turned over their power to the great nations of the world in crisis; today they fight fiercely to retain it by voting in blocks, changing allegiances and alliances as it suits their purposes. And there could be no chance of agreement today on who would have the veto power.

But even assuming a new world government were negotiable, how would it be structured? If it followed the "one man–one vote" principle, it would be dominated largely by Asian nations; under "one country–one vote," it would be run largely by the small states; and with "one dollar–one vote" it would result in domination by the United States, Japan, the Soviet Union, and Western Europe. All three options are unacceptable, and a compromise seems almost impossible. Under the circumstances, the Security Council is the best we have, and while a consensus by that body potentially could still have enormous impact (e.g., theoretically it is able to overrule national laws and possibly even the Constitution of the United States), it is unrealistic to expect a major and "binding" UN resolution on nuclear weapons to have much real-world significance.

As for total disarmament, there are almost 50,000 nuclear weapons in the world today; even if they were banned, not all would be destroyed.

And even if they were destroyed, there is still a large amount of weapons-grade uranium and plutonium available, plus the knowledge of how to turn these materials into nuclear devices. It would not be acceptable to have a disarmament "solution" that allowed those with hidden weapons or weapons-grade material to gain an extraordinary advantage over the rest of the world.

3. *Even if it cannot be total, the goal should be disarmament rather than arms control.* The objective of nuclear-weapons policy should not be solely to decrease the number of weapons in the world, but to make the world safer—which is not necessarily the same thing. World War I broke out largely because of an arms race, and World War II because of the lack of an arms race. Similarly, many scenarios for the outbreak of nuclear war which are now "implausible" would become "not implausible" or possibly even "plausible" if the existing U.S. and Soviet nuclear arsenals were reduced to very small, less intimidating, and probably more vulnerable forces.

Developments that contribute to a safer world need not be the result of negotiations to reduce the number of nuclear weapons. For example, between 1967 and 1983, the number of weapons in the U.S. nuclear stockpile actually declined by 30 percent. The aggregate megatonnage in the stockpile declined by 75 percent between 1960 and 1983. These changes are attributable more to narrow military considerations (e.g., improvements in delivery accuracies diminished the utility of multi-megaton warheads in many missions) than to arms-control influences. Nonetheless, the drop in the number of weapons and total explosive yield did lessen some of the dangers associated with nuclear war. Appropriate arms control could increase the trend toward decreased megatonnage and even toward fewer weapons, but unwise disarmament could set it back.

4. *There should be a total nuclear freeze.* A total nuclear freeze is counterproductive—especially now, when technology is rapidly changing and the Soviets have some important strategic advantages. An effective and verifiable freeze would worsen the U.S. position by "institutionalizing" apparent Soviet military superiority, and no freeze would be reliably verifiable, despite many claims to the contrary. More important, a freeze would prevent agreement on better arms-control measures by eliminating the incentive for useful negotiations and for the development of beneficial technology.

In fact, the most important reason for rejecting a freeze is that much of the weapons technology ahead is, relatively speaking, beneficial. Many people seem to believe that any change in weapons technology has to be for the worse, but that is demonstrably untrue. For example, almost all military analysts agree that the change from bombers to missiles in the early and mid-1960s made the world safer, since at that time missiles were much less vulnerable and accident-prone than the bombers. In addition, a freeze would preclude many adjustments and refinements that could make existing systems and forces safer. Nuclear-arms reductions or trade-offs are unlikely to take place under a freeze, but if our objective is to make the world safer, we must have the option of increasing, decreasing, or changing forces to achieve this goal.

As a first step toward a bilateral nuclear freeze, some antinuclear activists urge a unilateral halt to the development, testing, and deployment of U.S. nuclear forces. They believe this token of good faith will induce reciprocal restraint by the Soviet Union. Such support for a unilateral U.S. freeze betrays a gross ignorance of the history of the U.S.-Soviet arms competition for the last decade and a half.

From 1967 to 1983, the numbers of U.S. intercontinental ballistic missiles (ICBMs) and submarine-launched ballistic missiles (SLBMs) remained relatively constant, declining somewhat in the late 1970s and early 1980s. The number of U.S. strategic bombers decreased by 60 percent. During the same period, the number of Soviet ICBMs and SLBMs drew even with and then surpassed the inventories of U.S. ICBMs and SLBMs, while the size of the Soviet long-range bomber force grew slightly. In addition, the Soviets were very active in modernizing their strategic ballistic missile force. Over the sixteen-year period, the United States introduced two new or modified types of ICBMs; the Soviets fielded thirteen. The United States fielded two new or modified SLBMs; the Soviets deployed ten.

When in 1980 NATO withdrew one thousand theater nuclear weapons from Europe, in part to show good faith toward the upcoming negotiations on intermediate-range nuclear forces, no one paid much attention—least of all the Soviets. They increased, rather than decreased, the number of nuclear warheads trained on Western Europe. In short, the Soviets find it less than morally and psychologically compelling to match any unilateral U.S. efforts to dampen the arms competition. A unilateral freeze would most likely be exploited by the Soviets to augment their margin of military advantage over the United States and its allies.

But assuming a freeze were negotiated, it would not prevent either side from working on nonnuclear systems (e.g., modernized air defense networks, improved capabilities for antisubmarine warfare) which would not be frozen. Both parties would also have to worry about a technological "breakthrough" or a "breakout" by the other side.[1] Each side could justify its own attempt to achieve a breakthrough and then a breakout by "discovering" that the other side was cheating. New nuclear and nonnuclear systems could both be made extraordinarily effective against an opponent whose current systems were frozen.

As a political maneuver, the call for a nuclear freeze has turned out to be an effective way of telling national leaders in the West that something must be done to allay public fears of nuclear war. But it has also been counterproductive by sending Soviet decision-makers the message that they can gain more by manipulating Western public opinion than by making genuine attempts at arms control. As a national policy, however, there is simply no case for a freeze.

5. *Deterrence must be made 100 percent reliable.* This is a nonissue simply because there is no way to make any complex human (let alone technical) system 100 percent effective.

6. *Deterrence must fail eventually, and probably will fail totally.* There is no way we can ignore this possibility. But many doomsayers argue that since it might fail, it eventually has to fail. This is technically incorrect, but not entirely unreasonable (unless it assumes that the failure must be total). My guess is that nuclear weapons will be used sometime in the next hundred years, but that their use is much more likely to be small and limited than widespread and unconstrained.

Deterrence would then have failed—but not totally. This is why the following points are so important.

7. *Useful "damage limitation" in a nuclear war is infeasible;* or

8. *One can achieve totally reliable damage limitation.* If counterforce attacks and strategic defenses[2] could reduce damage in a nuclear war to, perhaps, 10 million to 40 million deaths instead of the 50 million to 100 million that might occur in their absence, and if various other measures could improve the effectiveness and rapidity of recovery from a nuclear war, then they would be worth the effort. Some people believe that the development of such capabilities would be reckless because they would encourage U.S. complacency about nuclear war and U.S. risk-taking in crises, and/or excessive Soviet fears which would lead them to preempt a U.S. strike. Others believe systems and operations intended for damage limitation must be made foolproof to be worthwhile.

There is no such thing here as total reliability, but if appropriate efforts could mitigate the effects of a nuclear war, then perhaps even an unprecedented catastrophe would not be a total disaster. There are many contexts in which even marginally effective damage-limitation programs might be very effective.

The usual discussion about counterforce wars and strategic defenses does not recognize this in-between position, i.e., that some reduction is better than none and that efforts to limit damage will not produce a material increase in the likelihood of nuclear war. I would argue that it is immoral for a nation not to take at least the relatively simple and inexpensive measures it can to achieve an "improved war outcome" in the event that deterrence fails.

9. *A nuclear war can be reliably limited;* or

10. *There is no possibility of a limited war.* No one can guarantee that either of these predictions would accurately describe an actual nuclear war. In

some circumstances, some kinds of limited nuclear war are clearly possible. There are very large and very clear "firebreaks" between nuclear and conventional war. In nuclear war, the primary firebreak might be "no attacks on the homeland," the next might be "no attacks on cities," and so on. Both sides may choose to observe these firebreaks, though no one can absolutely guarantee they will. But one also cannot be sure they will be totally flouted.

11. *There can be no victory in nuclear war* (i.e., "nobody wins a suicide pact"), or

12. *Either the United States or the Soviet Union could rely on victory.* These issues have become a morality test: to say that "a nuclear war might be limited" or that "there might be a victor in a nuclear war" is to label oneself as a nuclear war hawk (one who seeks to start a nuclear war) or a defender of similarly monstrous positions. To me, it is outrageous to make a morality test out of a realistic and important observation—and both of the quoted remarks are realistic and important.

It is incorrect to say that victory in nuclear war is impossible. It is especially possible if either side, or both, have low levels of nuclear forces that are vulnerable to destruction through creative or clever enemy tactics. Unfortunately, it is even quite conceivable at current levels of nuclear armament—but neither nation is likely to choose to go to war just because it has developed some ingenious war plan that might work; the risk is too frightening, and the present governments on both sides are too prudent and cautious. However, that differs from saying that victory could not happen. Indeed, some reasonable facsimile of victory could be achieved even by a nation forced into war. The Soviets, for example, won the war started by Nazi Germany despite suffering 20 million deaths and losing a quarter of their capital stock.

It is unwise to judge realistic analyses and preparations as a lust for war. There are no two sides to the nuclear debate: no one is "for" war; everyone is against it—some categorically so and others only to the degree that it does not result in an even less desirable alternative.

These twelve "nonissues" are important because many of them are deeply held beliefs and reflect genuine concerns. But they offer no substantive guidance in dealing with nuclear dangers, cannot be translated into constructive programs, and often stand in the way of serious discussions of useful and necessary programs.

TWELVE ALMOST NONISSUES

One step removed from these "nonissues" are twelve propositions that are equally popular, widely held, and emotionally defended, but offer almost as little practical guidance on how to make the world safer from the threat of nuclear war. The difference is that while we are comfortable in our belief that the first twelve are truly irrelevant, we are not as sure about these (i.e., they involve a "Scotch verdict").

1. *Nuclear war would result in the destruction of the created order,* and/or

2. *Nuclear war would result in the destruction of all human life.* There are no respectable objective analyses or calculations to indicate that either of these is likely. But the data and theory are so lacking one cannot be absolutely certain. From a scientific perspective there is some indication that a nuclear war could deplete the earth's ozone layer or, less likely, could bring on a new Ice Age—but there is no suggestion that either the created order or mankind would be destroyed in the process. From a religious perspective these assertions are almost heretical, since only God can fashion or destroy the universe (but some believe that He may choose nuclear war as His means of doing so). As a practical matter, however, these concerns do not offer any useful policy guidelines.

3. *The threat of a nuclear war would mean "everybody Red, dead, or neutral."* In Europe, when the only alternatives were presented as "Red" or "dead," the obvious choice was "Red." However, sophisticated Europeans are now formulating the choice to include "everybody neutral." A further revision of the slogan—"everybody Red, dead, neutral, or NATO"—is much more reasonable. Indeed, the purpose of the Atlantic Alliance is to make the last option the most attractive one.

4. *Nuclear weapons are intrinsically immoral.* Nuclear war is such an emotional subject that many people see the weapons themselves as the common enemy of humanity. Nuclear weapons are intrinsically neither moral nor immoral, though they are more prone to immoral use than most weapons. But they can be used to accomplish moral objectives and can do this in ways that are morally acceptable. The most obvious and important way is to use them or their availability to deter others from using nuclear weapons. The second—of much lower, but still significant priority—is to use them to help limit the damage (human, social, political, economic, and military) that could occur if deterrence fails. Anything that reduces war-related destruction should not be considered altogether immoral.

On the other hand, the position that nuclear weapons are "just another" weapon and therefore as moral as any other is not accurate either. I would judge them as moral when used solely to balance, deter, or correct for the possession or use of nuclear weapons by others, and immoral when deliberately used against civilians, for positive gains, or to save money and effort on nonnuclear military alternatives. This rule precludes the first use of nuclear weapons to defend Western Europe (current NATO policy), simply to avoid the more complicated capabilities, plans, and costs required for improved conventional defenses. It likewise stamps as immoral the targeting of enemy cities simply to avoid the problems of counterforce weapons and attack planning (countercity targeting is endorsed by many supporters of the nuclear freeze).

It is unacceptable, in terms of national security, to make nonuse of nuclear weapons the highest national priority to which all other considerations must be subordinated. It is immoral from almost any point of view to refuse to defend yourself and others from very grave and terrible threats, even as there are limits to the means that can be used in such defense.

5. *Expenditures for strategic nuclear forces are bankrupting the United States and the Soviet Union.* U.S. strategic expenditures are now less than one-tenth of 1 percent of the gross national product (and have been less than 2 percent for almost two decades), while Soviet expenditures are probably about 2 percent of the Soviet GNP. The cost of U.S. strategic forces represents only about 10 percent of total U.S. military expenditures; roughly 15–20 percent of the Soviets' defense budget is allocated to strategic forces. So while reducing the cost of arms is a desirable goal, it is simply not an overriding priority in terms of bringing about a dramatic turnaround in U.S. fiscal solvency.

6. *Defense expenditures should be reallocated to the poor.* A healthy and fully functioning society must allocate its resources among a variety of competing interests, all of which are more or less valid but none of which should take precedence over national security. This is not an argument for papering over instances of wasteful or excessive spending in the Department of Defense, but simply a recognition that national security programs have a legitimate and fundamental claim on the nation's resources. Furthermore, even if defense expenditures were cut, the savings would be divided along the lines of current federal fiscal allocations. Only those who are ideologically opposed to military programs think of the defense budget as the first and best place to get resources for social welfare needs.

7. *"War-fighting" measures are simultaneously too ineffective and too effective,* and

8. *"Deterrence only" is the least undesirable policy; any "war-fighting" policy is fatally flawed.* As used by most strategists, "deterrence only" implies an all-or-nothing strategy: first, a very strong belief that deterrence can and must be made to work for the foreseeable future, and second, that if it fails we are all doomed—because the cities on both sides would be deliberately and automatically destroyed at the outset of a war. The policy of "mutual assured destruction" (MAD) is the clearest form of "deterrence only."

It is often believed that any attempt to mitigate the damage a nuclear war would cause, or even to reinforce deterrence with "war-fighting" capabilities, is "destabilizing" or a waste of resources. For its supporters, a "deterrence-only" policy offers a simple, clear and, by itself, unaggressive "solution" to the threat of nuclear war. But the term "war fighting" does not mean one wants to fight a war: the position simply recognizes that deterrence can fail and says that it is prudent to have programs both to reinforce deterrence and to alleviate such failure should it occur. As I will argue later in more detail, these efforts are likely to be effective enough to be worthwhile (i.e., they could have a positive effect on the course and outcome of a war), but would not be likely to cause or contribute to an appreciable increase in the risk of war.

9. *No significant weakening of deterrence is acceptable.* In most situations, some small "destabilizing" or weakening of deterrence is not likely to be significant. In some instances, an intentional weakening might be an acceptable part of a trade-off for other gains. For example, a minor and relatively insignificant decrease in deterrence would be justified if it would bring about an enormous reduction in the damage done if deterrence failed. Deterrence itself is not a preeminent value: the primary values are safety and morality.

10. *If retention of nuclear weapons is unavoidable, then "simplistic stability" is preferable to "multistability."* If we recognize nuclear deterrence as a means toward attaining a safer overall security environment, then simplistic stability (stability only against a first strike) should not be the sole objective of strategic forces. In fact, it is not the only mission of U.S. forces: their purpose is multistability—i.e., to deter serious provocations against the United States (and its allies), as well as to prevent an actual first strike.

Multistable deterrence imposes much more stringent—and necessary—requirements on our strategic forces than simple deterrence. While the U.S. can no longer have the kind of extended deterrence that covers all areas where provocation is possible, it still needs a "not-completely-incredible" ability to punish an opponent for a variety of (extreme) provocations.

11. *Nuclear war would be fought mainly to achieve positive gains.* Both the Soviet Union and the United States are essentially very prudent and cautious—the Soviets probably even more than the Americans—and both are unlikely to risk a nuclear war for positive gains (i.e., to fulfill or advance national or personal ambitions), even if they think they can do it successfully. Neither the United States nor the Soviet Union believes in "war by calculation" (i.e., planned and carried out as scheduled), but rather by miscalculation (plans always go awry). Calculated wars have not worked in either country's history, leading both to the realization that even theoretically sound plans are almost certain to go astray. Consequently, only desperation could persuade the leadership of either country to initiate a nuclear war.

The belief that war has become virtually obsolete as an instrument for advancing positive ambitions (as opposed to averting disaster) is not completely the result of nuclear deterrence. It is also because, increasingly, the most effective and reliable way to achieve affluence, power, influence, status, and prestige is through economic development, and not through territorial or political gains. While war between two major powers may still be an important way for one or both of them to avoid what appear to be more severe alternatives (e.g., for the Soviet Union, the loss of political control), primarily it has become largely dysfunctional. And yet, maintaining a credible (or "not incredible") capability to resort to nuclear war remains basic to an adequate defense and foreign policy.

12. *Normally, there is an automatic and increasingly dangerous "arms race."* This concept is plausible and has sometimes been accurate—for example, the arms race preceding the outbreak of World War I. Post–World War II history has witnessed some automatic increases in armaments. New developments in weapon systems during the 1950s and early 1960s created a situation that was most dangerous, and even conducive to accidental war. In retrospect, we were fortunate that none occurred.

However, it appears that in both the United States and the Soviet Union the radical development of military technology since World War II has been a greater engine of weapons development than has any sense of detailed measure/countermeasure competition. A careful study of the development of Soviet and American strategic weapons suggests that in almost all cases weapons were developed in conformity with strategic and technological thinking that took remarkably little account of the other side's real or likely programs and other strengths and weaknesses. If each side must more or less commit itself to a weapon system as much as ten to fifteen years before it enters service in any quantity, then there is little chance that the concepts being developed in one country will serve as a guide for the other.

The world became much less dangerous in the 1960s because of improvements in equipment (e.g., submarine-launched ballistic missiles—SLBMs), tactics (e.g., alert procedures), and thinking (e.g., planning for limited counterforce campaigns). But even with advances in U.S. and Soviet weaponry and defense planning, there was no "arms race." For example, from 1963 to 1980, the U.S. defense budget was more or less constant (if computed in constant dollars, except for the operational expenses of the Vietnam War), while the Soviet budget increased by 4 or 5 percent a year—about the rate of increase for the Soviet GNP.

More accurate than the "race" metaphor is the observation that if it was a contest at all, the Americans walked while the Soviets trotted. There was no race—but to the extent that there was an arms competition, it was almost entirely on the Soviet side, first to catch up and then to surpass the

Americans. The United States barely competed: except for some retrofitting (e.g., equipping ICBMs and SLBMs with multiple warheads), the U.S. defense establishment languished. The present controversy over the expense and morality of "rearming" the United States is a result of two decades of a very lax U.S. defense effort; the controversy could largely have been avoided if a consistent pace and pattern of defense preparedness had been maintained all along. The United States and the world would be much safer today, and the current anxiety-provoking defense program would not be necessary. But even this recent attempt to redress the balance is very different from being involved in an inevitable and increasingly dangerous "arms race." In fact, as discussed later, many of the innovations in defense that we expect over the next decade or two are as likely as not to make the world safer.

The accuracy of these twelve oft-cited assertions is, then, dubious at best. Those who uncritically accept their validity are less likely to help make the world safer from the threat of nuclear war than those who question them. So while we doubt that these "givens" are relevant to government policy, they are less irrelevant than the first set of commonly held assumptions.

NOTES

1. In general, "breakout" involves the relatively sudden, explicit, and unilateral abrogation of an arms control agreement through the fielding of new or additional weapons that had been constrained by the broken treaty. With the illegal deployment, the violator hopes to gain significant military advantages or political.

2. "Counterforce" attacks are strikes directed against the enemy's military assets (e.g., land-based missiles, bombers, command-and-control facilities). "Strategic defenses" are systems providing protection against nuclear attack. Ballistic missile defense and air defense systems are "active" defenses; civil defense measures are "passive" defenses.

3

The Revolution in Warfare: Continuities and Discontinuities

This chapter considers some of the most important ways in which nuclear weapons have and have not changed the theory and practice of modern warfare and defense planning. We begin by noting that the idea that a "revolution" in warfare has taken place is imprecise; it gives the impression that the changes caused by the development of nuclear weapons occurred all at once. In fact, from 1945 to 1982, there were many "revolutions" in the technology and policies of nuclear warfare, bringing about changes as great as those that occurred between the Civil War and World War I, or between World War I and World War II.

The most fundamental of these "revolutions" clearly involves nuclear warheads and the increased efficiency in kilotons deliverable per pound of payload, going from .002 kt/lb for the Hiroshima bomb to a reported 2 kt/lb in the mid-1970s—a factor of 1,000 in thirty years, or ten in every decade, or more than three every five years. There have also been spectacular developments in ballistic missile technology, missile accuracy, nuclear submarines, antiballistic missile capabilities, cruise missiles, and so on. Piled one on top of the other, this progression has been so continuous it has appeared almost evolutionary.

The invention and development of nuclear weapons signaled the onset of the "nuclear era," but these revolutionary accomplishments would not have been nearly as dramatic had it not been for the many nonnuclear technological developments occurring at the same time. The debate over

---

[*Thinking about the Unthinkable in the 1980s* (New York: Simon & Schuster, 1984).]

precisely what and how much has changed in the nuclear era, and how much of the prenuclear military wisdom is still valid, does not usually allow for the "mixed" position we take. Some students of military science argue that nothing much has changed from the days of the Greeks and the Romans—that war is still war, and its basic principles are the same; in particular, the objective is to defeat the enemy and compel him to surrender or otherwise accede to your demands. To accomplish this, a nation employs many of the same tactics and strategies that nations have always used. The opposing argument holds that traditional military concerns with the detailed strategies and tactics of conflict are irrelevant in the nuclear age; they claim that the only valid strategy today is total deterrence of war.

An extreme variation of the first position compares strategic forces today with the six-gun fighter epitomized in an earlier culture of the American West—whoever draws first and fires accurately still wins. An extreme variation of the other view is illustrated by the metaphor of two scorpions in a bottle—the inevitable result of a struggle is mutual suicide. Such phrases as "nobody wins a suicide pact," and "mutual assured destruction" are the typical rhetoric of this last position.

We believe that both of the above positions are largely incorrect or out of perspective. There are significant continuities with prenuclear warfare that military planners must still consider. But there are also significant differences that will influence developments in military procurement, doctrine, strategy, and tactics. In particular, we believe there is perhaps even more to be learned about the potential use of nuclear force in terms of the historical role of war than about any new uses of conflict. More than ever, there are lessons in the application of the nuclear threat "as a continuation of politics/policy by other means" (Clausewitz) and as an instrument for advancing the national interest by deploying military forces, though some important caveats and modification are needed.

If this discussion appears biased in favor of the continuities (rather than the differences) between the nuclear and prenuclear era, it is because the Western world has generally adopted such an intense belief in the discontinuities. Most people simply accept as obvious the idea that a nuclear war would be the end of history, and that it is therefore unproductive (or even counterproductive) to think creatively about strategy and tactics. From this perspective, thermonuclear weapons are the equivalent of the doomsday machine, an attitude that, while exaggerated, highlights one of the most fundamental changes between the prenuclear and nuclear eras— the unprecedented destructive potential of nuclear warfare.

A nuclear war, even if limited in scope, could easily cause between 10 and 50 million immediate fatalities, plus millions more wounded or ill. Such casualty levels have been reached before, but over a long period of time and among many nations (the estimated number of military and civilian fatalities during World War II was approximately 50 million). Coping with such huge numbers of casualties all at once would place tremendous (and unprecedented) strains on the resources and very fabric of society. Moreover, since these figures are estimated only from the known effects of nuclear explosions, it is possible that unknown and unanticipated effects could make damage even greater.

Uncertainty is another significant new development of the nuclear age—the creation of weapons whose unknown effects may be more important, and more harmful, than the known ones. Except for Hiroshima, Nagasaki, and a limited number of nuclear tests, we have no recent or actual experience from which to make judgments or assessments regarding the use of these weapons, especially on the scale (thousands of megatons) that would be involved in a major war.

Because of the concentrated destructive power and instantaneous impact of nuclear weapons, the question of how a nuclear war begins is an important factor in determining its ultimate destructiveness. The initiation of the conflict is also a critical determinant of whether the attacked society can survive and ultimately recover. This, too, is a change from past eras when the outbreak of hostilities had little bearing on the war itself. If a nuclear attack were to come out of the blue, without any warning or opportunity for evacuation or other civil defense measures, the casualty figures could be far greater than if a nation's citizens were given time and opportunity to protect themselves. If a war were preceded by a period of heightened tensions or even conventional conflict, and if government leaders either officially ordered an evacuation of major urban centers or people spontaneously decided to take their own precautions, casualties could be reduced significantly.

The fear of nuclear weapons has prompted many dramatic slogans and rallies (as well as many fallacies and myths). In 1955, fifty-two Nobel Prize winners signed their names to the so-called Mainau Declaration, which stated that "All nations must come to the decision to renounce force or war as a final resort of policy. If they are not prepared to do so they will cease to exist." Such positions summed up the typical Western view that nuclear warfare was "unthinkable," and that the very survival of mankind was at stake as never before. A not uncommon thought, even among military generals, was that "if these buttons are ever pressed, they have completely failed in their purpose. The equipment is useful only if it is not used." [. . .]

All efforts, in other words, must be on prevention; none on fighting a war should prevention fail. Not surprisingly, advocates of this view believe that military preparations are stupid and dangerous. They scoff at attempts to reduce wartime casualties from, say, 100 million to 50 million, believing that any casualty level in that range is "unacceptable" and that the only acceptable option is the total elimination of war. They may disagree over which policies can best achieve this, but they share a horror and distrust for scenarios that suggest there could be a nuclear war in which one or both sides emerged with damage no greater than that suffered in wars of the prenuclear age.

Another position, which is not completely dissimilar but is much more acceptable to us, contends that in a reasonable world, the only rational and moral role for nuclear weapons is to deter, balance, and/or correct for the possession and/or use of nuclear weapons by an opponent. Unfortunately, the conclusion drawn from this defendable (if controversial) position often "degenerates" into a much less defensible assertion: that the only way to deter the use of nuclear weapons is through some form of mutual assured destruction. This deterrence-only position is actually quite close to that of the pacifists who also believe that war can be rationally eliminated—the former believe the constraint is fear, the latter believe it is a profound abhorrence of violence in any form. Both hope that the world eventually will disarm completely, but neither takes that possibility very seriously.

It is generally acknowledged that in the unlikely event nuclear weapons did become generally unavailable, a nation that somehow retained even a single weapon would represent a terrible threat to the rest of the world. Consequently, some supporters of disarmament simultaneously support a world government that would have a monopoly on nuclear weapons. The practical problems of this alternative, namely, the possibility that such a government itself could become oppressive, or could be taken over by an oppressive group, are rarely considered.

Another argument frequently made by nuclear pacifists and/or supporters of deterrence only is that war has become an inappropriate way to resolve international disputes in the nuclear age and an age of economic and technological interdependence. Modern developments have either obviated, lessened, or made transitory the strategic value of many geographic areas; nations can rarely gain wealth, commercial advantage, or political security by attacking a neighbor and conquering its territory. (The Middle East and to some degree the Soviet bloc nations, may be exceptions to the rule.) Power, prestige, and influence are today attained primarily through successful economic development, not through military might or aggressive expansion.

While all of the above observations are true, the pacifist conclusion that "war never pays" is simply not correct. Wars have paid and paid handsomely in the past and could again in the future. In addition, the mere belief in an ultimate world without war does little to help resolve the tensions and strains of the current international system. To arrive at any kind of utopian accommodation in the future, we still have to get through the rocky and unstable 1980s and 1990s and had best be prepared to do so.

Deterrence-only positions can be dangerous. The most obvious question is—what happens if deterrence fails? Equally troublesome is what happens if there is a significant imbalance in the reliance on deterrence—if one potential adversary believes in it much more strongly than the other? One of the biggest changes of the nuclear era is that such fundamental philosophical differences about the nature of war can exist—differences about its prevention, its consequences, and its likely outcome. Based on the available evidence, it seems clear that the Soviet Union does not accept the West's apocalyptic view of nuclear war, nor do they support deterrence-only policies. Soviet military writings depict nuclear war as a survivable experience, and back up their reliance on deterrence with war-fighting capabilities, that is, the ability to fight a nuclear war and defeat the enemy.

Yet a belief in deterrence—including reliance on some degree of unilateral restraint in the acquisition, deployment, and role of nuclear weapons—has been a great deal more successful than most "realists" thought it could be (realists tend to discount the importance of voluntary unilateral restraint). [. . .]

Deterrence has become the most basic politico-military strategy of the nuclear era. Bernard Brodie recognized that in the past the chief purpose of our military establishment was to win wars: "From now on its chief purpose must be to avert them" (*The Absolute Weapon*, 1946, p. 76). To be meaningful, however, deterrence must take place in a specific context: who deters whom, from what actions, by what threats and counteractions, in what situations, in the face of what counterthreats and counter-counteractions? Some analysts argue that since we can do unacceptable damage to the Soviet Union, they will not provoke us; in fact, the Soviets may be able to deter our response to their provocation through threats or counteractions.

Deterrence, therefore, is not just a matter of military capabilities; it has a great deal to do with perceptions of credibility, i.e., the other side's estimates of one's determination, courage, and national objectives. For example, in the early days of the nuclear era, the British nuclear force probably could have inflicted much greater damage to the Soviet Union in either a first or second strike than the Soviet Union could have inflicted on the United States in a first or second strike. However, we are reasonably sure the Soviets were not too concerned about the British, whereas we were very concerned about the Soviets. The reasons, of course, have very little to do with theoretical military capabilities—they are a function of political realities. If the enemy is (correctly) convinced that you will not use your weapons, then it does not matter how sophisticated or powerful your weapons are. In many cases it is what allies and others think, or what they think the main opponents think, or what the opponents think the allies and others think, and so on, that is decisive.

This issue of perception and credibility often comes up in reference to the American commitment to NATO to deter a Soviet conventional attack on Europe through the threat of strategic retaliation. While the U.S. is clearly capable of such a response, it is increasingly doubtful that the United States would actually resort to nuclear weapons. The force of U.S. deterrence in Western Europe has therefore been substantially undermined by a visible weakening of U.S. resolve, a weakening clearly related to the buildup of Soviet intercontinental offensive forces, hence a revision in the strategic balance. Yet the Soviets still could not be "sure" that we would refrain from strategic retaliation, an uncertainty that would probably be sufficient to deter the Soviets from an attack on Western Europe.

The emphasis on deterrence in the nuclear age has led to a decline in the study and formulation of appropriate strategies and tactics for using the special qualities of nuclear weapons in guaranteeing the security of the U.S. When the atom bomb was first invented, many people felt that military strategy and tactics had virtually become obsolete since the inevitable result of a nuclear war would be world destruction, and that destruction would occur no matter what tactics were used. Tactical theory was therefore considered irrelevant. In addition, since the annihilation of the nation or the world could not be a national objective (strategy), strategy has become equally irrelevant. Clausewitz's concept of war as an instrument of foreign policy was no longer valid if war would destroy humanity.

The invention of the atomic bomb, therefore, seemed to end any constructive thinking about strategy and tactics. Nuclear war was simply unthinkable—both literally and figuratively.

This phenomenon, known as psychological denial, meant that while one side (ours) did little or no thinking about nuclear weapons, the other side simply regarded them as "bigger bombs," or "higher-quality weapons," and also did not undertake any fundamental rethinking of classical political and strategic assumptions. Indeed, on both the U.S. and Soviet sides, strategic concepts and tactics remained almost identical to those used in World War II. Attempts were made to correct the mistakes of World War II (e.g., the Strategic Bombing Survey prompted the selection of power stations as high-priority targets), but these "corrections" merely emphasized the absence of any new and creative thinking about the possible military value of nuclear weapons.

In the early 1950s strategic thinking had a partial revival. There was some discussion of the options open to a potential nuclear attacker—threats the attacker might make, tactics he might use if the threats failed, and the counteroptions available to the defender. For a time, the discussion reached a relatively high level of sophistication as it considered mixtures and levels of active and passive defense and of counterforce and counter value targeting. But not for long. Strategic considerations came to an abrupt conclusion with the development of the H-bomb, which seemed so close to being a doomsday weapon that the details of war fighting really were irrelevant. Multimegaton weapons appeared to be unusable for any rational (and most irrational) purposes. There seemed to be no need for further strategic thinking.

In a well-known article, "Strategy Hits a Dead End," Bernard Brodie wrote:

> In a world still unprepared to relinquish the use of military power, we must learn to effect that use through methods that are something other than self-destroying. The task will be bafflingly difficult at best, but it can only begin with the clear recognition that most of the military ideas and axioms of the past are now or soon will be inapplicable. The old concepts of strategy . . . have come to a dead end. (*Harper's* magazine, October 1955)

If anything, this position has become more extreme over time. A more recent commentator expressed much the same position:

> . . . the sheer destructiveness of nuclear war has invalidated any distinction between winning and losing. Thus, it has rendered meaningless the very idea of military strategy as the efficient deployment of force to achieve a State's objectives. . . . (Leon Sigal, "Rethinking the Unthinkable," *Foreign Policy*, Spring 1979)

We would argue that both statements are incorrect. While both Brodie and Sigal admit that nuclear forces can and should be deployed for political and military purposes, they have difficulty seeing how a central nuclear war could achieve any policy objectives.

We believe the need remains for coherent and credible nuclear-use policies, including the need for clear and imaginative tactics. Terrible as nuclear weapons are, they exist and therefore may be used. Even if they are used only as a threat, such threats, if credible, in themselves represent a kind of use. When we deter the Soviets by the threat of escalation if they provoke a limited war, we are in fact using the potential application of our nuclear weapons. Even pure deterrence-only policies "use" nuclear weapons in the attempt to institutionalize a mutual paralysis through fear.

Military and civilian professionals understandably find it very difficult to deal with the impact of nuclear weapons on the actual waging of war and the handling of international crises. The uncertainty about nuclear war means that many alternatives and options have to be considered in the abstract. In addition, the complexity of nuclear issues and the awareness of the potential physical and political devastation caused by nuclear weapons have caused many strategic planners to opt out. But this is a mistake.

While nuclear weapons have certainly changed the ways in which wars will be initiated, fought, and won, they do not necessarily make war obsolete. As far as we can calculate, no plausible employment of current and likely future weapon systems would result in the end of the world or the end of the human race or anything close to it. But the fact that we have to add the caveat "as far as we can calculate"—and such phrases as "plausible employment" and "likely future weapon systems" is another example of how much has changed since these weapons were created. Nuclear weapons can do more damage than any other weapons in history, particularly if used in large quantities and in uncontrolled fashion.

But consider the possibility—both menacing and perversely comforting— that even if 300 million people were killed in a nuclear war, there would still be more than 4 billion people left alive. Studies of the likely casualty rates of nuclear conflict range from less than a million to some tens of millions (unless the war is totally uncontrolled, in which case the casualties might reach hundreds of millions). The worst-case scenarios of hundreds of millions dead and widespread destruction would be an unprecedented global calamity, but not necessarily the end of history. And a power that attains significant strategic superiority is likely to survive the war, perhaps even "win" it, by extending its hegemony—at least for a time—over much of the world. Indeed, throughout history there have been leaders who were willing to pay a great cost in national wealth and lives for a chance to take over the world.

While almost no one would take the position that thermonuclear weapons are "just another" advance in the technology of warfare, it is important to realize that these weapons, like others, may be fired. Accordingly, we would like to argue that one of the most important continuities of the nuclear era is that wars can still be fought, terminated, and survived. Some countries will win a nuclear conflict and others will lose, and it is even possible that some nuclear wars may ultimately have positive results (as World War II did). Reconstruction will begin, life will continue, and most survivors will not envy the dead. (Inhabitants of a country that loses a nuclear war and is very badly treated by the winner might envy the dead, but this, too, is nothing new in man's history.) It is important for people to continue to think of war as an experience that can be survived and recovered from if proper preparations are made, and important for national leaders to recognize that they will be judged by how well they exercise their responsibility to help their country prevail.

Like wars of the past, the extent and duration of nuclear wars could differ greatly, depending largely on the causes of the war and its political objectives. Nuclear war will not necessarily be an all-out strategic exchange, with each side firing most or all of its arsenal in a single spasm of destruction. It could well be limited, either by region and theater of battle or by constraints (either self-imposed or coerced) on the number of weapons used and/or the targets attacked. A conflict in the Middle East or Europe involving battlefield nuclear weapons would be a nuclear war, but would not be comparable to a nuclear war involving large-scale strategic strikes by the U.S. or Soviet Union against each other's territory. These two extremes, and the range of possibilities in between, require entirely different resources, planning, and preparations. None of them should be totally neglected if the U.S. expects to defend itself and its interests adequately.

Another similarity with wars of the past is that a nuclear conflict could occur over an extended period of time. History provides examples of extremely short wars (the Austro-Prussian War of 1866, the Arab-Israeli Six Day War of 1967) as well as extremely long ones (the Thirty Years War, the Hundred Years War and, though less prolonged, the two World Wars). The standard picture of nuclear war envisions a conflict of only a few hours or days, but it is possible that a war could last weeks or perhaps months. In fact, a number of military analysts are now arguing that a prolonged or protracted conflict with limited exchanges of nuclear weapons, followed by periods of bargaining and struggle for supremacy in limited theaters of operations, is a more realistic scenario. These analysts argue that neither side will use its entire strategic force in an initial attack, preferring to maintain a reserve force for post attack contingencies.

This new conception of nuclear war raises questions of command and control, as well as other aspects of endurance. It is not clear that strategic forces can be operated in a controlled and flexible manner in a poststrategic nuclear attack environment, nor is it clear that the forces can be maintained at high alert levels for long periods of time. However, the point we wish to emphasize is simply that, as with wars of the past, nuclear wars could last longer than generally imagined.

But issues of war fighting, termination, and recovery are much more complicated in the nuclear era than ever before. To a degree that really is unprecedented, the analysis of these issues depends on the examination of many different factors, as shown in table 3.1. In order to argue persuasively that it is possible to fight nuclear war, to survive, and to rebuild, one must be willing to argue that it is possible to handle every one of these issues in some adequate, or at least minimal, fashion. Many sober, competent, and distinguished observers claim this cannot be done, but what most of them probably mean is that they foresee terrible difficulties or problems in dealing with these issues. That is not the same as saying with certainty that survival is not an option.

An examination of the issues in table 3.1 should make clear why so much attention is paid to the range of uncertainty regarding the outcome of a nuclear war. The unknowns can both increase and decrease the leverage of nuclear threats in peacetime negotiations. Stressing the dangers of escalation and the need for restraint by the opponent becomes a standard tactic. But is also reassures the weaker side that the stronger side is not likely to put great faith in the flawless execution of its plans; there is no track record of the weapons working reliably. Thus, it is often pointed out that war planning (a) must deal persuasively and convincingly with every point raised in table 3.1; (b) will necessarily be both a difficult and complex process; and (c) is still likely to be highly speculative because of the uncertainties.

One typical ploy in a potential nuclear crisis is for one of the negotiators to point out the insanity of subjecting the entire world to the risks of nuclear war, regardless of the importance of the issues at stake to the two countries involved. Diplomats and military leaders have made antiwar arguments in the past, but the global dangers and risks are much greater in the nuclear age. The negotiator can urge a reasonable resolution by

---

Table 3.1. How Many Survivors? Would They Envy the Dead?

1. Prewar preparations (including lack of realistic "hands-on" experience)
2. Outbreak scenario
3. Immediate weapons effects such as:
   A. Blast and prompt radiation
   B. Thermal radiation and fire
   C. Acute effects of fallout, electromagnetic pulse, earth shock, etc., and the likelihood of some unexpected weapons effects (including difficult operational problems)
4. War-fighting and war-termination scenario
5. Postwar scenario:
   A. Reorganization period (including role of neutrals and developing countries)
   B. Medium-term environmental problems
   C. Rate and character of recuperation
   D. Social and political changes
6. Long-term effects:
   A. Medical aftereffects
   B. Genetic effects
   C. Long-term environmental effects
   D. Long-term political and cultural changes

pointing out the disparity between some immediate crisis-prone "minor" issue and the almost infinite risks of a major war. Then he can suggest that "one of us has to be reasonable, and it isn't going to be me." This could end the bargaining and lead to war if his opponent's response is, "It's not going to be me, either." Or it could lead to capitulation by the opponent who realizes that compromise, or concession, is the only sane option, especially if the balance of forces is not on his side.

Some analysts, however, argue that superiority in the balance of forces can easily be dismissed as irrelevant in a nuclear war. This is probably too glib. In particular, the side with the advantage can argue that his government spent a great deal of money on these forces, something it would not have done if it thought they were irrelevant. In fact, if one side firmly believes that it has significant superiority (whether or not it is actually true), then the perceived balance is indeed relevant. A successful negotiator must be able to persuade the other side (as well as his own allies and sometimes even neutrals) that he believes in his own superiority. One purpose of procuring nuclear forces is to be able to make such a point in a bargaining session, and one purpose of a bargaining session is to explain why one side should back down and not the other. The influence and importance of courage, commitment, morale, and perceptions of strength have not changed in the nuclear era.

And there may still be rational reasons for going to war in the nuclear age. Not all nuclear wars will be accidental, inadvertent, or unintended, though such wars are, of course, possible. In the prenuclear era, accidental war was not a realistic possibility; today it is. In the nuclear age, however, war may still result from many of the same causes for which wars have always been fought: For immediate national, ideological, or religious gains (where gains would outweigh possible costs, including consequences of mistakes, bad luck, and critical uncertainties); in the belief that long-range national, ideological, or religious prospects will be improved or for abstract motives such as glory, plunder, boredom, power. Under pressure to: (a) Preempt a potential first strike by the enemy; (b) Avert some other immediate disaster; (c) Resolve some ongoing but increasingly desperate crisis; (d) Avoid some long-range disaster by initiating a preventive war.

It is reasonably clear that the most likely reasons for a modern nuclear war are a or b above; indeed, these possibilities have been much discussed. Some observers also seem to believe that c and d are not unlikely, but there seems to be widespread agreement that ideological reasons recede into the background as a cause of nuclear war (but might play a critical role in tipping the balance when reasons listed in were not quite good enough by themselves). In that sense deterrence, especially deterrence because of uncertainty, seems to work quite well.

As noted earlier, few nations are likely to go to war for positive gain in the nuclear age. Wars are unlikely to be started deliberately, unless they result from efforts to avoid what is perceived as an even greater immediate disaster [. . .]. Nonetheless, in some cases war might still be viewed and/or used as a continuation of politics "by other means."

Although largely overlooked in modern defense planning, another continuity between the prenuclear and nuclear era is the potential value of a formal declaration of war. Such a declaration would make clear the extreme seriousness of the issue at stake without necessarily producing or requiring an immediate resort to armed conflict. But by keeping the casus belli open it would also prevent immediate de-escalation of the crisis. Once a war is formally declared, the crisis cannot be resolved until a peace treaty of some sort is signed. The resolution of the conflict remains pending until a response is made by the "wounded" party. A formal declaration of war could be an extremely important device for the U.S. if, for example, it were unable to respond effectively to serious aggression in a distant region. In such a case the U.S. would probably not want to initiate a nuclear war, but would want to declare its opposition and its determination to do something eventually. A formal declaration would give the U.S. time to mobilize its economy and its society.[1]

A declaration of war might be followed by a period of "phony wars" as happened in World War II. The U.S. and Soviet Union might, for example, have deployed their missile-carrying submarines, dispersed their strategic bomber forces, and placed their land-based missiles on high alert. An effective disarming counterforce attack would then be extremely difficult. And given the strength of the balance of terror and the fear of starting a major nuclear conflict, each side would be extremely cautious. They would seek to gain advantages through bargaining, threats, and harassment while avoiding a major confrontation that could easily lead to escalation. However, a "phony war" cannot last forever—either the crisis will be resolved (by negotiation or capitulation if one side is especially afraid of escalation) or it will escalate (to confrontation, as was the case during World War II).

A "calculated war" is another phenomenon that precedes the nuclear era and has not been conceptually affected by the development of nuclear weapons. A calculated war has at least four components: (1) An outbreak scenario (i.e., early stages of the war) that includes a variety of communication, bargaining, and tactical options that are dealt with rationally (even if the war starts irrationally). (2) If there is no rationality in the outbreak scenario, each side will still make rational attempts to protect its important values through: intrawar deterrence, self-restraint, counterforce, active and passive defense. (3) Either side would probably continue to bargain by: improving its threat position using abatement tactics special attacks and messages. (4) A more or less rational attempt at war termination by use of what might be termed "end game" tactics—particularly cease fires and ultimatums.

In many ways, the importance of the traditional options of warfare has not changed much in the nuclear era, except that many new problems have been added, particularly problems of timing and control. In the age of nuclear weapons, it is much more difficult to learn how to improve one's capabilities during a conflict, or to make the necessary corrections quickly enough to matter. The outcome of a nuclear war may well be determined in the first few hours, or on the first day, making the outbreak of a war much more important than it was in the prenuclear era.

A final continuity between the prenuclear and nuclear era is the need for realistic military preparations. The ability of a country to mobilize for war, to protect and defend its people to the fullest extent possible, and to develop plans and capabilities for postwar recovery, remains an essential fact of national life. It can mean the difference between a "successful" war outcome and national disaster. Advocates of deterrence-only strategies often argue that preparedness in the nuclear era is irrelevant because nuclear weapons will destroy everyone and everything no matter what precautions are taken. As noted, I disagree.

The evacuation of civilians from potential target areas and the construction of an adequate system of shelters could substantially reduce the number of casualties caused by a nuclear attack on the United States. Civil defense is also important to enhance the credibility of our deterrent threat—the United States cannot threaten to attack urban targets in the Soviet Union (in retaliation for some Soviet aggression) if a Soviet counter retaliation will kill huge numbers of unprotected Americans. But if they have been evacuated and have a reasonable chance of survival, our deterrent threat becomes far more believable.

Active defense, through the development of antiballistic missile systems, can also plan an important role in the protection of our military forces and (in the future) of our population centers. Defense against incoming missiles is difficult to achieve, and complete protection can probably never be guaranteed, but this does not make the effort any less valuable. If ten missiles are headed toward a city and eight can be destroyed before they explode, the level of damage done would be drastically reduced.

A final element of civil defense preparedness planning for postattack recovery—clearly a process that must be organized before a crisis occurs— should be designed to restore essential services as quickly as possible, including the ability to regain military strength if necessary. In a protracted nuclear war, where fighting would continue beyond the initial strikes, there would be a need for ongoing military production. Even with prior planning, recovery would require an enormous effort and probably take a fairly long time, but it could make a big difference.

In the nuclear as in the prenuclear era, the United States must still be able to fight and survive a war. It is not enough to take out insurance against nuclear war's occurring; the U.S. must also be able to stand up to the challenge of fighting. We must have a credible "alternative to peace," so long as the possibility of war—nuclear or conventional—remains. That possibility of war is one of the more important historical constants carried over into the nuclear era.

NOTE

1. No nation has declared war in the traditional manner since the end of WW II when the United Nations charter outlawed war. This being the case, a classic statement of intentions might be especially forceful.

4

———⊱⊰———

On Escalation

ESCALATION IN BRIEF

Escalation, in the sense used here, is a relatively new word in the English language.[1] In a typical escalation situation, there is likely to be a "competition in risk-taking"[2] or at least resolve, and a matching of local resources, in some form of limited conflict between two sides. Usually, either side could win by increasing its efforts in some way, provided that the other side did not negate the increase by increasing its own efforts. Furthermore, in many situations it will be clear that if the increase in effort were not matched and thus resulted in victory, the costs of the increased effort would be low in relation to the benefits of victory. Therefore, the fear that the other side may react, indeed overreact, is most likely to deter escalation, and not the undesirability or costs of the escalation itself. It is because of this that the "competition in risk-taking" and resolve takes place.

There are many reasons why a nation might deliberately seek to escalate a crisis. Each of the criteria given later to measure the degree of escalation might also be a means or objective that one side or the other seeks. That is, one side might wish to escalate specifically to threaten the other side with all-out war, to provoke it, to demonstrate committal or recklessness, and so forth.

A nation may also escalate for prudential as well as coercive reasons: to prevent something worse from happening, to meet a problem, to prepare

[*On Escalation* (New York: Praeger, 1965; Westport, Conn.: Greenwood, 1986).]

for likely escalations on the other side, and so on. A nation might evacuate its cities simply because it wished to protect its people, without necessarily thinking through or even facing the thought that by making its people less vulnerable it increases its bargaining and military power, perhaps to such an extent that the other side may feel under pressure either to take some direct action or to back down. Sometimes the reasons for escalation, whether prudential or pressure-producing, will affect the technique and consequences of the escalation, and other times they will not.

THREE WAYS TO ESCALATE A LIMITED CONFLICT

There are at least three ways in which a would-be escalator can increase, or threaten to increase, his efforts: by increasing intensity, widening the area, or compounding escalation. For example, let us assume that there is some kind of limited conflict or "agreed battle"[3] going on. The most obvious way to escalate is by a quantitative increase in the intensity of the conflict by doing more of what one already is doing—perhaps using more equipment, using new equipment, or attacking new targets such as the enemy's logistics. A large intensive increase, or escalation, would be the use of nuclear weapons against these targets. The area of the conflict may also be increased; in particular, some local sanctuary could be violated. This could mean taking such actions as "crossing the Yalu," retaliatory raids or bombings of North Vietnam or hot pursuit, or other violations of geographical sanctuaries. It could constitute a permanent widening of the area of conflict or simply of the area of a local battle. In almost all the intense conflicts and crises that have occurred since World War II, there have been important local sanctuaries. There have also been pressures—usually one assumes, on both sides—to violate such sanctuaries.

Finally, one can escalate by precipitating a new crisis or conflict elsewhere than in the local area. This "compound escalation"[4] could consist of an attack on an ally or client of the principal opponent—though it could also be an attack on troops or colonies of the principal, but geographically outside the central sanctuary. The compound escalation might also violate the central sanctuary, but in the case of such opponents as the Soviet Union and the United States, this would be a very high-level escalation. Even in a conflict between, say, the Soviets and a powerful country such as Japan or a West European nation, this would be considered a high escalation.

Thus, in any escalation, two sets of basic elements are in constant interplay: the political, diplomatic, and military issues surrounding the particular conflict, and the level of violence and provocation at which it is fought. The latter merges with those considerations raised by the possibility of escalation to higher or more extensive levels of violence, including the possibility of a deliberate, provoked, or inadvertent conflict eruption[5] leading directly to central war.

Just as there are two basic sets of elements in the escalation situation, so there are two basic classes of strategies that each side can use. One class of strategies makes use of features of the particular "agreed battle" that is being waged in order to gain an advantage. The other class uses the risks or threat of escalation and eruption from this agreed battle.

Users of the second class of strategies can deliberately try to eschew the ultimate eruption threat by establishing a fixed limit on how high they will go. This limit can be kept secret, in which case one side may run some risk of a full-scale preemptive eruption by the other side; or it can be announced in advance, with varying degrees of solemnity and credibility.

Strategies that emphasize the possibility of escalation or eruption are associated with the term "brinkmanship." (We will sometimes refer to the game of "chicken" when the brinkmanship is overtly two-sided.) They include strategies that use the risks of escalation to induce an opponent to let one maintain a position that cannot be maintained solely by use of local capabilities and actions. But whatever is emphasized, some mixture of both classes of strategies is combined in almost any move by either side.

Thus, the conditions of two-sided escalation situations can be summarized as follows:

1. Either side can usually put enough into the particular battle to win if the other side does not respond.
2. The value of victory is usually great enough so that it would be worthwhile for either side to raise its commitment enough to win the escalation if it were certain that the other side would not counter the rise.
3. Upper levels of escalation are both dangerous and painful, and each side wishes to avoid them. Therefore, the risks of escalation even to limited heights, as well as to undetermined heights, and the risks of direct "eruption" to general war are all major deterring elements in almost all decisions about escalation or de-escalation—even when one expects to be able to "prevail" at the upper levels.
4. Typically, both sides are interested in "systems bargaining" in preserving precedents (thresholds) that reduce the likelihood of escalation, eruption, or other undesirable long-term effects.
5. There are two basic types of escalation strategies that each side can follow:
   a. strategies based on factors relating to particular levels of escalation (agreed battle) or the specific situation.
   b. strategies based on manipulation of the risks of escalation or eruption.

6. Generally, each side will attempt to avoid looking like a cool mathematician or cynical blackmailer in its tactics, and will emphasize the
   agonistic, stylistic, or familial aspects of its behavior.

Escalations are thus relatively complex phenomena. They are not to be
ordered in a simple fashion, yet for some purposes we wish to do exactly
this, even if it does some violence to reality.

Very roughly, at any particular instant in a crisis or war, the degree of
escalation might be measured by such things as:

1. Apparent closeness to all-out war
2. Likelihood of eruption
3. Provocation
4. Precedents broken
5. Committal (resolve and/or recklessness) demonstrated
6. Damage done or being done
7. Effort (scale, scope, or intensity of violence)
8. Threat intended or perceived

In practice, the "measurement" of the degree of escalation at any particular instant will depend on the criteria used. Thus, there is no objective
reason why the apparent closeness to all-out war (as measured by popular concern) need be a very good measure of the objective likelihood of
eruption. This is clearly true for accidents "out of the blue," and it may be
true for many other situations. In fact, in a crisis, concern over the possibility of eruption may make the probability of eruption very much less.
There may also be a great deal of provocation without much likelihood of
eruption or much apparent closeness to all-out war. In general, the criteria given above measure different things, but all have been used by various authors as measures of escalation. For our part, we will be deliberately vague and not usually specify the criteria being used to determine
the degree of escalation. However, in most situations the context (or the
correlation between the possible criteria) will be clear enough to avoid
confusion.

THE STRIKE AND "CHICKEN" METAPHORS

There are two interesting analogies, or metaphors, that one can apply to
escalation: the strike in labor disputes and the game of "chicken." Neither
of these analogies is entirely accurate, but each of them is useful in explicating the concept of escalation and in conveying a feeling for the nuances
and tactics.

The strike analogy operates primarily on the lower levels of escalation. In a strike situation, labor and management threaten to inflict harm on each other, do so, and under pressure of the continuation of this harm, they seek agreement. It is usually assumed that events will not escalate to the limit (i.e., erupt): we do not expect workers to starve to death or businesses to go bankrupt. In a strike, each side is expected to hurt or threaten to hurt, but not to "kill" or even permanently injure the other side. Under pressure of continuing threats of harm, it is assumed that some compromise will be arrived at before permanent or excessive damage is incurred. Occasionally, these expectations are not fulfilled; a business does go bankrupt, or the workers do look for jobs elsewhere. But this is rare. Usually, the strike is settled long before such limits are approached.

In this context, the question immediately comes up, "Why go through this expensive, dangerous, and uncomfortable route to settle disputes? Why have a strike at all? Why not settle the dispute?" The answer is obvious. In the absence of enforceable or acceptable adjudication, the side most afraid of a strike will tend to get the worst of the bargain. A "no strike" policy—the analogy, in labor disputes, to nonviolence—rarely works for any length of time. And even when it seems to work for some years and disputes are settled without strikes, a strike situation or a serious strike threat may eventually arise. The threat of a strike or a lockout is ever present as a last-resort pressure for compromise.

Escalation has one major feature that is not present in most strike situations—the possibility of eruption. In the usual strike, the maximum punishment that the workers can inflict on the management is to deny it one day's production at a time. The maximum punishment that management can ordinarily inflict on the workers is to deny them one day's wages at a time. There is, therefore, a natural limit to the rate of punishment—an accident or spasm of anger is not likely to force either side over the brink. Escalation in international relations is quite different, since each side decides at what rate it wishes to inflict harm on the other side. This makes escalation incomparably less stable than the strike situation. A moment of anger, a surge of emotion, a seemingly innocuous miscalculation or accident, or a "wrong" decision can have catastrophic consequences.

Another useful—if misleading—analogy which brings this aspect to the fore is the game of "chicken." While it is a very popular metaphor, particularly with peace groups, the analogy to the game of "chicken" greatly oversimplifies international conflicts. "Chicken" is played by two drivers on a road with a white line down the middle. Both cars straddle the white line and drive toward each other at top speed. The first driver to lose his nerve and swerve into his own lane is "chicken"—an object of contempt and scorn—and he loses the game. The game is played among teenagers for prestige, for girls, for leadership of a gang, and for safety (i.e., to prevent other challenges and confrontations).

Escalation is much more complicated than this game. Still, the game provides a useful analogy because it illustrates some aspects of international relations that are important and should be emphasized—for example, the symmetrical character of many escalation situations. Some teenagers utilize interesting tactics in playing "chicken." The "skillful" player may get into the car quite drunk, throwing whisky bottles out the window to make it clear to everybody just how drunk he is. He wears very dark glasses so that it is obvious that he cannot see much, if anything. As soon as the car reaches high speed, he takes the steering wheel and throws it out the window. If his opponent is watching, he has won. If his opponent is not watching, he has a problem; likewise if both players try this strategy.

One of the reasons people do not like to use the "chicken" analogy is that it emphasizes the fact that two sides can operate in the same way. It seems to me that some who object to this label want to play a limited game of "chicken," but do not like to concede that that is what they are doing. I believe it is a good thing to label the tactics, and I also think that, under current conditions, we may have to be willing to play the international version of this game whether we like it or not.

It is clear from the above why many people would like to conduct international relations the way a teenager plays "chicken." They believe that if our decision-makers can only give the appearance of being drunk, blind, and without a steering wheel, they will "win" in negotiations with the Soviets on crucial issues. I do not consider this a useful or responsible policy. We may be willing to run some risks, and we may not want to hem ourselves in tactically by seeming completely sober, clear-visioned, and in full control of ourselves, but we will obviously benefit by having a reasonable degree of sobriety, a reasonable degree of clear vision, and a reasonable degree of self-control. The Soviets are likely to pursue a similar policy.

But escalation often has a crucial point of similarity to the game of "chicken": one side must convey the impression to the other side that the opponent must be the one to give way, or at least accept a reasonable compromise, yet both sides are trying to get this message across.

The strike and the game of "chicken" both cast some light on the concept of escalation. But almost any analogy can be misleading, and these cases are not exceptions. Therefore, although we will use both analogies, we must now consider some points at which these analogies break down.

In the case of the strike in labor disputes, both sides are likely to recognize their absolute need for each other, and this basic community of interest will tend to dominate the negotiations. There will be no attempt by one side to eliminate the other. In fact, no strategy that envisages a great possibility of grievous harm to the other side is likely to be acceptable. Thus, while we will point out later that "familial" considerations may play an important part in escalation situations, the strike analogy probably overstates the shared sense of a community of interests in international conflict.

In the "chicken" analogy, the difficulty is the exact opposite. This involves no give-and-take bargaining. There are no natural pauses or stops, or even partial damage—only all-out collisions. Even more important, the primary objective of the game is the total humiliation of the opponent. There can be no possibility of compromise or face saving. In international relations, escalation is used to facilitate negotiations or to put pressure on one side or both to settle a dispute without war. If either side wanted a war, it would simply go to war and not bother to negotiate. For this reason, the common observation that "neither side wants war" is not particularly startling, even though it is often delivered with an air of revealed truth. Neither side is willing to back down, precisely because it believes or hopes it can achieve its objectives without war. It may be willing to run some risk of war to achieve its objective, but it feels that the other side will back down or compromise before the risk becomes very large.

"Chicken" would be a better analogy to escalation if it were played with two cars starting an unknown distance apart, traveling toward each other at unknown speeds, and on roads with several forks so that the opposing sides are not certain that they are even on the same road. Both drivers should be giving and receiving threats and promises while they approach each other, and tearful mothers and stern fathers should be lining the sides of the roads urging, respectively, caution and manliness.

There is another way in which escalation differs from these analogies. In escalation situations, both sides understand that they are likely to play repeatedly. Therefore (as discussed below), "systems bargaining" is important. Neither side wishes to gain an advantage at the cost of creating a psychological or political situation that will make eruption probable on the next play. Indeed, both sides may become anxious to work out some acceptable methods of adjudicating the game or to adopt general rules embodying some principles of equity or fairness. In fact, both sides may become so interested in getting such rules of procedure or rules of adjudication accepted that either side might be willing to lose a particular issue occasionally simply because trying to win that issue would set a precedent that would reduce the applicability of the basic rules.

In any case, the balance of terror is likely to work well enough to induce some degree of restraint and prudent behavior on each side. Precisely because both sides recognize that deterrence strategies are unstable, they are likely to refrain from testing the stability of the situation too often or too intensely, and to avoid the kind of behavior that might provoke an imprudent response from the other side. Both sides will understand that a strategy of deterrence requires the support of precedents and depends on widely understood and observed thresholds if it is to be reliable for any length of time.

One may still ask why we are buying this time. Why don't we settle these matters now, without running such great risks? Unfortunately, in this respect, the situation is much like the "chicken" and strike analogies. There is no reason, in principle, why manufacturers and workers should not be able to reach settlements without threatening or undergoing the great mutual harm of the strike. But, unfortunately, if either side desperately desires to make a settlement without harm or risk of harm, it is likely to get a very bad bargain. In fact, if one side does this repeatedly, it is possible that both sides might suffer harm: the manufacturer might go bankrupt through repeated concessions, or the workers might receive such low wages that they would be forced to leave the industry. The analogy in escalation would be to one side or the other becoming rigid or desperate as a reaction after having made repeated concessions, even though these were made in the hope of conciliation. In the absence of accepted or compulsory peaceful methods of adjudication, both sides must be willing either to escalate or to endure the settlements imposed upon them.

Thus, even if a nation is not willing to run great risks to achieve positive national goals and objectives, it may be willing to run great risks in order to prevent disasters or costly imposed settlements. In general, it is easier for a community to agree on what it is against, even if it cannot agree on what it is for. But we need alternatives other than all-out spasm war or peace at any price—i.e., war or surrender.

Conceding all the above, we see that the probability of war eventually occurring as a result of "chicken" being played once too often may be very high. In particular, in any long period of peace, there may be a tendency for governance to become more intransigent as the thought of war becomes unreal. This may be the case especially if there is a background of experiences in which those who stood firm did well, while those who were "reasonable" seemed to do poorly. After a while, the hypothetical danger of war may look less real than the tangible gains and the prestige that are being won and lost. It may turn out that governments learn only after peace has failed that it is not feasible to stand firm on incompatible positions. Today there is reason to hope that we can reduce the dangers of the game of "chicken" by considering carefully how wars might start and how they might be fought. Thus, our serious study of escalation. But escalation obviously is dangerous. Unless workable arrangements are made for effective adjudication, someone may play the international analogue of this game once too often. To rely even on slow, rung-by-rung escalation in international crises is a dangerous strategy.

No nation wishes to play the game of "chicken" in the same spirit as teenagers play it. One major alternative is to have sufficient capabilities on the lower escalation levels so that the opponent is not tempted to play even a limited game of "chicken." One side must not be given reason to believe that he can outdo the other in low-level escalations since this might tempt him to risk such escalations in the belief that the other side will capitulate before it escalates higher. And indeed the alternative to having significant capabilities for low-level escalation is to make sufficiently credible threats of going higher. However, there is a temptation to rely on this tactic too heavily, and it may be well to remind ourselves that in dealing with violence there is a tendency in the United States to take strong moral stands and then, because we have defined the issue as a moral one, to make excessive threats and take excessive risks.

It is because of this tendency that I have been so blunt in referring to the use of threats of escalation as playing or intending to play some version of the game of "chicken." To the extent that we are serious, or to the extent that our pretense creates seriousness, we will have to face the consequences of being on the escalation ladder. And when one competes in risk-taking, one is taking risks. If one takes risks, one may be unlucky and lose the gamble. It may be that, unilaterally or bilaterally, we should agree not to play the game of "chicken." This could be encouraged by increasing the instrumental, agonistic, or familial restraints against eruption, thus converting escalation into something more like a labor strike, and by reducing the role of escalation threats in settling international disputes. But there are likely to be limits as to how far we can go in this direction.

NOTES

1. It is not found at all in the *Oxford English Dictionary* (1961), and *Webster's New International Dictionary* (3rd ed., 1961) defines it only in the non-international sense. Yet the word is now familiar and can be used without apology to describe an increase in the level of conflict in international crisis situations.

2. I believe this is Thomas C. Schelling's phrase (though he does not recall inventing it).

3. Max Singer's term. It emphasizes that in an escalation situation in which both sides are accepting limitations, there is in effect an "agreement," whether or not it is explicit or even well understood. Thus the term does not have any connotation of a completely shared understanding, an intention of continuing indefinitely with the limitations, or even a conscious quid pro quo arrangement.

4. The focus of our analysis is on deliberate compound escalation. But it must be remembered that in a tense situation or a confrontation, the whole relationship

of the contending states is specially charged and acts no longer will necessarily be accepted by an opponent at their "normal" valuation or significance. A "normal" troop or fleet movement, a conventional and unrelated diplomatic act by one party may be interpreted by the opponent as an escalatory act. Moreover, third parties may take advantage of a tense situation to gain ends of their own and in fact escalate the big-power crisis. The British-French-Israeli attack on Suez in 1956, while not planned to take advantage of the Hungarian crisis, actually affected the behavior of the U.S. and the U.S.S.R., and itself was affected by the crisis situation of the great powers. The Turkish air action against Greek Cypriots in August, 1964, was probably influenced in its character and timing by the crisis between the U.S. and North Vietnam and was probably made more "acceptable" because of the precedent set by the U.S. in striking against North Vietnam a few days before. The importance of such precedents will be discussed later. If the Cyprus crisis had continued—had escalated—with greater Soviet involvement, this crisis could have constituted an inadvertent compound escalation of the great-power crisis.

5. Morton H. Halperin has suggested (in his *Limited War in the Nuclear Age* [New York: John Wiley & Sons, 1963], p. 3), that two terms should be used to describe different kinds of escalation: ". . . *explosion*—the sudden transformation of a local war into a central war by the unleashing of strategic nuclear forces . . . and *expansion*—a gradual increase in the level of military force employed."

He then points out: "These two processes, 'explosion' and 'expansion,' are frequently discussed together as 'escalation.' However it is important to keep the two processes separate. The considerations that go into the decision to begin a central war would be very different from the considerations that have gone and will go into decisions to expand a local war. These latter decisions will be influenced by a number of factors, including the foreign-policy objectives of the two sides, their estimate of the risk of central war, their images of the role of force, and their domestic political objectives."

Our term "escalation" covers Halperin's terms "expansion" and "escalation" (according to context), and our "eruption" is similar to his "explosion."

5

⟨⟨⟨⟩⟩⟩

Seizing the Moral, Political, and Strategic High Ground

Four decades into the nuclear era, nuclear weapons seem to have taken on a new and immoral life of their own. They are alternatively cited as the harbingers of an almost certain Armageddon or as the last stop on the way to the redemption of mankind. There is a constituency for every antinuclear position, and a coalition of concerned doctors, lawyers, mothers, actors, and so on, for every antinuclear rally. But the real issue is how to achieve national security and international order within a morally and politically acceptable framework.

THREE POPULAR (BUT FLAWED) ANTINUCLEAR POSITIONS

Under the circumstances, that becomes a very difficult task. Probably as much as any other single book, Jonathan Schell's *The Fate of the Earth* raised the antinuclear consciousness to the point where anything short of the elimination of all nuclear weapons (and all conventional forces) becomes morally and politically unacceptable. However, one of his fundamental arguments—that all values and interests must be subordinated to avoiding nuclear war—is impractical, illusionary, and dangerous.

If we take the position that Schell takes, that nuclear war clearly threatens the existence of humanity, that nuclear war has some significant probability of ending all human history, and that as far as humans are

[*Thinking about the Unthinkable in the 1980s* (New York: Simon & Schuster, 1984).]

concerned "peace" has to be the overwhelming value and that there are no other values that in any way can compete with this, then we can get into quite a lot of trouble. Focusing our attention solely on "peace" (defined simply as the absence of nuclear war) can lead to weakness that creates opportunities for smaller scale (but nonetheless dangerous) aggression that threatens peace. There are two great defects in Schell's position: one of them is that you simply cannot afford to make any single value overwhelming. One must assign some kind of finiteness to any value because society cannot let one priority dominate everything it does. The second and more important issue is that making one value infinite still does not give a nation any direction—it does not tell government officials how best to preserve this value.

In order to establish the transcendental value of avoiding nuclear war at any cost, Schell describes, in graphic (and often exaggerated) detail, the incredibly horrible consequences of a nuclear war. The emotional impact of the book is apparently so powerful that very few readers (and very few reviewers) ever notice the book's substantive inadequacies and inaccuracies—e.g., the author's highly selective and tendentious use of evidence, or the distortions that necessarily follow from exaggerated assumptions about the dangers and risks of a nuclear war.

And yet, if it is necessary to overstate the case in order to focus public attention on the nuclear threat, then Schell and the authors of many other recent antinuclear books may be serving a useful purpose. Nuclear weapons exist, they will not go away, and one day they might even be used. What happens then, however, is an issue that none of the volumes are willing to deal with in any useful or reasonable way. Schell's utopian solution envisions some kind of world government where sovereign nations cede their political authority and military power to an unclearly defined global order. How we get to there from here is one of the many "awesome, urgent tasks"—"the political work of our age"—that Schell says he has "left to others."

The nonsolution that has captured the greatest popular attention is the freeze. According to most advocates of this impressively widespread movement, both the U.S. and the Soviet Union should agree to halt any further testing, production, or deployment of nuclear weapons.

In a vision that is almost as romantic and simplistic as Schell's, they believe a freeze would automatically end what they fear is an "inevitably spiraling arms race." Perhaps. But while it may prevent further growth in the U.S. and Soviet nuclear-weapon stockpiles, it would also prevent unilateral measures by the U.S. (or the Soviet Union) to lessen the dangers of nuclear war breaking out (e.g., through the deployment of more survivable nuclear forces) or to make nuclear war less horrible (e.g., through the development of lower yield, more accurate warheads). Like any across-the-board limitations (e.g., rent control and wage-and-price controls), the freeze is an indiscriminate restraint that is only a partial remedy at best and creates adverse side effects.

Further, a freeze would codify the current Soviet edge in nuclear forces (just as SALT was a formal acknowledgment by the U.S. that it accepted Soviet achievement of strategic parity and recognized the Soviet Union as a superpower). Granting the Soviets this edge now could have deleterious political implications for the U.S. and its allies.

Because there is popular support for a freeze in the U.S. and not in the Soviet Union, the freeze movement imposes asymmetric pressure on U.S. negotiators to reach ill-conceived agreements at the Geneva talks. And assuming a satisfactory bilateral freeze could be negotiated, what guarantees are there that the Soviets would in fact honor it? There is some evidence that they may have violated certain provisions of the SALT agreements (agreements with a relatively limited arms-control ambit), and even with relatively sophisticated verification techniques, human ingenuity can always devise ever more sophisticated ways around limitations.

Nor would a nuclear freeze preclude nonnuclear weapon system breakthroughs—potentially devastating developments that could be in the making even as a freeze is put into place, to be exploited against an opponent at the first signs of tension. A freeze would not have helped lessen any dangers at all if a crisis situation arose to cancel it—no arms reduction talks would have taken place, no further safeguards (political or technological) would have been worked out; in short, no meaningful arms control would have been achieved. The stagnation fostered by a freeze could only bring about a false sense of security that would be exposed as soon as the popular pressure subsided and a hostile confrontation seemed imminent.

The extreme wing of the freeze advocates goes so far as to advocate unilateral reductions in nuclear armaments, either regardless of the consequences or hopeful that such a show of good faith and honorable intentions would shame the other side into a similar position. Many proponents of unilateral disarmament believe in the so-called demonstration effect, i.e., if the United States refrains from deploying the MX ICBM or Pershing II missiles, or other new nuclear weapon systems, the Soviets will exercise similar restraint. Unfortunately, the history of U.S. unilateral restraint in its nuclear-weapons programs is a sorry one, best characterized by former Secretary of Defense Harold Brown: "When we build, they build—when we stop, they continue to build."

In many ways, the Green Movement in West Germany is the European counterpart of the freeze campaign in this country. (The label "Greens" stems from their initial concern with environmental issues.) The reasons for the strength of the movement in the Federal Republic are not hard to understand: most of the members are fairly young, postwar children of affluence. They have no experience with economic hardship or hostile geopolitical realities. Their personal satisfaction does not derive from material progress (they are all overprivileged), but from participation in "meaningful" social causes. In some ways they are the most protected, naive, and illusion-prone young people in the West today.

Add to this the fact that West Germany today is without nuclear weapons and therefore without the means of self-defense against Soviet nuclear coercion or attack. Moreover, the world's largest concentrations of conventional military forces face each other on either side of its border. Indeed, most scenarios for a serious confrontation or war between the U.S. and the Soviet Union evolve out of the potential for conflict between these two forces. In most situations, therefore, West Germany would be the battlefield (at least initially) in any war between NATO and the Warsaw Pact. [. . .] Quite understandably, then, West Germans feel most at risk and have very little interest in pursuing confrontational policies. The Greens' call for West German neutrality (or reunification with East Germany) and the elimination of nuclear weapons from German (and European) soil is understandable within this context.

The morality of any of the above positions—Schell's vision of a nonnuclear utopia, support for a nuclear freeze, opposition to European-based nuclear weapons and the existing European military alliances—is self-evident to their adherents; it escapes others entirely. I, for example, fail to recognize any redeeming higher value in a stance that places an entire nation at any greater risk than necessary. Flaunting one's vulnerability (which is essentially what a freeze would do) is neither morally nor militarily useful. Politically, it is primitive. A much more responsible posture would be to do as we are and have been doing—namely, to pursue bilateral arms reductions seriously (e.g., the ongoing Strategic Arms Reduction Talks [START] and the Intermediate-Range Nuclear Force [INF] Negotiations), while continuing to improve our national defense through a rearmament program. The principal moral obligation of a government in the nuclear age is to make every effort to enforce deterrence or, should deterrence fail, to limit as much as possible the damage to its citizens and its economy and to enhance the prospects for postwar recovery.

"NUCLEAR MORALITY" AND THE PASTORAL LETTER ON WAR AND PEACE

Taking somewhat of a middle ground between the nonnuclear extremists and the more moderate antinuclear realists are the American bishops of the Roman Catholic Church. Their Pastoral Letter (drafted by the Committee on War and Peace of the National Conference of Catholic Bishops) attempts to provide spiritual guidance on how to reconcile the existence of nuclear weapons with traditional Church doctrine—and concludes that such a conciliation may not, in fact, be possible.

The bishops have attempted to apply the criteria for a just war to nuclear war. They conclude (with insufficient supporting evidence and analysis) that a just nuclear war is practically impossible because of the "overwhelming probability that a nuclear exchange would have no limits" and would therefore violate two of the major principles of the doctrine, namely, "discrimination" and "proportionality." By proscribing first use of nuclear weapons and the deliberate targeting of civilians, the Pastoral Letter also (correctly) condemns any attempt to gain security "on the cheap."

Contrary to the bishops' assessment, I would argue that the nuclear age has not rendered the doctrine of a just war obsolete. While it is true that no war can be reliably limited, it is not at all certain that all nuclear wars will escalate. An attempt to fight a limited nuclear war may be the least desperate choice in a future U.S.-Soviet conflict. Moreover, it has become more imperative than ever to meet the highest and most stringent criteria of justification for waging war, and—equally important—to strengthen both the effectiveness and the morality of deterrence.

In this regard, the Church makes an important contribution to the nuclear debate by endorsing no first use and by stressing the prohibition against the targeting of civilians and their property. I began advocating no first use about twenty years ago, and have continued to support it ever since. But the Pastoral Letter stretches no first use to a practically no-use-at-all position (basically nuclear pacifism) that I believe is unnecessarily dangerous and, for those of us who are not religious or philosophical pacifists, probably immoral. The letter explicitly calls for no first use but implicitly goes beyond that position to a no-use posture. It proscribes attacks against cities; it rules out attacks against many military installations because the collateral damage, even in limited nuclear wars, would be "disproportionate"; and it condemns counterforce weapons as "destabilizing." No recommendations are offered as to what targets the U.S. should threaten to strike in retaliation for Soviet first use, or what military capabilities would be required for these retaliatory attacks. A U.S. nuclear-war plan informed by the directives contained in the Pastoral Letter would have no direction or purpose. The credibility of an effective U.S. reprisal for the most serious Soviet aggressions would be severely undercut. This, in turn, could result in Soviet provocations that might precipitate nuclear war—the abhorrent act at the center of the letter's concern.

An appropriate no-first-use policy implies a willingness, if necessary, to resort to a justified second use. That justification, as noted, would be only to deter, balance, and correct for the possession or use of nuclear weapons by others. Under such circumstances, appropriate second use would be a justifiable moral action. But no-first-use can also weaken deterrence if it results in a significant lessening of the possible risks confronting a potential aggressor. I would accept some such weakening, if necessary, but would prefer to see governments adopt this policy in a way that strengthened deterrence, i.e., by accompanying it with a credible ability to counter conventional attack with nonnuclear forces, and to alleviate the consequences of a nuclear conflict if deterrence fails. The Pastoral Letter condemns most possibilities for doing this on the basis of some very dubious strategic judgments.

Similarly, one wonders about the bishops' opposition to any efforts by the United States or NATO to gain nuclear superiority. If we knew clearly what superiority meant, this might be a reasonable position (although I would probably be opposed to it). But the fact is that superiority depends upon assumptions about the causes, conduct, and consequences of nuclear war—i.e., on the context in which one makes the estimate. If one has the unalterable conviction that any nuclear war would be the end of history, then the concept of superiority is meaningless. The only harm done by its proponents would be the misutilization of resources, or a very remote possibility that some people might believe in nuclear superiority to the extent they might be willing to risk or actually wage nuclear war; or, alternatively, that the potential enemy would believe in the superiority of the other side and be "provoked."

The letter of course does accept deterrence, but what it calls a "conditioned moral acceptance." According to the letter:

> . . . we cannot approve of every weapons system, strategic doctrine or policy initiative advanced in the name of strengthening deterrence. On the contrary, these criteria require continual public scrutiny of what our government proposes to do with the deterrent. Nuclear deterrence should be used as a step on the way toward progressive disarmament. Each proposed addition to our strategic system or change in strategic doctrine must be assessed precisely in light of whether it will render steps toward "progressive disarmament" more or less likely. Progress toward a world freed of dependence on nuclear deterrence must be carefully carried out. But it must not be delayed. There is an urgent moral and political responsibility to use the "peace of a sort" we have as a framework to move toward authentic peace through nuclear arms control, reductions, and disarmament.

The letter is correct in arguing that we should seek to reduce the nuclear threat in the time afforded by deterrence. (I have made this same point for many years.) However, to put pressure on the government to justify every "strategic system or change in strategic doctrine" in terms of its contribution to the nebulous concept of "progressive disarmament" and to achieve quick results in Geneva would place the United States at an enormous disadvantage in negotiating with the Soviets. In essence, U.S. negotiators would labor under a new timetable, while their opposite numbers would not. If the antinuclear groups in the United States and the other NATO countries pressure their governments for quick results in the INF and START talks, they make progress less likely by making the negotiations hostage to Soviet intransigence. When the talks flounder on genuine mutual disagreements between the two parties, the Soviets can nevertheless publicly accuse the U.S. and NATO of "lack of good faith." The letter would then seem to advise that the U.S. make some unilateral reduction in its forces in order to induce a reciprocal Soviet action. As noted above, this displays a gross ignorance of the history of the U.S.-Soviet arms competition over the last ten to fifteen years.

Furthermore, it is simply not at all clear that the aim of negotiation should be disarmament "for its own sake," as opposed to arms control, to make the world safer. It ought to be quite clear that to cut down to very small forces on both sides could be quite dangerous (perhaps making them more vulnerable than present arsenals and less capable of supporting severely damaging retaliatory attacks).

The Pastoral Letter is, however, clearly on moral and political terra firma when it notes that there must be no use of nuclear weapons solely or mainly against civilians. But as a strategist, I would add "except as a last resort or in very special circumstances." For example, imagine that (as in one of our Gedanken experiments) a powerful enemy nation destroyed a U.S. city just to teach us some kind of lesson, but otherwise used no additional nuclear weapons. We might not be willing to launch a major nuclear war in response, but might instead choose to retaliate according to the talionic law of an "eye for an eye and a tooth for a tooth," a doctrine that permits—even mandates—proportionate retaliation while it forbids escalation. A more likely situation would involve the withholding of U.S. forces during a war (probably submarine-launched missiles) for retaliation against Soviet cities if the Soviets attacked U.S. cities. But here again, they would be used only in a more or less talionic fashion—and only in the absence of other possibilities for punishing the individuals or group that had ordered the attack on U.S. cities. (In contrast, the bishops' letter even forbids "retaliatory use of weapons striking enemy cities after our own have already been struck.")

Living with nuclear weapons means making sure that they are never thought of as "just another" military option or "just another" way of resolving serious conflicts. But it also means that they are available as a credible last resort. This is what is generally called a war-fighting position.

[. . .] War-fighting strategies, like deterrence-only strategies, advocate measures to reduce the possibility of accidental war; advocate the maintenance of survivable forces; and support the transmission of reliable "go-ahead" orders. But they add to this an emphasis on how the war is waged and how it might be terminated should deterrence fail. Thus, according to strategists' use of the term "war fighting," the Pastoral Letter's concern with avoiding cities, and with the moral question related to the use of weapons, makes it a war-fighting doctrine. This, of course, is not the same as accusing the bishops of wanting to fight a nuclear war (nor should this accusation be leveled against strategists who favor a war-fighting doctrine).

As noted, the bishops state that "we cannot approve of every weapons system, strategic doctrine, or policy initiative advanced in the name of strengthening deterrence." Neither can we. But we can approve of some of them and can give good reasons for supporting them. A categorical statement such as the above, without adequate amplification, reflects a sincere concern but an unenlightened simplicity—perhaps even an evasion of some central (however difficult) moral and strategic issues.

Similarly, it is counterproductive to issue a facile judgment that the United States must not have any weapons with counterforce ability because such weapons would be "destabilizing." The incorrect idea that the limited measures now being considered by the government to minimize damage are inherently destabilizing, dangerous, and falsely reassuring runs through the Pastoral Letter. In fact, given the bishops' injunction (and my belief) that civilians are not an appropriate routine target, enemy weapons should be targets and the system must be designed for the task. And if the lives of Soviet citizens cannot be endangered for the sake of deterrence, then surely the U.S. government has a related moral obligation to protect its own citizens from nuclear attack—through programs like the civil defense measures I advocated [. . .] . (The clear moral imperative to provide adequate protection for civilian populations is one of the issues the Pastoral Letter delicately sidesteps.) "Damage limitation" can be sought through a combination of offensive nuclear forces (e.g., the MX ICBM, the Trident II submarine-launched ballistic missile) and strategic active and passive defenses (e.g., ballistic missile defense, civil defense). These are the very systems the bishops oppose (or at least fail to endorse), and in doing so they create a significant contradiction in their position. The destabilization effect, if any, might or might not be significant, but might still be morally and politically acceptable as an unavoidable cost of preparing for the possible failure of deterrence.

[. . .] Most of the problems I have with the document stem from seemingly uncritical acceptance of many currently popular (and seemingly plausible) but largely emotional arguments. Because of its tremendous influence and prestige, the Church must be prepared to reconsider technical and strategic judgments that are either unproven or clearly wrong, and to defend as strongly as possible those moral canons on which there can be no compromise. (The authors of the letter made a commendable effort to do this by writing that "the application of moral principles does not have, of course, the same force as the principles themselves and therefore allows for different opinions.") It would be immoral and unwise to jeopardize our national security interests and the values of most of the world on the basis of a strongly held but emotional evaluation of basically technical and strategic issues. However sincere, the accuracy of these strategic judgments is at best uncertain, at worst incorrect.

The Pastoral Letter seems to me to come too close to jeopardizing U.S. and global interests. If it is intended as an enduring statement on war and peace in a nuclear age, then the implications of war-fighting doctrines and enhanced strategic defenses must be considered much more carefully and objectively than the bishops have done so far. I am not suggesting that the Church should take my judgments (or those of my colleagues) as authoritative. I am suggesting only that many of these issues are more controversial or uncertain than many of the assertions by the bishops would seem to indicate. My views are almost certainly not wrong on any of the issues raised here (I have carefully restricted my comments so that I can make this remark quite responsibly), though others might not agree that they are entirely right. I believe the bishops also must have a high level of integrity in trying to arrive at defendable positions and must be prepared to drop or qualify positions that are undefendable, however fashionable they may be (particularly in liberal and leftist circles). The message of the Church leaders must be valid and persuasive enough on its own merits to impress even those outside the circle of "friends and relatives" in the "peace" movements and other dovish or individuals and groups.

Assuming the intention of the bishops is not to preach to the converted, they must offer more persuasive arguments to back up the moral validity of their position, or they must be more guarded and limited in their strategic and political judgments. For example, the letter's argument that the costs of the "arms race" divert resources that could be better spent on curing the world's social and economic ills may be true, but the same could be said for money spent on tobacco, liquor, space exploration, or anything else. If we are to have a morally acceptable posture, it is most unlikely that it will come for free; it is more likely that it will cost more: intellectually, financially, and perhaps politically.

I do not challenge the right or even the duty of the Church to take positions that are controversial in secular terms but well founded on religious terms. Accordingly, if the Pastoral Letter supports the concept of "no first use" and "no targeting of civilians" (or, better, "no routine targeting of civilians") but recognizes the security value of deterrence, then I think that the Church will be endorsing policies that are strategically as well as morally supportable, even if it might mean a more expensive and complex defense establishment for the United States and its allies. A great opportunity to seize the moral high ground would be lost if, in the long run, the bishops' efforts came to be seen as just another (misguided) commentary on the strategy and tactics of nuclear war.

A LONG-RANGE ANTINUCLEAR POLICY

The position I have taken for many years on the moral aspects of nuclear use (and nonuse) comes as close as any to putting nuclear arsenals into a proper ethical context. The strategy and tactics of nuclear war become secondary (but still very important) concerns. The primary focus is on the rationale for maintaining a force of nuclear weapons: the only justification for ownership is to deter, balance, or correct for the possession or use of nuclear weapons by others.

"Deter, balance, or correct" is a very important phrase, and one I use often. The first word, of course, means to dissuade by terror, and in fact "deter" might be changed to "dissuade" because we are interested in dissuading by any means that work, that are appropriate, and that will do the least amount of evil. So in many cases we may choose methods of dissuasion that are not by terror (e.g., by confronting the enemy with the fearful prospects of military defeat, revolution at home, or the "cost ineffectiveness" of his own attacks).

There are all kinds of subtle ways to use nuclear weapons. For example, by advocating no first use the United States is also giving up the right to threaten to use them in certain circumstances. We would, of course, still need to have the capability to enforce the ban on no first use; for this, a credible capability to initiate thermonuclear war would be required—a concept many people would deplore. But whatever limited bargaining power in crisis diplomacy may be lost by renouncing first use is regained in the morality of our effort to limit the influence of nuclear weapons (their actual and potential use) to as small a sphere as possible. We seek to eliminate any fringe benefits of simple possession, especially by smaller countries. But we have to have them, to "balance" the nuclear power of others.

By "correct" I mean that if somebody actually uses nuclear weapons, then something has to be done. The most basic correction is retaliation designed to make clear that an aggressor cannot get away with a violation of the moral principal of no first use, then to limit and alleviate the damage (to ourselves as well as to our opponents' populace) through U.S. civil defense, ballistic missile defense, air defense, and very careful and limited (in many cases "limited" only in the sense of less than all-out) second use of nuclear weapons against the aggressor. [. . .]

For the past twenty years I have been concerned with how best to reduce this potential for nuclear war. Certainly the instincts of the utopian (Schell) and religious (bishops) antinuclear advocates are right; even the revised "Establishment" position (Bundy et al.) comes much closer to the mark than their positions two decades ago. But it was around that time that I suggested a "long-range antinuclear policy" (with no first use at its core), which I still believe (indeed, am more convinced than ever) constitutes the only politically, morally, and militarily defensible nuclear policy for the long run. Specifically, a nuclear policy should accomplish the following objectives:

1. It should make nuclear weapons be and seem to be virtually unusable—either politically or physically.
2. In particular, it should prevent nuclear intimidation (except for the threats needed to preserve nuclear deterrence).
3. It should decrease the prestige associated with owning nuclear weapons (perhaps by limiting proliferation to regional military organizations whose purpose would be to provide for a nonnational tit-for-tat retaliation, or by a more or less explicit U.S. or Soviet talionic guarantee to various nonnuclear areas).
4. It should limit proliferation without necessarily freezing the nuclear status quo (nations should not be put into an unnecessarily vulnerable security position).
5. If nuclear weapons are used, it should limit the damage that is done—it should not rely on deterrence working perfectly (an explicit policy of proportionate retaliation, or lex talionis, would impose intrawar limits on escalation, while strategic defenses would provide an important degree of direct protection against attack).
6. It should be competent (i.e., resilient and flexible enough) to withstand crises, small and even large conventional wars, and even some nuclear breaches and violations.
7. It should be responsive to national interests, sentiments, and doctrines, and should be negotiable.
8. It should improve current international standards, but should not require thoroughgoing reform (a responsible nuclear policy is not a

moral mission to redeem mankind, but a program to reduce the risks and costs of war among nation-states).

9. It should be potentially permanent (i.e., not designed as a transitional arrangement) and yet be flexible enough to constitute a hedge against events and opportunities in both negotiation and operation—it should allow for major or basic developments and changes.

Some of these objectives may appear to be almost as utopian as those Schell-like visions I have rejected as unrealistic and unrealizable. But in fact, most of them should not present insurmountable obstacles, and if such arrangements are successful, they could limit the further spread of nuclear weapons and increase the credibility of a talionic response to a nuclear provocation—and therefore the deterrence of provocation. Alternatively, if deterrence failed and weapons were used, the result would not inevitably be Armageddon but would be limited to whatever destruction was entailed in the tit-for-tat exchange. After that, there would presumably be a return to some previous status quo.

The objective of proportionate retaliation is to bring the violence to a rapid conclusion and to create precedents that prevent recurrence; it is not to determine who was "right" or to consider other abstract points of law. (In this sense, the talionic rule is conceptually akin to the role of many UN peacekeeping operations.) As has been true for lex talionis arrangements from the most primitive cultures on, their primary objective is to restore equilibrium.

And yet there are certain objections that can be made to the basic tit-for-tat doctrine. For example, the idea of "an eye for an eye" might be manifestly unjust when it actually means "a city for a city," and when the city attacked in retaliation is inhabited by persons with no special responsibility for the initial nuclear attack. Serious ethical and political questions are raised, which depend in part upon empirical, analytical, and technical considerations, such as what response is proportionate or whether a talionic doctrine would be more unjust or unstable than alternative doctrines. The injustice and other defects of inflexible tit for tat must be compared with the possible infeasibility, risk, or even immorality of some counterforce or massive city attacks, and other more or less flexible, ambiguous, or unpredictable doctrines, as well as the possible consequences of not retaliating at all or not retaliating in a manner that deters further attack. None of these questions can be answered simply or dogmatically. In any case, some allowance might be made for responsible authorities to avoid at least the most rigid kind of city-for-city retaliation.

To prevent misinterpretation of an intended tit-for-tat response, slight underescalation might be advisable. Furthermore, within the limits of technical capabilities and political circumstances, it might be advisable to select on an ad hoc basis a different kind of target in retaliation—say, an isolated military installation for a city—or indeed, in certain special circumstances, to use nonnuclear means to enforce the lesson that nuclear weapons are not to be used.[1] In practice the lex talionis need not be absolutely inflexible in order to be effective; the doctrine of "justifiable reprisal," often invoked in the nineteenth century, offers better analogies than does the literal practice of eye-for-an-eye retaliation among some primitive peoples.

This long-term antinuclear policy would build upon the common revulsion at the thought of using nuclear weapons. For example, "imperialism" and "racism" were operative and even acceptable theories several decades ago, but they are now "out." I believe it is not impossible that sometime in the next few decades the illegitimate possession of nuclear weapons (i.e., possession other than to deter, balance, or correct for their use by others) will seem equally reprehensible. Antinuclear sentiment will flourish (but not as it does today in an emotional, partisan, or counterproductive manner). Creation of a durable antinuclear taboo requires the joining of the popular psychological and moral abhorrence of nuclear weapons with the policies outlined above. People must be not only opposed to nuclear war, but ready to foreclose the possibilities for nuclear intimidation and to correct for nuclear use. Otherwise, the widespread fear of nuclear war will be manipulated by parties not sharing the taboo to forestall opposition to military aggression. Without tying antinuclear sentiment to a sound long-term antinuclear policy, there is a risk that a nation that legitimately had to resort to nuclear weapons for its self-defense might become a pariah.

No scheme can completely assuage the multifarious fears that arise as a consequence of the existence of nuclear weapons; for even in the case of total disarmament, fears will remain that the weapons might again come into existence or that disarmament was not complete. Nor will any scheme completely eliminate nuclear weapons from the calculations of statesmen, and in fact, it might be undesirable to try to go that far. The major, perhaps sole legitimate function of nuclear weapons should be to deter—to answer the threat or use of nuclear weapons. Aside from this the world should psychologically be relatively close to a situation in which nuclear weapons did not exist.

The reason for the emphasis on the word "relatively" may need clarification. A widespread belief that the world was completely nonnuclear would clearly result in some undesirable effects. For example, nations today are very careful in nonnuclear confrontations simply because they fear escalation to nuclear weapons (or the procuring of nuclear weapon systems by their opponents). These inhibiting fears have some desirable consequences. But we may be able to eat our cake and have it too. Such fears of nuclear escalation or production will still exist despite measures that successfully limit proliferation and reduce the likelihood of the use of nuclear weapons.

A declaration of no first use (as part of a long-term antinuclear policy) is not a panacea, nor is total trust in religious credos, nor is an underlying faith in the ultimate goodness and rationality of mankind. Spiritual and moral values certainly inform practical and secular ones, but they cannot substitute for them. Even the most devout and pious practitioners have to live in the real world, and almost all religions accept the basic notion that the Lord helps those who help themselves. In terms of seizing the moral, political and strategic high ground, this means that a nation, in addition to relying on God's good will and aid, is entitled to use force in defense of the lives, property, and values of its citizens if it is attacked. In fact, we would argue that anything less would be immoral and irresponsible behavior.

NOTE

1. Even in the event cities were to be destroyed under the talionic rule, precautions could be taken to lessen the human suffering by a significant degree. For example, evacuation of the targeted cities could be permitted prior to their attack. (In some conceivable conflicts, enraged survivors in the aggressor nation might attempt to overthrow the regime that had caused them such tremendous hardship. The prospect of this kind of internal disorder could be a more powerful deterrent threat to the regime than that of counter population retribution.)

II

A WORLD TURNING POINT: ECONOMIC GROWTH, CULTURAL CHANGE, AND THE LONG VIEW

6

---∞∞∞---

The Big Picture—and Some Details: Watersheds of History

Excluding great religious events, there are two great watersheds of civilized history. The first was the agricultural revolution that started in the fertile crescent of the Middle East some ten thousand years ago and took about eight thousand years to spread around the world. The second was the Industrial Revolution. It can be argued that the first watershed, the agricultural revolution, created civilization—civic culture. It created a relatively high standard of living for elites and made possible the survival of many more people. However, it did not greatly change the standard of living of the world's masses. No agriculturally based society ever dropped much below the equivalent of $100 GNP per capita or exceeded the equivalent of $500 per capita for any lengthy period.[1]

It was not until the Industrial Revolution began in Holland and England about two hundred years ago that a sustained growth occurred in the average level of income. Since then, the average income of about two-thirds of the population of the earth has increased by factors of from five to twenty. We suggest below that by the end of what we call the Great Transition, average world per capita income will increase from current levels by a factor of about ten. This change and all that is associated with it will alter the basic character of world civilization.[2]

The Great Transition, which includes the Industrial Revolution, encompasses roughly the last two hundred years and the next two hundred years. Many of its aspects are not spread evenly over the entire four-hundred-year

---

[*World Economic Development: 1979 and Beyond* (Boulder, Colo.: Westview Press, 1979).]

period; rather, they are mostly contained within the second half of the twentieth century—"the half century of rapid and worldwide transition." This period is so dramatic and so startling that we may usefully think of it as almost by itself encompassing the historical watershed we have called the Great Transition. Earlier and later periods of the Great Transition can be seen respectively as a sort of takeoff or preparatory period and an aftermath or consolidation period.

For almost ten millennia the total number of people in the world oscillated between 10 and 500 million, with a very slowly increasing long-term trend (less than 0.1 percent per year). Around the seventeenth century A.D. there was a dramatic increase in the rate of population growth, which became almost explosively rapid (about 1 percent) in the middle of the second half of the twentieth century. The rate probably peaked in the early 1970s at below 2 percent. It will almost certainly stay over 1 percent for the rest of the century. Most demographers believe that the rate will decline quite rapidly, dropping even faster than it rose until it reaches a fairly slow pace (a fraction of a percent) in another century or so. Barring some great change, world population eventually will again become relatively static.

One of the other dramatic events in the half century of rapid worldwide transition was the introduction of nuclear armaments and other weapons of mass destruction. While it is probably not yet true that all human life could be destroyed by a large nuclear war, this capability may be approaching and clearly illustrates the potential consequences of bad luck or bad management. As additional inherently dangerous technologies become developed, such potentialities seem likely to increase.

On the positive side, the scientific innovations in computers, communications, and other technological areas are equally or more significant. Some single out the spectacular feat of space satellites and vehicles exploring the solar system—of human beings and their artifacts leaving the world's surface—as a truly dramatic new kind of event. Others stress the emergence of a true world economic and intellectual ecumene and universalization of the Industrial Revolution. A quite different perception puts the primary emphasis not so much on the transition but on the emergence of physical or social limits to growth and the consequent transformation to a "sustainable world economy"—however this may be defined.

To some degree, we are entering virgin territory. We are discussing a process affecting the dynamics of an industrial culture that in many respects is unprecedented in history. Fortunately, we believe that there is more continuity than discontinuity. If true, this improves our ability to understand these trends. We disagree with those who argue that useful comprehension requires a major breakthrough in sociological or anthropological theory or in philosophy or religion. We are not attempting such a breakthrough.

Teilhard de Chardin, William Thompson, Charles Reich, Marshall McLuhan, Willis Harmon, François Revel, Abraham Maslow, and Jonas Salk, among others, believe that a mystical or spiritual transformation is associated with this half century, and is driving the trends and forces. We do not accept the concept of a mystical or spiritual transformation as the driving force, but we do agree that something exciting is happening. Nineteen fifty to two thousand is surely not just another half century in humanity's long history. During this half century the world should go from almost 2.5 billion people to about 6 billion; from about $2 trillion of gross world product to $15 trillion to $20 trillion; from mostly poor to mostly middle income or rich; from mostly rural to mostly urban; from mostly preindustrial and illiterate to mostly industrial and literate; from mostly ill-fed, ill-housed, ill-clothed, and short-lived to mostly well-fed, well-housed, well-clothed, and long-lived.

The picture that has just been presented is one of relatively smooth development, the reaching of a goal, and roughly speaking, staying with that goal for the rest of history. This is most implausible because history is not likely to be like that for one, much less for many, millennia. History always shows change: rise and fall; reformation and counter-reformation; disruption and reconstitution; decline and renaissance; extension and diminution; other internal or external contradictions; or mutations causing conflict and change, defeat or victory. We do not dwell on such possibilities, though, for they are not relevant to our three immediate concerns: to present images of the next few centuries that reflect current and emerging trends, to analyze the present and the next decade or two, and to proffer some prescriptions for today.

One of our most important aims is to study some of the discontinuities within the continuities, and vice versa. We tend to emphasize continuities more than discontinuities because we believe that history is relatively continuous, that institutions and other social constructs are grown rather than created overnight, and that almost every aspect of tomorrow's society will have historical roots. If we slightly overemphasize the continuities, we offer a useful balance to the prolific literature that rejects and ignores the historical past to argue for a pervasive and sharp break—a viewpoint we consider almost totally unjustified.

In much the same way that the agricultural revolution spread around the world, the Industrial Revolution is also spreading and causing permanent changes in the quality and characteristics of human life. Instead of taking eight thousand years, however, this second diffusion is progressing with incredible speed and will probably be largely completed by the end of this century. Two more centuries should see almost all countries become postindustrial—or at least attain or pass the level of the current Advanced Capitalist nations.

THE GREAT TRANSITION

Images of the long-run future will hold true only if other things are more or less equal. If basic assumptions change, projects may have to change accordingly. But even if the images do not turn out to be valid, they can still be realistic—that is, providing a reasonable picture of the basic trends of our time. Thus, such images may still be useful as a context for short-range planning. The age-old question: "When will this accelerated economic and population growth end, and how?" often dominates discussion of longer-range planning. People have asked this since the beginning of the Industrial Revolution, with virtually all observers agreeing that such rapid expansion could not continue indefinitely; the high growth rates of the Industrial Revolution must represent a transitional period in history. However, there has been no agreement about when or how the transition will end, or where it will lead.

There have always been some people who expected the end would be disastrous. Until recent years this was a distinctly minority opinion, only occasionally in vogue. An increasing number of people—especially among literate and academic elites—has come to believe that rapid exponential growth may be humanity's greatest tragedy rather than its greatest triumph; that human beings are on the verge of a catastrophic collision with reality. Our view of the likely future is very different.

To characterize the economic changes that seem likely, we distinguish among primary, secondary, tertiary, and quaternary kinds of economic and quasi-economic activities. Primary activities are extractive—principally agriculture, mining, forestry, and fishing. A preindustrial society focuses on these activities. Basically, the society is organized to "play games with and against nature."[3] Before the Industrial Revolution, for every person who lived in a city, perhaps twenty people labored elsewhere, supporting the city dwellers by pursuing primary activities.

The principal secondary activities are construction and manufacturing. The corresponding society is organized mostly to "play games with and against materials." The culture is primarily urban, characterized in our time by the nation-state and by a relatively sharp distinction between the city and the countryside.

Tertiary activities are services to primary, secondary, or other tertiary activities emphasized in an emerging post-industrial economy. These are services to society; hence the term service economy. Such services include transportation, communications, insurance, finance, management, engineering, merchandising, aesthetic design, advertising, many governmental activities, and much education and training. In emerging postindustrial societies, even those engaged in primary and secondary activities find themselves closer to white collar tertiary activities than to the traditional primary and secondary blue collar interactions with and against nature or materials. The society is organized to "play games with and against organizations." It is characterized by organizational and professional pluralism, particularly in the distribution of power and prestige and is probably more suburban than urban. Its business activities may be dominated more by transnational corporations than by purely national corporations or indigenous individual proprietorships. The emphasis is on the "knowledge" industries and the growth of bureaucratic and intellectual elites.

Early in the twenty-first century, a partial transition to a different kind of service economy should occur, at least in what we call the Advanced Capitalist countries. This is what we call a quaternary or true postindustrial economy—a tentative concept subject to many caveats. Basically, it holds that primary, secondary, and tertiary activities will eventually constitute only a small part of human endeavors. The strictly economic tasks of furnishing the material and commercial needs and mechanical services of a society will require fewer and fewer people. At the limit, these tasks will be carried out largely by highly automated equipment and complex computers. The small professional group needed to operate the equipment may not, despite its seeming critical importance, be the elite of their society just as farmers, even big landholders, are not a very special elite in today's society. As the average income and welfare benefits increase, low-level service jobs will disappear, become high-level jobs, or become completely or partially voluntary. For example, full-time maids have already almost disappeared in the Advanced Capitalist countries.

Such high-level personal service roles as teacher, psychiatrist, doctor, author, priest, and public entertainer will increase. Both consumers and producers will pursue these activities for their own sakes—that is, for relatively noneconomic or personal reasons and not because they contribute to the performance of primary or secondary activities. Much basic research would be included in this category. Means as well as ends will be evaluated in terms of their wider social, personal, and cultural implications, rather than by narrow cost-benefit calculations. An activity will be judged as much by what kind of people it produces and how it affects the individual and the community as by narrow profit and loss calculations. Economic and technical efficiency will be deemphasized in favor of concepts of the good and the beautiful according to cultural and personal criteria. Such a society can be characterized as playing games "with and against people, with and against communities, and perhaps with and against oneself." Indeed, the use of the word game will probably become less metaphoric and more literal.

This image of postindustrial society is not idiosyncratic. Many great thinkers speculating on what the Great Transition of the Industrial Revolution would bring have envisioned similar outcomes. Karl Marx's vision is probably the most renowned of these scenarios. Marx believed, as we do, that the Industrial Revolution would usher humanity into a new era. Although Marx first thought that only a violent revolution would remove the capitalists, he believed that the era after their demise would be far better than the past and that the ordinary human being would reach new heights surpassing those achieved by the elites in fifth-century-B.C. Athens or during the Italian Renaissance. Marx foresaw a society in the distant future where "nobody has one exclusive sphere of activity but each can become accomplished in any branch he wishes, [where] society regulates the general production and thus makes it possible for me to do one thing today and another tomorrow, to hunt in the morning, fish in the afternoon, rear cattle in the evening, criticize after dinner, just as I have a mind, without ever becoming hunter, fisherman, shepherd, or critic." J. M. Keynes put forth remarkably similar images of a rapid Great Transition to a quaternary society in an essay published in 1930. Keynes clearly foresaw a better world where the values and priorities of the capitalist system would ultimately be rejected, and where humanity would be free to pursue nobler goals.

In contrast with Marx and Keynes, our scenario does not anticipate a future utopia. We are skeptical or agnostic about this. Indeed, the world of one or two hundred years from now may not be a very happy place— at least by present standards. Instead of harmony, the future might be plagued by disorder and unrest or subjected to regimentation. The visions of both *1984* and *Brave New World* seem genuine possibilities, even if not inevitable or even likely.

A century from now, much relative poverty and perhaps even major pockets of absolute poverty will probably still persist. The arithmetic (but probably not geometric) gap between the richest 10 percent and the poorest 10 percent of the world's people will almost certainly be greater than today. But unless the future is marred by a major nuclear war or other disaster, almost all of humanity will be materially better off. The traditional grinding absolute poverty, famine, pestilence, disease and incapacity, illiteracy, and backbreaking toil, all of which have been humanity's lot throughout history, should be almost gone, and with luck for once and for all. What the majority of people will do in such a world is an open question and may be a serious problem.

The opportunities for both good and evil will be enormous. If all goes well, the centuries to come could well be when humanity's true history begins. If, as seems reasonable, technology continues to advance and wealth accumulates and spreads throughout the world, the global society might eventually become largely posteconomic as well as postindustrial. There is no intrinsic reason why consumer goods, such as the twenty-second-century equivalents of houses, automobiles, and television sets, should not become almost infinitely durable. Very likely, rapid obsolescence or deterioration of many products would no longer occur. Industry's tasks would be limited to gradual replacement. Overall production might substantially decline as the world's people became satisfied with the existing stock of physical goods. And given the probable high level of automation, the workers required to maintain the stock might be only a small percentage of the world's population. Business, as we know it, might even disappear. (In a way this is exactly the social system or society which many in the New Class believe is coming, but at a much higher level of affluence and technology than they envisage. Our major quarrel with their vision is with its premature quality rather than with its contents.) If these visions materialize, the quaternary culture would be strongly reminiscent of many aspects of the richer and more stable preindustrial cultures that included many of these "mundane" activities: Reading, writing, painting, acting, composing, musicianship, arts and crafts—done for their own sake or as a part of a larger context. Tourism, games, contests, rituals, exhibitions, and performances. Gourmet cooking and eating, an aristocratic and formal style of life. Epicurean and family values (including visiting, entertaining, and "togetherness"). [. . .]

There could also be activities of a sort usually judged as more significant, or at least less private than those listed above: Public works and public projects—some done more for propaganda, morale, interest, amusement, ceremonial, or ritualistic reasons than for "cost-effective" economic or research objectives [. . .] openly ceremonial, ritualistic, and aesthetic activities [. . .] evoking of images or feelings of splendor, pride, pomp, awe, and communal, ethnic, religious, or national unity or identity; oneness with nature and the universe, and various "explorations in inner space" or other forms of emotional or spiritual self-fulfillment, the creation of taboos, totems, demanding religions, traditions, and customs; arbitrary pressures, constraints, and demands; moral and social equivalents of war; some other pressures and risks, including those involved with some of the more bizarre forms of "discretionary behavior" and the "testing" of one's abilities and limitations.

Finally, the concept of quaternary culture includes mystical and "inner space" activities. Many writers on this subject assign a much higher role to these activities than we do, although we concede that they may be significant and perhaps even dominating. This quaternary culture is already emerging in many Advanced Capitalist nations, largely among what we will call the New Class. In fact, one way of defining the New Class is as people who have mostly upper-middle class backgrounds and who have been raised in or live a more or less quaternary culture or in the more analytical, aesthetic, symbolic, or intellectual parts of the tertiary sector. One of our major themes will be the social, intellectual, and cultural difficulties that the largely New Class quaternary culture will have in dealing with the more mundane and practical aspects of the world.

Some people may feel that this future quaternary economy is in some sense unreal—a bit like a play-world or a play-acting world. We do not deny this observation and emphasize that it may be very difficult to think of certain traditional issues seriously in this kind of quaternary economy. There may indeed be a lack of contact with traditional reality, which nonetheless may remain important, if only latently.

This transition would mark the completion of the Industrial Revolution, the second great watershed of human history. Still more distant societies will probably consider these centuries of industrialization to have marked humanity's journey from a world that was basically inhospitable to its few dwellers to one that was fully commanded and presumably enjoyed by its multitudes.

If we place ourselves in the year 5000 or so and look backward, we might recognize three stages separated by two narrow, almost instantaneous, periods of transition. The first stage is the period before 8000 B.C. of hunting bands and tribes. We might shorten the process we call modernization or the Great Transition—that is, from 1800 to 2200—into a single line at about the year 2000. From this perspective, that 400-year period might be seen as almost instantaneous termination of the so-called civilized era and the creation of something new. After all, the agricultural revolution is usually seen in a similar way, even though in fact it took thousands of years to spread around the world.

We do not have a good idea of what we mean by postindustrial. The term itself is negative, describing what will not be rather than what will be. There are, many other possible terms. Postcivilized implies that our ideas of civilization have thus far been largely determined by traditional society, but they will no longer hold. Posteconomic implies that the behavior of most human beings most of the time will not be simply determined by cost-effectiveness. For example, even today, whether an affluent American travels three hundred miles or three thousand miles to a vacation spot may not be much affected, much less determined by the distance or airfare. For all practical purposes, the person thinks of the two distances as about the same. Similarly, future income will be so high and costs so low that most individuals will be indifferent to the prices of their various options.

We do not know exactly what we mean by truly human and post-human, but they seem like usefully provocative phrases. Faustian connotes making a pact with the devil to gain power, wealth, and secular knowledge. (In the legend the devil eventually claims Faust's soul, but this need not happen; in fact it does not happen in Goethe's version.) Promethean is intended to emphasize knowledge and progress; no pact with the devil is involved, though of course Prometheus was grossly punished for his temerity in giving fire to humans by being bound to a rock and having his liver eternally gnawed by a vulture. We do not claim to know much about the long-term outlook for humanity, except that we believe it will probably be incredibly affluent by current standards and that the accompanying technology can give the average individual capabilities that have previously been reserved for gods or magicians.

WHY MORE ECONOMIC GROWTH?

[. . .] We firmly believe that despite the arguments put forward by people who would like to "stop the earth and get off," it is simply impractical to do so. Propensity to change may not be inherent in human nature, but it is firmly embedded in most contemporary cultures. People have almost everywhere become curious, future oriented, and dissatisfied with their conditions. They want more material goods and covet higher status and greater control of nature. Despite much propaganda to the contrary, they believe, almost certainly correctly, that it is technologically and economically possible for them to achieve these goals.

We are not arguing that humanity's desires are open-ended. But the rewards of economic growth and advanced technology—however flawed and problem-ridden—are not illusory. The social limits to growth are simply not, for the time being, likely to be as restrictive as much current discussion suggests. At least 90 percent of the world's population reject such arguments. As these people become more affluent and as their children adopt new values, their opposition to growth may increase—why not? As the world gets richer, the marginal utility of increased wealth will probably diminish.

Even if much better arguments were advanced in favor of social limits to growth, most people are willing to take chances. It is probably a waste of time to think ideologically about stopping progress (much less social change) and foolish to regret that much of the physical environment and many established institutions must change. Much may be protected or preserved, and many aesthetic, environmental, and conservationist values may be furthered and enhanced. Nonetheless, some basic and irrevocable changes will occur. There will probably be many gradual changes in the direction of less "creative destruction" and slower growth.

Serious discussion should start with some common sense, widely accepted assumptions about growth and change in order to waste less energy and time on utopian, ideological, or impractical issues. Eight of these sensible assumptions are:

1. Modernization in one form or another is now both natural and inevitable—though the rate may vary enormously and there may be hard core pockets of resistance. There is also much argument over what modernization means. (Many do not accept our definition that it is equivalent to participating in the Great Transition.)
2. Change always involves risk, pain, dislocation, and doubt. The objective should be to alleviate these symptoms rather than to eliminate them. It is especially wrong to increase the amount of pain by counterproductive digressions.
3. How change occurs is subject to some degree of intervention. Intervention may not always be knowledgeable and may not always achieve what it sets out to do, but it can be useful. It can also be counterproductive.
4. Nothing can prevent further change—for good or evil. Therefore, it is probably best to try to direct change toward the good or at least the less evil. This assumes that even if we cannot always agree on a long list of things we would like to have, we can usually agree on a long list of things we would like to avoid.
5. Modernization no longer means Americanization—or even Westernization—though much can still be learned from the West, Japan, South Korea, Taiwan, Singapore, Mexico, and Brazil may be more useful examples than some currently affluent countries. Each country will have to find its own way and will have to decide which mountain it will choose to climb, by what road, and with how much of the "old baggage and possessions" it wants to retain for sentimental or other reasons.
6. The trip will be much easier and safer if there is a relatively unified commitment to the trip and its objective and if skilled guidance and direction are available to help the travelers avoid becoming lost or trapped.
7. While not all the experience, path breaking, and equipment of those who have gone first is useful, much is and should be exploited.
8. It is simply untrue that there is no possibility of having an attractive, human, high quality, affluent technological society.

NOTES

1. All dollar figures are quoted in the equivalent of fixed 1978 U.S. dollars. While this concept of a fixed United States dollar immutable over time and space stretches both imagination and theory to the limit, we judge it to have enough meaning and relevance to be useful. A 1978 dollar is ⅔ as valuable as a 1972 dollar and ⅘ as valuable as a 1958 dollar. We note this since so much data appear in fixed 1972 or 1958 dollars.

2. We often refer to the very long-term future, the centuries or millennia ahead. We do not pretend to predict these; usually, these statements about the very long-term future simply show, looking at all current trends as well as we can, what we conclude will happen if these trends continue indefinitely.

3. The term *playing games with or against nature* and other uses of game metaphors emerge from the extensive literature of gaming, simulation, and role playing. They should be thought of partly literally and partly metaphorically. The idea is that the major roles of the individual in a primary society involve activities that can be characterized as "interacting with and against nature" rather than, as in the other cases, "with and against materials," "with and against organizations," or "with and against communities." The word *game* introduces the concept that much as in a game, human economic activities are governed by many formal and informal rules and customs, and that rational tactics and strategies can be important in making more probable the achievement of desired goals. The inspiration for this terminology (and of the term *postindustrial*) comes from the American sociologist Daniel Bell. See Daniel Bell, *The Coming of the Post-Industrial Society* (New York: Basic Books, 1973). Some readers may be offended at our applying such a seemingly trivial word as *game* to the long record of human heroism and disaster. As noted above, the word *game* is not intended to detract from the seriousness or significance of the activities, but rather to relate them to the large and complex body of formalistic rules that govern human behavior and to the complex interplay of means and ends in purposive human actions. For a classic discussion of the role of play and games in human societies, see *Homo Ludens: A Study of the Play Element in Culture* by Johan Huizinga (London: Routledge, Kegan Paul, 1949). As we mention later, it is only in the quaternary society that the word *game* is likely to apply literally.

7

—⊗⊗⊗—

Viewing Growth in Context

THE CURRENT HOSTILITY TO ECONOMIC GROWTH

[. . .] After an excessively optimistic phase early in the post–World War II period, the intellectual climate surrounding the concept of modernization through economic and technological advancement has, until recently, tended to be excessively pessimistic. To the extent that the very legitimacy of the goal of development is now called into question, this negative climate has been strongly reinforced. It is a climate that can have pervasive, if often subtle, destructive effects. Belief in the ultimate desirability of economic development and technological advancement is a powerful force for constructive efforts, especially for obtaining foreign and domestic political and moral support. Conversely, the belief that modernization is harmful, illegitimate, or largely a failure erodes national as well as international development efforts and undermines foreign aid programs designed to encourage, extend, and protect development. It also undermines the willingness to tolerate some of the bad effects of modernization for the good it produces.

These doubts and concerns, intensified by a new focus on pollution and quality of life issues, do not spring from failure or disasters in recent years. In fact, much of the disappointment and disillusionment comes from success. By its nature, success may create, reveal, or exacerbate many

[*World Economic Development: 1979 and Beyond* (Boulder, Colo.: Westview Press, 1979).]

problems. Good results are taken for granted, while bad results are judged intolerable. We have compared many of the costs of development with its benefits and are prepared to justify our support for what we call modernization. We are convinced that economic development, industrialization, and the application and use of intermediate and advanced technology will—by and large and under current conditions—be judged desirable by our culture and by most other cultures. Moreover, we believe that one need not share our enthusiasm for many of the things we advocate to recognize them as the preferred options at present. This does not imply that we are confident that the worldwide movement toward modernization must turn out well—only that it is a good gamble.

All consequences of modernization and progress will be neither wildly successful nor universally desirable. Even if they are beneficent in the medium run, the question of their capacities for good and evil over the long run still remains open. Despite these concerns, we give little credence to the negative attitudes toward economic growth so prevalent in recent years. Many of these activities are excessive, elitist, romantic, self-serving, or based on false information or absurd theories.

Indeed, self-interest and self-indulgence—especially the narrow biases and interests displayed by many upper and upper-middle class people in affluent countries—have dominated recent discussions of economic and social problems to a degree that is seldom acknowledged. Three subgroups comprising what we call the Anti-Growth Triad. Listed in order of increasing importance to our concerns, they are: (1) affluent radicals and reformers; (2) Thorstein Veblen's "leisure class"; and (3) a subgroup of upper-middle class intellectuals we refer to as neo-liberal members of the New Class.

Members of the Anti-Growth Triad have typically enjoyed the benefits of economic growth and modernization since their childhood, but as adults they are now disillusioned with further growth for reasons that run the gamut from admirable to unreasonable to selfish. They try to discourage others from gaining what they have enjoyed and now disdain. Some of their points, such as possible misuses of affluence and advanced technology, are valid; others are gratuitous or just wrong. Mostly, the Anti-Growth Triad seems likely to create diversions that greatly increase the costs and difficulties for the upwardly mobile but that are unlikely to change the basic trend of the world as a whole.

[. . .] Some observers have suggested that, since both the advocates of early or forced limits to growth and we believe in some limits, our debate is purely technical and the differences in our viewpoints hold little interest for the general public. Actually, the differences are fundamental.

The common concern that dangerous mistakes can result from rapid growth is definitely justified. The following table summarizes some pros and cons of economic and technological growth. As the economic and technological scale and pace of development have increased, the likelihood has also increased that major dangers can arise too suddenly to be dealt with in time to avoid disasters. Rapid growth may increase the possibility of serious imbalances but it can also create situations that make it easier to deal with such imbalances. Industrial pollution, for example, reached high levels in some developed countries, but these countries have been able to use their resources and technological capabilities to avert disasters, if not all serious problems, by dramatically reducing the rate of pollution while there was still time.

**Some Pros and Cons of Economic and
Technological Growth**

Basic Argument: Affluence and technology are good things, both as ends and means.

Basic Caveat: But not always and not everywhere—there are many bad aspects (e.g., often excessively encourages materialistic values).

Basic Argument: In any case, economic wealth and technical capability provide security and insurance1—and can be essential to survival.

Basic Caveat: May also create excessive dependence on wealth and technology—can make life too easy and unchallenging, in any case not really essential unless competing in material terms with an "advanced" culture (either militarily or commercially).

Basic Argument: Provides a base for power and influence.

Basic Caveat: To do bad as well as good—creates a need for more power and influence, can also lead to arrogance, carelessness, and callousness.

Basic Argument: Gaps help make the poor rich.

Basic Caveat: But not all of them, may damage their self-respect and status, seduce them into giving up more than they gain, and lead to feelings of injustice, envy, guilt, and contempt.

Basic Argument: Rapid growth facilitates the Great Transition and early achievement of affluence.

Basic Caveat: But can also be excessively destructive of existing values and assets and may even help precipitate the kind of disaster one is trying to insure against.

Basic Argument: Growth facilitates adaptation to change and fulfillment of economic aspirations.

Basic Caveat: But it causes too rapid change and arouses excessive economic and other aspirations.

The necessity for dealing with these kinds of problems has been widely recognized. Regulatory agencies have tightened their requirements, in some cases excessively. Effective programs to protect the environment have already been institutionalized in North America, Japan, Australia, and northwestern Europe. In the years to come, almost all highly industrialized nations are likely to have much less pollution than they now have, despite the widespread impression that these problems are getting worse. Pressures for high standards must be maintained, but here as elsewhere overly zealous crusaders have sometimes done more harm than good. This is a learning process automatically involving much wasted motion and inefficiency, unfortunately tragically excessive at times. One reason for such excesses in coping with pollution is that many people are upset about dangers that are either exaggerated or already handled satisfactorily.

While the danger of mistakes, imbalances, and major new problems (many as yet unperceived) can be overstated, it should not be dismissed. The danger is serious enough to justify more effective study, planning, and research, including greater efforts to establish safeguards. However, we do not believe that the danger can be avoided or even significantly reduced by misguided attempts to mandate a lower rate of economic growth across the board. The most sensible opponents of growth call for caution. They say, "Why take a chance?" or "Why not stop growth, at least in the developed world, until we are more sure of the consequences?" This position may seem reasonable enough, but generally it is motivated by a distaste for an ever-wealthier world. Many upper and upper-middle class people correctly perceive that while growth was helpful to them at one time, it now often hurts their personal and class interests.

Most lower income people in the developed world have their basic material needs satisfied (often through welfare programs), while many upper income people are satiated by a vast variety of material goods. The result is that an emotional appeal for a simpler and less materialistic way of life is gaining favor among many of the affluent, and the middle class is increasingly losing its motivation to strive for further economic gains. Few lower income people take this position; nor do most relatively wealthy people agree—at least not yet.

If opposition to growth were primarily a genuine appeal to caution, it could help reduce pollution and waste of resources and stimulate greater care in innovation and expansion. Unfortunately, however, when they are not pushing some narrow class or personal position, most opponents of growth often are excessively eager either to maintain the status quo or to "junk" the entire world economic system—or sometimes, paradoxically, both. The typical limits to growth advocates do not have a tenable middle ground position. If finite limits to growth do exist (because of insufficient resources or excessive pollution), then the proper focus for the world's economy would be to curb growth to bring about a sustainable steady-state economy as soon as possible. Such a world would have to maintain an acceptable standard of living more or less indefinitely. This would probably require a dramatic cut in production and consumption levels in the developed world. It would also mean much less willingness to protect uneconomic endangered species, ecology, and the environment. Even a modified version of most resource limit positions requires radical and immediate changes that would not favor many of the shibboleths of "the environment" and "the ecology." No genuinely poor society would even consider putting aside 100,000,000 acres in Alaska or otherwise worry about preserving in perpetuity pristine wildernesses almost equal to France in area, a proposal that almost passed the U.S. Congress in 1978 and that remains very alive.

A fundamental tenet of modern Western culture until recently has been that the secular trend of technological and industrial progress will lead to better standards of living and a better quality of life for more and more people. The anti-growth movement challenges this concept. The idea of progress goes back about two or three hundred years and is thus a relatively new idea in human affairs. There is no overwhelming a priori reason to believe that it is necessarily correct. Still, the concept became so firmly embedded in Western culture that as recently as the mid-1960s, historians and social scientists believed that the commitment to economic and technological progress was virtually unchallengeable. After World War II the commitment was globally recognized under the banner of the "revolution of rising expectations." Few countries in the world have consciously and explicitly resisted economic and technological progress as too destructive of old and valued institutions and traditions.

The belief that progress is inevitable and generally beneficial has come to be considered as a "natural" worldview. It is rarely regarded as an artificial philosophy or ideology, except by the limits-to-growth movement. We agree with the historian Sidney Pollard that: The idea of progress is, in this modern age, one of the most important ideas by which men live, not least because most hold it unconsciously and therefore unquestionably. It has been called the modern religion, and not unjustly so. Its character, its assumptions, have changed with time, and so has the influence exerted by it, but at present it is riding high, affecting the social attitudes and social actions of all of us.

THE NATURE OF THE CHALLENGE

Challenges to the concept of progress are not new. What is new is the effectiveness of today's challenge and its broad support by the upper-middle class and professional elites. These groups have an essentially modern outlook, have benefited most from technology and industrialization, and presumably understand and appreciate the modern industrial world. In the past, challenges to modernity have come from romantics, reactionaries, aristocrats, aesthetes, and various religious and ideological groups. Many of these people, too, have jumped on the Club of Rome bandwagon. However, the basic impetus for the campaign against economic growth still comes from "modern," "progressive," and "enlightened" individuals and groups with much greater than average education and affluence.

The various attacks on and negative prognoses about current capitalist industrial cultures encompass many themes, old and new, most of which have some validity. The list below gives a sense of the variety of perspectives that the anti-growth movement draws upon to rationalize, exploit, and promulgate its message.

Those who argue that the capitalist industrial culture is now historically obsolete and is or soon will be due for the trash heap of history: Older Marx, Lenin, old left generally; Younger Marx, Marcuse, Reich, Revel, new left or humanist left generally; Keynes (effect of affluence via compound interest); Schumpeter (the failure of success); Modern postindustrial formulations (some views of the service economy and knowledge society, Maslow/Reich self-actualizing society, our view of some possible quaternary cultures); Many macro-historicist prognoses (Spengler, Toynbee, Sorokin, etc.). Some miscellaneous traditional critiques: Anti-bourgeois/secular humanist criticism; Reformist-welfare/humanist/conservationist groups; Heroic/religious critique; Technocratic/socialist/central planner critique. Other more modern critiques: The Galbraithian institutionalization analysis; Arguments and perspectives based on the liberal crisis; Moral deterioration possibility; "Future Shock" thesis; Zero growth/"anti-progress"/pollution/ecology perspective.

For many people the anti-growth arguments prove the evils or impending collapse of the capitalist and private enterprise way of life. People who already believe, for other reasons, that the current system is wrong welcome supporting evidence from these new perspectives. Most of the diverse limits-to-growth arguments provide what purports to be "scientific evidence" for reforming our ways and reversing current trends. The combination of many disparate points of view strengthens opposition to growth. As a result, during the last decade the anti-growth syndrome has become dominant among intellectuals and educated elites all over the world, especially in the affluent countries [. . .]

THE GAP BETWEEN THE RICH AND THE POOR

Unlike others who discuss the popular concept of the "widening gap" between the rich and the poor, we focus on the positive aspects of the gap. The increasing disparity between average incomes in the richest and poorest nations is usually seen as an unalloyed evil to be overcome as rapidly as possible through enlightened policies by the advanced nations and international organizations. If this occurred because the poor were getting poorer, we would agree, but when it occurs at all, it is almost always because the rich are getting richer. This is not necessarily a bad thing for the poor, at least if they compare themselves with their own past or their own present rather than with a mythical theoretical gap.

In contrast, we view this gap as a basic "engine" of growth. It generates or supports most of the basic processes by which the poor are becoming rich, or at least less poor. The great abundance of resources of the developed world—capital, management, technology, and large markets in which to sell—makes possible the incredibly rapid progress of most of the developing countries. Many of these poorer countries are also developing relatively autonomous capabilities at an increasing rate.

Current attitudes toward the gap illustrate the worldview of many modern liberals. The dramatic increase in the disparity of per capita income between the wealthiest and poorest nations would have been a cause for self-congratulation by the fortunate wealthy nations at an earlier time in history—whether Roman, Greek, Chinese, or Indian. Indeed, when the colonial powers expanded their dominion, their affluence was largely accepted by all parties as a sign of their inherent superiority. Today, however, it is more a source of guilt than of pride for descendants of those same high morale colonialists. Yet such guilt is even less justified today than a hundred years ago.

It is still not widely understood that in light of eventual modernization colonial rule was likely to produce more advantages than disadvantages. Moreover, in much (but not all) of the Third World, the European expansion was more just and humane than most previous conquests by expanding cultures. Without condoning the evils of colonialism, one can nonetheless say that conquest is not an international crime invented by the European peoples. The poverty that exists in the Third World was not caused by European colonization, nor can the current problems of the poor nations be solved by fostering a sense of guilt in the rich nations. The modern liberal view holds that an international system that perpetuates inequalities among nations is morally unacceptable. This attitude is indelibly Western in origin and is most prevalent among citizens of what we call the Atlantic Protestant culture area. The affluent minority of humanity has a genuine responsibility to aid the poor, but largesse dispensed because of guilt is likely to produce counterproductive and self-righteous expectations and attitudes in developing countries.

NOTE

1. By "insurance," we include having economic and technological flexibility to react to problems, whether caused by people or nature (e g., oil shock or climate changes), toughness of the system, and capability to prevent, influence, correct, or alleviate the impact of harmful events on oneself and others.

8

Four Characteristic Views of Two Basic Images of the Earth-Centered Perspective

There are two basic and totally different images (or models) of the earth-centered perspective, which we have labeled the neo-Malthusian and the technology-and-growth positions. The first is a modern version of the analysis of the nineteenth-century English economist Thomas Malthus, who argued that population would eventually grow faster than food supply, thus implying that starvation would soon become mankind's perennial lot, at least for the poor.[1] The opposite image stems from the premise that in the next one hundred years material needs can be met so easily in the currently developed world that the more advanced nations will develop superindustrial and then postindustrial economies, and that the rest of the world will soon follow. Obviously these two basic images encompass a range of differing views and concepts, so to represent them fairly and without exaggeration, we have developed two detailed views for each of the two models—one of which in each case is a relatively extreme position, the other a moderate one. Thus, the neo-Malthusian model includes the views of a strong neo-Malthusian and a moderate neo-Malthusian (that is, a guarded pessimist); and for the contrasting model, we describe the positions taken by a moderate (or guarded optimist) and an enthusiastic advocate of technology and economic growth. Both of the moderate positions argue that we can expect serious problems in energy shortfalls, resource scarcities and food distribution.

[Herman Kahn, Leon Martel, and William M. Brown, *The Next 200 Years: A Scenario for America and the World* (New York: Morrow, 1976).]

Both also raise the real possibility of cataclysmic or irreversible environmental damage. But both hold open the possibility (in one case barely and in the other relatively clearly) that with technological progress, wise policies, competent management and good luck, mankind can deal with these problems and survive into a future where, at the least, opportunity is not foreclosed and disaster is not foreordained.

FOUR VIEWS OF THE EARTH-CENTERED PERSPECTIVE

1. Basic World Model

A. Convinced Neo-Malthusian

Finite pie. Most global nonrenewable resources can be estimated accurately enough (within a factor of 5) to demonstrate the reality of the running-out phenomenon. Whatever amounts of these resources are consumed will forever be denied to others. Current estimates show we will be running out of many critical resources in the next fifty years. The existing remainder of the pie must be shared more fairly among the nations of the world and between this generation and those to follow. Because the pie shrinks over time, any economic growth that makes the rich richer can only make the poor poorer.

B. Guarded Pessimist

Uncertain pie. The future supply and value of both old and new materials are necessarily uncertain. Past projections of the future availability of materials usually have been gross underestimates. One can concede this could happen again, but current estimates seem relatively reliable. Current exponential growth clearly risks an early exhaustion of some critical materials. Prudence requires immediate conservation of remaining resources. Excessive conservation poses small risks while excessive consumption would be tragic.

C. Optimist

Growing pie. Past technological and economic progress suggests that increasing current production is likely to increase further the potential for greater production and that progress in one region encourages similar developments everywhere. Thus as the rich get richer, the poor also benefit. Higher consumption in the developed world tends to benefit all countries. Excessive caution tends to maintain excessive poverty. Some caution is necessary in selected areas, but both the "least risk" and the "best bet" paths require continued and rapid technological and economic development.

D. Technology-and-Growth Enthusiast

Unlimited pie. The important resources are capital, technology and educated people. The greater these resources, the greater the potential for even more. There is no persuasive evidence that any meaningful limits to growth are in sight—or are desirable—except for population growth in some LDCs. If any very long-term limits set by a "finite earth" really exist, they can be offset by the vast extraterrestrial resources and areas that will become available soon. Man has always risen to the occasion and will do so in the future despite dire predictions from the perennial doomsayers who have always been scandalously wrong.

2. Technology and Capital

A. Convinced Neo-Malthusian

Largely illusory or counterproductive. Proposed technological solutions to problems of pollution or scarce resources are shortsighted illusions that only compound the difficulties. Even on a moderate scale this approach would only further deplete crucial resources while avoiding the real problems and prolonging the poverty of the LCDs. Any future economic development should be restricted to the Third World and should include some transfer of existing capital assets from the overdeveloped nations. A completely new approach is needed for the long term.

B. Guarded Pessimist

Mostly diminishing returns. Generally, despite many exceptions, the future will bring diminishing marginal returns from new investments, and the effort required for economic gains will increase dramatically. The technology, capital equipment, and other efforts required to obtain minerals and food in increasingly marginal situations will accelerate the approaching exhaustion of many resources and substantially increase pollution and shortages possibly to lethal levels. Until practical solutions to these problems have appeared, we must turn away from technology and investment.

C. Optimist

Required for progress. Despite some dangers, only new technology and capital investment can increase production; protect and improve the environment; hold down the cost of energy, minerals and food; provide economic surpluses with which to improve living standards in the LDCs; and prepare prudently for any potential unexpected catastrophes. We must be alert for problems resulting from adequately understood innovations, inappropriate growth, and/or natural causes. However, we should proceed with energy and confidence even while exercising great caution and constantly reassessing future risks and benefits.

D. Technology-and-Growth Enthusiast

Solves almost all problems. Some current problems have resulted from careless application of technology and investment, but none without a remedy. It is not paradoxical that technology which caused problems can also solve them—it only requires mankind's attention and desire. There is little doubt that sufficient land and resources exist for continuous progress on earth. Most current problems are the result of too little technology and capital, not too much. In any case man's desire for expansion into new frontiers will lead eventually to the colonization of the solar system and effectively unlimited Lebensraum.

3. Management and Decision-Making

A. Convinced Neo-Malthusian

Failure is almost certain. The complexities, rigidities, and ideological differences among nations and their institutions—make it inconceivable that present human organizations, even with computer assistance, could sufficiently comprehend and effectively act to solve our most important problems. A drastic redesign is needed to circumvent the thrust toward bigness, to permit much more local and decentralized decision-making, and to live and work on a manageable human scale. More emphasis is needed on the community and regional level—much less on big business, big government and big organization generally.

B. Guarded Pessimist

Likely failure. The rapidity of change, growing complexity, and increasing conflicting interests make effective management of resources, control of pollution, and resolution of social conflicts too difficult; some slowdown and simplification of issues are imperative—even if they require drastic actions. If we don't reform voluntarily, more painful political and economic changes may be imposed on us by the catastrophic events made inevitable by failure to act soon. (Note that there is a wide range of attitudes hcrc toward central planning and local decision-making, but almost all of them mistrust the current "unfree market.")

C. Optimist

Moderately successful. Systematic internalization of current external costs and normal economic mechanisms can make most private organizations adequately responsive to most problems. A practical degree of public regulation and a low degree of international cooperation can handle the rest, if somewhat awkwardly. Outstanding management is rare but usually not essential as most institutions learn from experience—if often slowly and painfully. (But good management can reduce the number and intensity of painful experiences.) Except for wars, shocks as great as the oil shock and other 1973–1974 experiences are rare, and yet existing systems reacted adequately—and survived.

D. Technology-and-Growth Enthusiast

Not a serious problem. We flatter ourselves that current issues are more important and difficult than ever. Actually there is usually nothing very special happening. Mankind always has faced difficult and dangerous problems and poor solutions resulted in high costs. Sometimes there is even a Darwinian selection—the successes surviving and the failures disappearing. Progress has made the stakes today less dramatic. Modern communication and information systems and sophisticated organization provide a capability for rapid adjustments to reality whenever changes are required and government interference is not counterproductive.

4. Resources

A. Convinced Neo-Malthusian

Steady depletion. Mankind is steadily, and often rapidly, depleting the earth's potential resources for foods, fuels, and minerals, and overwhelming its capability to absorb or recycle pollutants. Catastrophic results for some of these resources may be postponed until the twenty-first century, but food, energy, and some minerals already appear to be critically short for the near term. All signs point to catastrophe for the medium- and long-term future.

B. Guarded Pessimist

Continual difficulties. The basic problem of limited resources may be insoluble, even when sufficient resources exist; politics, incompetent management, poor planning, and slow responses make effective solutions difficult under conditions of exponentially increasing demand. Where resources are becoming scarce and unrelenting demands for growth are coupled with incompetence, intolerable pressures are generated and disaster becomes probable. A more cautious approach to growth seems clearly desirable.

C. Optimist

Generally sufficient. Given slow but steady technological and economic progress and an ultimate world population below 30 billion, it should be feasible to attain economic living standards markedly better than current ones. With rapid progress and good management generally, even higher economic levels and an outstanding quality of life become possible. Economic success enhances national capabilities to resolve specialized resource issues as they arise. However, the tendency toward cartels coupled with political conflicts could create occasional short-term problems in maintaining adequate supplies at reasonable prices.

D. Technology-and-Growth Enthusiast

Economics and technology provide superb solutions. The earth is essentially bountiful in all of the important resources. Sudden large price fluctuations tend to be "self-correcting" within a few years although they can be misinterpreted as basic shortages (as in 1973–1974). Near-term prices are certainly important, but we have often lived with short-term problems. Trust in the economics of the market system, confidence in emerging technological solutions, and a little patience will remedy the current resource issues just as they have in the past.

5. Current Growth

A. Convinced Neo-Malthusian

Carcinogenic. Current population and economic production are akin to a spreading cancer. They are already more than the earth can sustain in a steady state. Future economic or population growth will hasten and increase the magnitude of the future tragedy. The current demand for continued economic growth and the likelihood of a greatly increased world population only imply a steady worsening of the present extremely dangerous conditions.

B. Guarded Pessimist

Large potential for disaster. Even if roughly current levels of production could be indefinitely sustained, continued exponential growth in population and production eventually must lead to exhausted resources and hazardous pollution. Few positive human values would be served by continued mindless growth. We must learn that demand is not need. Unless drastic voluntary reforms limit future growth, catastrophes stemming from limited resources and high pollution levels are likely to make these reforms mandatory before long.

C. Optimist

Probable transition to stability. Although current projections are uncertain, social and cultural forces inherent in both developing and affluent societies appear likely to limit the world population to about three times the current level and average per capita production to about two or three times the current U.S. level. There seems to be more than enough energy, resources and space for most populations, assuming that a relatively small number of people put forth the necessary efforts and others do not interfere.

D. Technology-and-Growth Enthusiast

Desirable and healthy. No obvious limits are apparent. Even with current technological potential, growth (except perhaps in a few of the poorest nations) is and will be purely a matter of human choice, not of natural limitations. Probabilities always exist, but solutions always emerge—often as a result of the dynamism of growth. We do not know man's ultimate fate, but truly fantastic economic and technological capabilities are likely to be included as both a means and an end (e.g., they probably include self-reproducing automation and space colonization in the next century).

6. Innovation and Discovery

A. Convinced Neo-Malthusian

A trap. New discoveries of resources, new technologies and new projects may postpone the immediate need for drastic actions, but not for long. Such postponement will make eventual collapse earlier and more severe. Prudence demands immediate restraint, cutbacks, and a basic change in values and objectives. The time for short-run palliatives is past.

B. Guarded Pessimist

Increasingly ineffective. The basic solution is to increasingly limit demands, not to encourage a desperate search for new inventions that might suffice temporarily but would exacerbate long-run problems by increasing environmental damage and depletion of resources, while encouraging current growth and deferring hard decisions. Although technological solutions may buy some time, it has become increasingly important to use this time constructively and avoid the undue economic expansion that new discoveries encourage.

C. Optimist

Usually effective. New resources, new technology and economic growth often produce new problems, but they still do solve current problems, improve efficiency, and upgrade the quality of life. Also, they increase the toughness and flexibility of the economy and society (i.e., provide insurance against bad luck or incompetence). With good management, they also can help to reduce population growth, conserve expensive minerals, improve nutrition within the poorer countries, and generally improve future prospects.

D. Technology-and-Growth Enthusiast

Mankind's greatest hope. New and improving technologies (agronomy, electronics, genetics, power generation and distribution, information processing, etc.) aided by fortuitous discoveries (e.g., ocean nodules) further man's potential for solving current perceived problems and for creating an affluent and exciting world. Man is now entering the most creative and expansive period of his history. These trends will soon allow mankind to become the "master" of the solar system.

7. Income Gaps and Poverty

A. Convinced Neo-Malthusian

Destined to tragic conclusions. The major consequences of industrialization and economic growth have been to enrich the few while exploiting and impoverishing the many. The gap between rich and poor as well as the total misery in the world are at all-time highs—and growing. Meanwhile natural resources, the heritage of the poor countries, are being consumed by the rich, thereby denying the poor any real hope for better living conditions—even temporarily.

B. Guarded Pessimist

Increasing and threatening. Income gaps have been increasing and may lead to dangerous responses. A drastic decrease in income among the poor may even be likely soon. Worldwide class warfare may emerge following a series of desperate political crises. These are not only possible but may be imminent as a consequence of the gaps and the exploitation of the mineral resources of the LDCs. A more equitable income distribution has become a most urgent matter.

C. Optimist

Declining absolute poverty. Worldwide, the threat of absolute poverty (i.e., possible large-scale famine) is likely soon to be forever abolished. Some income gaps may increase during the next century, but some will decrease. Generally, incomes of both rich and poor will increase. Both the gaps and improving technology will tend to accelerate development in poor countries. Attempts to force a rapid equalization of income would guarantee only failure and tragic consequences.

D. Technology-and-Growth Enthusiast

A misformulated problem. Western civilization required about two hundred years to change from general poverty to general affluence. Because of their success and continuing advances in technology, many of the current LDCs will be able to make a similar transformation within fifty years. All countries can be expected to become wealthy within the next two hundred years. Any lesser scenario would be unreasonable or simply an expression of some exceedingly bad luck and/or bad management. The gap is a false issue possibly conjured up by neurotic guilt.

8. Industrial Development

A. Convinced Neo-Malthusian

A disaster. Further industrialization of the Third World would be disastrous and further growth of the developed world even worse. The rich nations should halt industrial growth and share their present wealth with the poor. The poor nations should husband their precious natural resources, selling some of them only at prices much higher than those prevailing today.

B. Guarded Pessimist

A step backward. The LDCs should avoid the mistakes of the developed nations. They should instead seek smaller, more human and more community-oriented enterprises appropriate to their needs. They would be better off preserving their cultural, environmental, and ecological values than entering headlong into destructive polluting industrialization, sacrificing thereby both their current values and any long-term potential for a peaceful world.

C. Optimist

Should continue. Industrialization of the LDCs should and probably will continue. The rich nations will probably help with technical assistance, but would be unlikely to share their output to the extent of serious deprivation. Also the natural resources of the LDCs are at most of limited benefit even to those richly endowed. Their only real hope for affluence lies in economic development.

D. Technology-and-Growth Enthusiast

Necessary for wealth and progress. During the last two hundred years progress has been identified mostly with chronological innovation and economic development. Despite the current outcries, this view is and will be substantially correct. All those who wish to, can and should share in the benefits offered by modern civilization.

9. Quality of Life

A. Convinced Neo-Malthusian

Ruined. Through excessive growth, mankind has become the most destructive species in history and may yet increase the extent of this damage manyfold. Indeed, a point of no return may have been passed already, mostly because of the persistent and growing potential for nuclear warfare. In any event, the values that lead toward a satisfying and wholesome life have already been largely destroyed in the developed nations.

B. Guarded Pessimist

In conflict with much growth. Continued economic development or population growth might well mean further deterioration of the environment, overcrowding, suburban sprawl and a society suitable more for machines than human beings. Priorities must change; market demand is not the same as need; GNP is not wealth, high technology not the same as a good life; automation and appliances do not necessarily increase human happiness.

C. *Optimist*

More gains than losses. If environmental protection, health, safety and other considerations are neglected, growth would be accompanied by an unnecessary destruction of important values. However, much of what some elites claim to be destructive others consider constructive (e.g., a pipeline). With adequate internalization of the appropriate costs (by society's criteria), complaints from unhappy factions might still be loud or visible but would be generally inappropriate.

D. *Technology-and-Growth Enthusiast*

A meaningless phrase and issue. Disgruntled or unhappy people often oppose real progress for romantic, class, selfish or other reasons. They are not representative of the nation and need not be taken at face value. In a changing world, some elites may not benefit much or may even lose somewhat. But most people would benefit and gain expectations for an even better future.

10. Long-Run Outlook

A. *Convinced Neo-Malthusian*

Bleak and desperate. Unless revolutionary changes are soon made, the twenty-first century will see the greatest catastrophe of history resulting from large-scale damage to the environment and to the ecology of many areas. Billions will die of hunger, pollution, and/or wars over shrinking resources. Other billions will have to be oppressed by harsh authoritarian governments. Grave and even draconian measures are justified now to alleviate the extent and intensity of future collapse.

B. *Guarded Pessimist*

Contingent disaster. Although it is not possible to predict which disaster is most imminent, many possibilities exist even if we are careful and prudent today. Unless we take drastic actions soon, mankind may be overwhelmed by climate changes, destruction of ocean ecology, excessive pollution, or other disasters. Society must not challenge the environment and ecology so recklessly any more. We must also manage our resources and population more prudently—at least after the next disaster, if not before.

C. Optimist

Contingent success. The twenty-first century is likely to bring a worldwide postindustrial economy in which most problems of poverty will be largely solved or alleviated. Most misery will derive from the anxieties and ambiguities of relative wealth and luxury. Some suffering and damage will mark the historical transition to a materially abundant life, but the ultimate prospect is far superior to a world of poverty

D. Technology-and-Growth Enthusiast

High optimism and confidence. We cannot know mankind's ultimate goals, but they include a solar civilization and a utopian notion for the quality of life on earth. The potentialities of modern technology and economic progress are just beginning to be visualized. Dangers exist but they always have and always will. There is no need for faint heart. Man should face the future boldly and openly because the future is his to determine—and to enjoy.

The guarded optimist's view goes even further, holding that we may still avert ultimate disaster even if the policies are not so wise, management not so competent and luck not so good, but the worse the policies, management and luck, the greater the potential for tragedy along the way and even for final cataclysm.

The four views, as they relate to ten different issues, are summarized above. A and B list the typical neo-Malthusian concerns about the limited potential of the earth and the likelihood of greatly diminishing returns on future investments, rapid depletion of resources and uncontrolled exponential or cancerous population growth. In this image, innovation and discovery are seen as traps and further industrial development is expected to hasten the approaching disaster; growth of either the population or the economy is considered antithetical to a high quality of life. In short, the long-term outlook is grim. The two views of the technology-and-growth model, listed as C and D, argue that because of the evolution of knowledge and technology, resources are increasing rather than fixed; more technology and more capital are vital; decision-making will probably rise to the occasion, despite some incompetence or bad luck; enough resources will be available at reasonable costs so that reasonable rates of growth can be achieved; current exponential population growth will make a natural transition to stability; innovative discoveries will yield great improvements; and although absolute income differences could increase for a while, current levels of absolute poverty will decrease almost everywhere (the rich will not get richer while the poor get poorer, but both will become richer). Thus, in this view, all things considered, the long-range outlook is quite good.

In this study we are more interested in the differences between B and C than in the gross differences between A and D, even though B and C come rather close to merging on some issues. Current advocates of B (formerly closer to A) originally emphasized the sheer physical impossibility of the earth's supporting 10 or 20 billion people and often stated this claim in an extreme form. Today many of them take a relatively moderate position, but one still strongly colored by their past beliefs. Rather interestingly, many of the followers of these less extreme advocates have not shifted with them and talk as if those they support still hold A rather than B beliefs.

B and C advocates represent two of many possible middle positions. They project that in some places and at some time there will be too many people for available food supplies and that considerable suffering will result, but in the long term they see the rate of population growth slowing and world population eventually stabilizing—but for different reasons. The B position is remarkably close to the C position, but it tends to emphasize conscious and drastic efforts to reduce demand as the basic method of solution rather than major efforts to increase supply. Indeed, B advocates argue that unless there are very intense and dramatic programs to cut demand and limit it permanently, the situation will turn out much as anticipated in A. Those who favor C, on the other hand, see the situation as rather close to the D view. However, they also believe that there are both more natural limitations to demand and more dangers in growth than the D people might concede. The C people also depict some few resources as fixed, limited, and nonrenewable, but they argue that the growth of knowledge and technology will normally make available—though not always without problems and difficulties—new sources and substitutes. Acknowledging that there will be incompetence and bad luck, causing serious problems, they doubt that these will be fatal. They visualize much more demand than A and B believe can be tolerated, but not so much more that it could not be met, even if it required expanding supply capabilities somewhat.

In the last several years, the neo-Malthusian attitudes outlined in A and B have gained great influence. Not too many years ago—not more than a decade—most educated Americans would have placed themselves in C, leaning toward D. Today they tend to be in B and leaning toward A, and many unreservedly support its full neo-Malthusian conclusions. It has become increasingly fashionable, especially among intellectuals at prestige universities and among spokesmen in the most respected newspapers and journals as well as on television, to attack economic growth, capitalism, industrialization, the consumer society and related values. Casual references are made to our vanishing resources, the end of the "energy joyride," our increasingly "suicidal" pollution, our "self-destructive materialism," the poverty of our emotional and aesthetic lives, the disease of "consumeritis" and the need to "kick the energy habit." The United States is usually singled out as the prime culprit in this indictment: It has only one-sixteenth of the world's population, yet with incredible selfishness and shortsightedness, it has been allocating to its own use about one-third of the world's nonrenewable resources.

We believe that the movement toward A—propelled by a combination of compassion and guilt for the plight of the world's poor and the coincidental occurrence of worldwide crises in the supply of food and energy—has gone too far. Spurred now by well-publicized studies, it has acquired a momentum of its own which, if continued, will only deepen the malaise it depicts and make longer and more difficult the recovery that is required. We believe that plausible and realistic scenarios can be written consonant with a view that sees the world moving from C toward D. We argue that there is both need and opportunity for growth, and that because America and the rest of the nations of the developed world do use resources so intensely, there will be stimulation, not depression, for the economies of the less-developed countries. In fact, the clearest moral and political argument for further growth in the developed world (and against artificial and forced limitation) is that it aids the poor both within and outside the developed countries.

Despite the confident tone of these last few pages and some of our earlier discussion, we would like to stress that in no sense do we wish to play down the importance of the issues raised by the neo-Malthusians or to assert that there are no serious problems. While we generally tend to be optimistic about many of them, we recognize that very unpleasant situations can arise—possibilities, which must be dealt with competently and responsibly. We also believe not only that this can be done, but that in many cases it already is being done. Finally, we feel that even though the costs and risks are great, the effort to achieve a postindustrial society is on balance a worthwhile one; and further, that priorities which emphasize technological advancement and economic growth, but with prudence and care, are likely to be acceptable and largely beneficial.

Thus our disagreement with advocates of the limits-to-growth positions sometimes is that they raise false, nonexistent or misformulated issues; equally often, perhaps, they pose as being basically insoluble real problems for which we believe rather straightforward and practical solutions can be found in most cases. In our view, the more intractable and basic difficulties usually lie much less in the nature of things than in recent or current policies, in unnecessarily poor administration or sometimes in just plain bad luck. Most important of all, if successful programs are devised to deal with old problems, then inevitably new problems are uncovered and new goals are set; to those who take the initial success for granted, it may then seem as if nothing has been accomplished.

NOTE

1. Scholarly integrity and concern for the somewhat maligned memory of Malthus compel us to note that this best-known conclusion of his was an early view which he tempered and amended in his later work.

9

Some Current Cultural Contradictions of Economic Growth: The New Emphases

The world is now at a critical point in the history of economic growth and modernization. In the Advanced Capitalist nations, the growth orientation of Western societies, a relatively unquestioned guiding light for the last two centuries, is under direct challenge by advocates of limits to growth and by other groups. At the same time the middle income and some of the poor nations are in a takeoff stage.

Thus, many of the values that underlie growth are now being challenged by the wealthy—possibly with decisive effects for the wealthy. It is too early to predict reliably how much confusion this will cause in the developing nations, but we think that while it will lower the potential growth rate of almost all nations and create some real problems in special cases, it will not change overall trends much. In some cases, it will add to the incentives to grow; the prospect of catching up becomes easier and more exciting.

Economic historians have always identified a clear correlation between past economic growth and such underlying cultural elements as the "Thirteen Traditional Levers" listed below.

1. Religion, tradition, or authority. Automatic and perhaps unthinking, respect for the legacy of the past, for continuity, for the existing "social contract," and for persons in authority (e.g., parents and teachers).

[*World Economic Development: 1979 and Beyond* (Boulder, Colo.: Westview Press, 1979).]

2. Biological and physical realities (e.g., respect for and acceptance as more or less normal and to some degree inevitable of the pressures and dangers of the physical environment, the frailty of life and health, the more tragic aspects of the human condition, and the basic and natural "unfairness" of any feasible social order and of life itself, etc.).

3. Defense of frontiers (territoriality).

4. Earning a living—obtaining the five guarantees Chinese communes often explicitly promise to their members: (1) adequate food, (2) adequate clothes, (3) adequate shelter, (4) adequate medical care, and (5) adequate funeral expenses. Sometimes they add: (6) adequate education and (7) adequate pregnancy leave and expenses.

5. Defense (by the nation, business, or family) of vital strategic and economic interests.

6. Defense (again, by the nation, business or family) of vital political, moral, and morale interests.[1]

7. Other appeals to economic or technological rationality and efficiency.

8. The "manly" emphasis—in adolescence: team sports, heroic figures, aggressive and competitive activities, rebellion against "female roles"; in adulthood: playing an adult male role (similarly, a womanly emphasis).

9. The "Puritan ethic" (deferred gratification, work-orientation, advancement-orientation, sublimation of sexual desires, sobriety, good work habits, etc.).

10. A high (perhaps almost total) loyalty, commitment, or identification with nation, state, city, clan, village, extended family, or secret society.

11. The "martial" virtues—duty, patriotism, honor, heroism, glory, courage, loyalty, and pride.

12. Other sublimation or repression of sexual, aggressive, aesthetic, or "other instincts."

13. Other "irrational" or restricting taboos, rituals, totems, myths, customs, and charismas.

The traditional values embodied in these societal levers and binders are still held by a majority of the American people—perhaps even by most of the working and middle classes in the United States, Western Europe, and Japan. However, a relatively "new" emerging set of emphases is becoming increasingly influential and threatens to slow or even stop economic growth in the affluent market-oriented countries. These New Emphases are listed below. Although the values and preferences outlined there have existed for a long time, they are now beginning to play a much more intensive, pervasive, and overwhelming role.

1. Selective risk avoidance (innovators, entrepreneurs, businessmen, and "do-ers" generally must bear all risks and the burden of proof as if only they and not society as well benefited from their profits and efforts).
2. Localism ("ins" vs. "outs," no local disturbance or risks because of needs of external world).
3. Comfort, safety, leisure, and health regulations (often to be mandated by government regulation—sometimes approaching "health and safety authoritarianism").
4. Protection of environment and ecology (at almost any cost to the economy or other programs).
5. Loss of nerve, will, optimism, confidence, and morale (at least about economic progress and technological advancement).
6. Public welfare and social justice (life must be made to be "fair"— equality in result, not of opportunity—justice should not be blind).
7. Happiness and hedonism (as explicit and direct goals in life).
8. General anti-technology, anti-economic development, anti-middle class attitudes ("small-is-better" and "limits-to-growth" movements, but enormous resources can be allocated or great economic costs accepted to further points 1–7 above).
9. Increasing social control and "overall planning" of the economy (but mostly with new class values and attitudes and by "input-output" theorists).
10. Regulatory attitudes that are adversary or indifferent to the welfare of business (the productivity and profitability of business are taken for granted).
11. "Modern" family and social values and a deemphasis of many traditional (survival and square) values.
12. Concern with self (often accompanied by an emphasis on mystic or transcendental attitudes and values or an expression of the "me generation").
13. New rites, ceremonies, and celebrations (both against and instead of traditional ones).
14. New sources of meaning and purpose; of status and prestige.

A quick glance may not reveal just how critical their relationship is to economic growth, but a closer look almost certainly will. It makes a difference whether these Fourteen New Emphases are held as a "discretionary choice" (caused by changes in levels of affluence or awareness or other changes in the world external to the individual), or because of preferential values and moral imperatives. Whatever their source and intensity, the New Emphases can create the "cultural contradictions" referred to in the title of this section.[2] Indeed, growth as we have known it in Western history would not have begun or continued if these New Emphases had existed previously as strongly and widely held values.

We are not arguing that they are all to be deplored. Most are clearly desirable, at least in moderation. Many adjustments are certainly and undeniably necessary if growth is to evolve healthily. Eventually economic growth may cease, but this will probably occur when economic activity reaches a plateau at a very high level or when our culture enters some other stage of history. The question of whether the New Emphases are desirable is not clear-cut; rather, it is mostly a matter of timing, intensity, tactics, and other subtle distinctions.

We expect that as more nations move into—or further up—the declining part of the S-shaped curves for population and gross product, the conflict between the "new" culture exemplified by the New Emphases and the traditional culture will grow in intensity and scope. (As always, this is both cause and effect. The New Emphases aid or force the decline in the rates of growth and the erosion in dynamism; this in turn reinforces the New Emphases.) We therefore now turn to a discussion of the important issue of the social limits to growth. This discussion will provide the necessary context for our [understanding] of each of the Fourteen New Emphases.

THE SOCIAL LIMITS TO GROWTH

An expanding literature devoted to the so-called social limits to growth holds, we believe correctly, that the main limits on economic growth will be caused by decreasing marginal utility for more production per capita and by increased difficulties resulting from the Fourteen New Emphases. Both should lead to a gradual deemphasis on the production of material goods—or even to a deliberate negative emphasis including hostile attitudes toward innovation, genuine antipathy to business, extreme opposition to Schumpeter's "creative destruction," fear of technology, and so on. Even though we share some of the ideas and values of the New Emphases, when we judge that they are being carried to excesses we refer to "putting sand in the gears."

All of this has been discussed for a long time, but until recently it has not been understood that a diminishing drive for growth, increasing emphasis on other values, and a greater tolerance for sand in the gears might be caused by a near crusade against growth by certain elite groups rather than by the general public. Indeed, such a crusade is often carried out against the public's wishes and deeply held interests. We did not fully grasp the extent and speed with which these new attitudes could become influential, but we now expect that a relatively few influential opponents of growth will exert an increasing leverage that will hinder the operation of business in our society.[3]

There is a reasonable basis for the current, much advertised lack of business confidence. It follows that at this critical juncture society should not add any more sand to the gears than is absolutely necessary. In particular, the Fourteen New Emphases seem to be having an extraordinary impact on the costs and risks of doing business in almost all advanced affluent countries. We use the United States (and, subsequently, Japan) as the major referent for discussion of these trends because we are better informed about recent American and Japanese experience. However, we are convinced that these New Emphases represent important social limits to growth in all the affluent OECD nations. Something similar to the Fourteen New Emphases may well turn out to be a basic internal contradiction of capitalism. As capitalist countries become rich, these Emphases may emerge as powerful forces that, if given sufficient priority, eventually slow down or stop further economic growth and perhaps technological advancement as well.

Very different attitudes ranging across a broad spectrum can be adopted toward these Emphases. At least six different attitudes can be discerned. (In discussing these attitudes, we will use attitude toward ecology and environment as a typical issue.)

Traditional Attitudes

A Matter of Indifference. The traditional attitude of Western culture and of the Jewish, Muslim, and Christian religions is that nature exists to be used or conquered. In harsh climates or environments it is often thought of more as an enemy than as a friend. Whenever ecological values have clashed with other important values, the latter have normally been given priority. The Old Testament gives human beings "dominion over the fish of the sea, and over the fowl of the air, and over the cattle, and over all the earth and over every creeping thing that creepeth upon the earth." Neither the Koran nor the New Testament stresses ecological values for their own sake.[4]

A Discretionary Choice. These are "more or less" changes in priorities caused by increased affluence, changing awareness and information, technological and social innovations, and other new pressures or opportunities. Relatively narrow cost/benefit criteria can be very important in affecting these choices. People are now seldom really indifferent to the environment, but, until recently, few have felt rich enough to sacrifice much to preserve it. The Advanced Capitalist nations are now so well off by historical standards that clean air, clean water, and aesthetic landscapes are being given much higher priority than previously. However, for most people in most places, they still don't come ahead of enhancing prosperity and security.

A Preferential Value. These are basic changes in likes and dislikes, tastes, attitudes, values, and customs. For example, French people have traditionally placed a much higher value on taking an annual vacation away from home than have Americans. But younger Americans tend to be closer to the French in this respect than they are to their own parents. Both would make sacrifices for vacations which would be considered ridiculous by the older American.

Emerging Attitudes

Proper or Meritorious Behavior. More than a preferential value but less than a moral imperative. A good example of proper behavior is the pressure not to pick your nose in public or to belch after a meal. (The latter, of course, varies among cultures; in China belching after a meal shows proper appreciation for its high quality.) It is obviously not immoral to belch or pick your nose, but it does show that you have been badly raised if you do so; they are "wrong" things to do. Meritorious or proper behavior is also not a moral issue. For example, in many religions, one is supposed to give 10 percent of his income to charity. A practitioner of the religion is under no compulsion to give more than 10 percent, but it is meritorious to do so; it is good behavior and one gets credit for it. We believe that the attitude that will eventually be adopted by most Americans toward the Fourteen New Emphases will place them in the category of proper or meritorious behavior. They will be more than preferential choices but less than moral imperatives or matters of central importance.

Matter of Central Importance (e.g., An Issue of Physical Survival; Grave Hazard to Health, Economic, Cultural, or Other Values; or An Issue of Psychic Survival; Aesthetic Imperative). Many people argue that the New Emphases may not be moral imperatives but that they are still very important for other reasons, so much so that they simply do not wish (or cannot) live in a world in which the relevant New Emphases are not given an appropriate priority. Sometimes their reasons are romantic, sometimes stylistic, sometimes semi-religious. Much of the small-is-beautiful movement or the current emphasis on solar energy partake of this perspective, as do many of those who are participating in the current revolt against the "excessive materialism" of our culture.

Sometimes this belief is held as a literal issue of survival for one or another of the New Emphases (a currently common one is preserving the environment). Often people who really take the moral position given below understand that others do not share their moral values; therefore they switch to the survival issue as more persuasive. Still others take the attitude that the society has become too unpleasant in one way or another: therefore survival is not worthwhile. Even if one did not take such an extreme position, one could still feel it is of the utmost importance that current developments be checked or changed, that the New Emphases be emphasized. Many people who so view preserving the environment are also convinced that they are living in an era of limited resources. Surprisingly, most of these people do not note that in many cases preserving just the appearance of the environment (as in strip mining) does not raise any survival issue but is instead a luxury that can only be indulged by a society with excess resources. Whether or not they make this mistake they typically argue that all ecosystems should be protected, either because they are unique or are part of a larger whole whose interactions are never completely known. They think of the ecosystem as similar to a watch; any interference with the inner works is likely to be disastrous.

Moral, Ideological, or Religious Imperative. Does not allow for give-and-take bargaining, easy compromise, or normal narrow cost-benefit analysis. It is often thought that the issues are obvious and controversies are often thought of as being conflicts between morally secure positions based on higher values and positions that are morally indifferent, or based on lower or vulgar values.

The attitude of discretionary choice is basic. Once a person has many material goods, the marginal utility of having more of them usually goes down and he will not work as hard to get more. Also consider what happens when the welfare state expands. People are still concerned with basic needs, but they depend less on their own efforts because they know the state will provide. They can thus afford to put less emphasis on fending for themselves, on savings, and on insurance. Poor people usually do not object much to pollution if it means more jobs. Richer people feel they can afford to have clean air and clean water, even if it costs them something. None of these new attitudes necessarily represents a change in available information (e.g., attitudes toward some food additives). For most older adults in the United States, these changing conditions are more important than any change in values.

However, changing values per se are important for many people—particularly younger groups. As parents become better off they tend to shift the emphasis in the training and education of their children away from economic growth toward other values, many of which are either indifferent or hostile to economic growth. These children grow up with few direct experiences that emphasize and reinforce many of the work-oriented, advancement-oriented, survival-oriented values of their parents.

Sometimes the new values are held as moral imperatives rather than as strongly felt preferences that do not raise issues of right and wrong. The difference between preferential values and moral imperatives is important.

Assume that an individual informs the authorities that he or she intends to kill two people a year, but offers to make up for this by turning over to the state enough money to save at least twelve lives a year (perhaps by preventing other murders or by better health and safety precautions). The net effect would be to save ten lives a year. Thus, the self-appointed killer argues persuasively (and inaccurately) that if the authorities care about human life, they will surely accept the offer. However, the injunction against murder is an absolute moral imperative and not just a preference. The state simply will not bargain about the issue. It is not interested in this kind of cost-effectiveness analysis. It wants instead to make clear that murder is an abhorrent crime that will not be tolerated.

Let us assume now that an individual goes to the authorities and says he or she would like to dump a certain amount of pollutants into a river because it is convenient for a specific operation to do so. The person offers to give the state enough money for every pound of pollutants dumped to enable the state to remove or prevent the spread of two pounds of pollutants elsewhere in the river. Therefore, the more the person dumps, the cleaner the river. Almost everybody who is interested in a clean river will accept this offer. Those who hold traditional values will say if we are affluent enough to afford clean water, then let us have it. Those who value clean water over economic growth will also accept the offer even when they are relatively poor. Only those who feel too poor to afford clean water and would therefore prefer that the money be applied to "more urgent tasks" and those who think of preventing pollution as a moral imperative (perhaps almost as strong as that against murder) will find the proposition unacceptable. However, many of these people will not accept an offer to save ten other rivers for permission to dirty one river. They see this as a moral rather than a cost effectiveness issue.

THE ANTI-GROWTH TRIAD

The most intense support for the New Emphases comes from the upper and upper-middle classes. Within this group there are three subgroups that advocate the New Emphases with a special, indeed in some cases an almost manic crusading zeal. These subgroups we labeled the Anti-Growth Triad. We sometimes refer to the more extreme members of the Triad as Crusaders for the New Values or Secular Evangelists. To elaborate our earlier discussion, we see the Anti-Growth Triad as composed of:

Affluent Reformers (or Radicals). It is a familiar paradox of politics that members of the upper classes and the aristocracy often lead or work with reformist or even revolutionary groups, sometimes even attacking the society that has been so benevolent to them—at least in material terms and status. Such people are sometimes referred to pejoratively but accurately as "parlor pinks," "limousine liberals," or devotees of "radical chic." Some, however, genuinely dedicate themselves to these movements in a competent and effective way. (Friedrich Engels and Franklin Roosevelt are good examples.)

Thorstein Veblen's "Leisure Class." According to Veblen: The leisure class is in great measure sheltered from the stress of those economic exigencies which prevail in any modern, highly organized industrial community. The exigencies of the struggle for the means of life are less exacting for this class than for any other; and as a consequence of this privileged position we should expect to find it one of the least responsive of the classes of society to the demands which the situation makes for a further growth of institutions and a readjustment to an altered industrial situation. The leisure class normally does not have to make "agonizing compromises" because of economic or occupational pressures or to associate closely with the middle class or working class. This is truer today than it was at the end of the century—and also applies to the other two members of the Triad.

Neo-Liberal Members of the New Class. We will consider the New Class first. Mainly of upper-middle class origin, the New Class derives its status and occupation from possession of considerable education. Its members actually earn their livings through their linguistic, symbolic, analytic, aesthetic, and academic professional skills. They are more or less intellectual or artistic—or are dropouts from such a life into bohemian or voluntary simplicity lifestyles. The New Class comprises a large part of academia, the media, most "public interest" groups, and many philanthropic, public service, and social service organizations—all of which not only have been growing in size, but are gaining influence in the Western industrial countries and in Japan. While it is not easy to define the New Class precisely, it was once equally difficult to delineate the aristocracy, the bourgeoisie, and the proletariat with great clarity. Each of these classes also contains important sub-classes, new arrivals, and dropouts. Initial analysis suggests that the New Class can be defined in terms of: high, or potentially high (i.e., students) formal education; professional occupational status, with an emphasis on the "soft" sciences and arts; high (but not the highest) income, often derived from professional activities or non-market sources (government or nonprofit salaries, grants, and contracts); and relative youth.

The last criterion is important. Because the New Class is "emerging," its attributes should be most obvious among the young. In this connection, Karl Marx's insight that a class does not exist unless it is self-conscious is instructive. This kind of consciousness has appeared only recently among members of the New Class. Some intellectuals and bureaucrats have always behaved like the New Class, but perhaps only within the past decade have its members become numerous enough to achieve the critical mass to break out of a subordination to other groups and strike out on their own.

WHO IS IN THE NEW CLASS AND WHAT ARE THEY UP TO?

The New Class is a cultural, social, and economic concept rather than a political, ideological, or ethnic concept. Nevertheless, in the United States it can be conveniently divided into five main political groups. A relatively large group, perhaps about a third of the New Class, has traditional liberal attitudes. These people largely agree with or follow in the tradition of Roosevelt, Truman, Stevenson, Jackson, Meany, and Humphrey. (They should not be confused with so-called nineteenth-century liberals who espoused the laissez-faire economics of Adam Smith.)

A second group, probably not as large, but at the moment much more self-confident and active, is now frequently called neo-liberal. These people are heavily influenced by the counterculture of the late 1960s. They provided much of the constituency for Eugene McCarthy and George McGovern and almost all of the active members and supporters of such public interest groups as the Sierra Club, Common Cause, and Nader's Raiders.

The remaining third or so of the New Class can be divided into three fairly equal groups: traditional conservatives, neo-conservatives, and the more or less humanist left. Speechwriters for Reagan and Goldwater or the staff of the National Review would be typical traditional conservatives. The neo-conservatives would typically include such people as Irving Kristol, Daniel Bell, Nathan Glazer, and James Q. Wilson. The magazine *The Public Interest* is almost a trade journal of the neo-conservatives (and one of the best sources for high quality discussions about United States domestic issues).[5] Traditional conservatives tend not to trust neo-conservatives because the traditional conservatives cannot always predict their reactions or stands on specific issues. Important differences in values and positions often distinguish these two groups.

The humanist left tends to be closer to the traditional liberals than to the neo-liberals, but they are much more radical in their politics and much more concerned with "human" than with material issues—i.e., with preserving spontaneity, creativity, and "doing your own thing" rather than with trade unionism, social security, income redistribution, or regulation of the stock market.

At the moment, neo-conservatives are relatively "in," and the influence exerted by neo-liberal members of the New Class is no longer as pervasive as it once was. In the 1976 United States presidential election, for example, neither party emphasized neo-liberal New Class issues except for those with very wide acceptance, such as environmental protection. (More than 90 percent of the American public are for protection of the environment—but only at reasonable cost and with reasonable tactics and objectives.) Yet the neo-liberals of the New Class still tend to be extremely important because of their domination of middle-level regulatory agency staff positions, their highly effective use of the law and the courts, their tremendous influence in the media, and their skilled use of public interest organizations, demonstrations, and lobbying campaigns.

A strong case can be made that in the late 1960s and early 1970s, the humanist left and the neo-liberal members of the United States New Class, taken together, largely controlled or dominated the following groups and institutions: the humanities and social science faculties of almost all leading universities (both private and public), professional schools, and teachers colleges; most national media organizations (i.e., the influential daily newspapers, most of the periodical press, the book publishing industry, the commercial television networks, recording, films, and most educational media); the fine arts; the establishment foundations and other non-profit eleemosynary institutions concerned with influencing public opinion; many research organizations; a large part of the staffs of liberal congress and the federal social welfare bureaucracy; and the apparatus of the new government regulating agencies.

While this domination has weakened, neo-liberal values and sensibilities are continuing to penetrate additional United States institutions and groups, including natural science faculties, business schools, rank-and-file school teachers, state and local government bureaucracies, the clergy, advertising, trade union staffs, salaried professionals of all kinds, and even business corporations, especially in departments of public relations, long-range planning, and internal education. Private companies have increasingly adopted the expedient of hiring people of this type precisely because they have verbal and analytic skills. Sometimes these people are co-opted by the companies they work for.

The New Class is likely to be in staff rather than line or substantive positions and to produce or deal in ideas or words, holding their jobs because of analytic and literary skills. They are not usually involved in the commercial and administrative aspects of an operation. Thus we do not think of the chief executive officers of these organizations as New Class people. By using the phrase "largely controls or dominates," we mean that they set the basic tone of an organization and its basic policies toward the information it deals with.

[. . .] For some time we have expected compromises resulting from changing emphases and shifting values eventually to lead to a leveling-off or plateau of economic growth—perhaps until something new intervenes—long before the world encountered physical limits (resource shortages or pollution), that might prevent further growth. But we underrated the degree of hostility to growth that would be displayed by the leading edge of the opposition movement. Instead of encouraging or tolerating a gradual shift to values that are hostile or indifferent to growth, the New Class, or certain parts of it, is taking a much more activist and political role—espousing low growth directly as a value in itself (indeed sometimes as a moral imperative) or as an urgent necessity, often throwing sand in the gears of the whole system and in any case impeding it, we believe, too suddenly and too violently. To use Marxist terms, we do not really challenge their historic role, but we do fear that they are going too far too fast.

Why do they do this? We believe that this is best understood by thinking of their position as arising out of a very intense change of values—so intense that it is better thought of as the creation of "moral imperatives." The neo-liberal New Class in fact takes many of the Fourteen New Emphases as moral imperatives. Many people in the Anti-Growth Triad think of the New Emphases as a form of modernization more in tune with current realities than traditional concepts of modernization, i.e., economic development and technological advancement. In the very long run (fifty or so years from now), they may be correct, but we believe that they are, to say the least, premature.

Many New Class people, particularly the neo-liberals, sense that further economic development works against their interests. For example, as the size of the upper-middle class increases, dilution of the benefits of being upper-middle class occurs, as does increased competition for these benefits. Furthermore, increased affluence decreases the availability of many other benefits, such as competent, inexpensive services (e.g., maids). Consequently, the upper-middle class finds itself threatened if, with further modernization, large numbers of people move into the upper-middle class or become affluent enough to crowd them.

Recent books have discussed these phenomena in some detail, but often from a misleading perspective, by assuming that the interests of the existing upper-middle class are the same as everyone else's. They do not recognize that middle class individuals who move up benefit from substantial improvements in their standards of living. Those who have already achieved the higher status feel that they lose something when others join them, a loss usually greatly exaggerated. What is in reality little more than an annoyance hardly justifies the "Third Dismal Theorem" coined by E. J. Mishan: "The more science, technology, and the gross national product grow, the more nasty, brutish, vile and precarious becomes human existence."

Most analysts concerned with the future of the developed nations believe that in the next century New Class "brain workers" of all political complexions will play central roles in influencing the direction of the societies they live in. If so, much of this influence seems likely to be in the direction of the Fourteen New Emphases. Additional support for neo-liberal positions will come from the rich and from the leisure class, as well as from the upper-middle class—generally from all groups who believe they gain from maintaining the status quo and slow growth. It will also come from those who are genuinely concerned about specific issues. (The two groups often overlap.) Thus, support for any of the New Emphases can in various circumstances, come from a wider constituency than the Anti-Growth Triad.

NOTES

1. Many of those who oppose the Thirteen Traditional Levers would be willing to allow almost any excesses in the defense by a minority or dissident group of its vital political, morale, and moral interests, at least if they are sympathetic with this group's view of its vital interests. They do not, however, allow this privilege to the nation, the business firm, the WASP family, or the square individual.

2. The term is adapted from Daniel Bell's *The Cultural Contradictions of Capitalism* (New York: Basic Books, 1976). Bell's book focuses mainly on numbers 3 and 6 of our New Emphases.

3. Many of these were either nonexistent a decade ago or have become much more extreme and exaggerated than they used to be. Most of these issues or trends are accidental or unplanned. Some, even though they entail significant costs and risks, are desirable if implemented in a reasonable fashion. But the people who crusade for these reforms often have very narrow ideological or class interests and consequently do not understand or even care about the problems they create. In some cases their tactics are actually counterproductive. Thus, they can cause a backlash that leads to an excessive rejection of their values and programs. Alternatively, the tactics can be really designed to accomplish the reformers' hidden agendas or real objectives, which may include self-serving, prejudicial, or ideological goals.

4. See Lynn White, "The Historical Roots of our Ecological Crises," *Science Magazine*, March 10, 1967, p. 1203.

5. Almost all other organizations with the term "public interest" on their mastheads are largely dominated by the Anti-Growth Triad.

10

---ͦ888ͦ---

Economic Development: Economic and Cultural Parameters

POLITICAL INFLUENCES ON ECONOMIC DECISIONS

One trouble with a centrally managed economy is the political nature of much economic decision-making. For example, the government may tell some people to use less and tell others to use much less of some resources. Those with political clout argue that they do not want to make the adjustment being asked of them. Those without such clout resent the government's "tyranny" or "political decision-making" and try to evade the regulations. These political discussions—or the revolts against such discussions—can be very wasteful and counterproductive. The market place has the great virtue of being self-enforcing. Those with the economic power generally give full weight to economic considerations and command the necessary resources to implement the decisions made on such grounds.

In socialist or other governmentally controlled economies, this behavior does not occur. There is usually no genuine comparison from the viewpoint of the user of the best way to do something, but rather a judgment by a remote governmental bureau about what is best for the country, the ruling political party, or the bureaucrats concerned. These bureaucratic judgments are usually based on limited knowledge and concern, the prejudices of the decision makers, and the political and economic power of the recipients of the largesse.

[*World Economic Development: 1979 and Beyond* (Boulder, Colo.: Westview Press, 1979).]

Many years ago I wrote, I have attended many committee meetings of governmental advisors in which decisions involving hundreds of millions of dollars were taken or recommended. In most cases, many of the people present, perhaps all, spent less time and effort on the decision than they would on buying a new suit. And very few of them were well-dressed. The attention given to various decisions is likely to be proportional to the personal stake that the individuals who are making the decision have in its consequences.

While the central planners have an overall view that the individual planners lack, private individuals and organizations have a variety of local and personal perspectives that are at least as important as the special knowledge and perspectives of public officials. One moral is that central planners should rely as much as possible on the intelligence and understanding of the individuals personally concerned about what is best for them. But what if these individuals are perverse, ignorant, dumb, or just do not know what is good for them? Even planners who appear competent and professional can be perverse, ignorant, dumb, and not know what is good for others—and also be more prone to "educated incapacity."

Complexities in the real world sometimes contradict these elementary concepts of planning and economic decision-making. Nevertheless, the concepts are usually sufficiently correct to be put into practical use—and to put the burden of proof on those who would violate them. We stress these simple ideas because some of our readers may have been overly exposed to elegantly argued ideological polemics that ignore the fundamental logic of practical experience. No system works perfectly. However, we should normally be willing to risk mistakes by allowing individuals to pursue their own judgments of their own interests. We know of many counterexamples but these exceptions do not occur nearly as often, nor are they as important, as most advocates of central planning believe. Of course, "professional" information and analysis should also be provided where useful.

We believe that a market free enough to communicate useful information through prices, and to utilize that information through decisions made by highly motivated and knowledgeable people (at least at the margin), is likely to operate relatively effectively and smoothly. This concept has been dimmed by a flood of anti-growth, anti-business, anti-middle class, and elitist attitudes. Members of the New Class usually lack the practical experience that good planning needs so badly.

The operation of the "invisible hand of the marketplace," reflected in the structure of prices and the decisions of various personally involved individuals and groups, produces a more satisfactory result than can normally be obtained by centrally managed economies. The market does not have to be very free nor individuals very well informed for this use of prices and price-motivating actions to work extraordinarily well—on the average and over the medium run and perhaps over the long run as well.

The marketplace is flexible, effective, and efficient in making realistic adjustments. A government planner who had to decide where adjustments would best be made simply would not have the information or calculating ability—even with current computing techniques—to do so as quickly or effectively as market forces. Thus, if there is a decrease in the availability of copper or an increase in its demand, the market tells every user of copper overnight that copper has become a little more scarce (i.e., expensive), and therefore should be used more economically. It communicates precise and usable information to users as to how much more economical they should be without any political influence and without involving any personalities. The signals are quick, sure, unequivocal, and unarguable. The price is what the price is.

Basic and general principles are not destroyed just because they do not hold precisely and universally in every single instance. They are not supposed to. Their function is to give general guidance about and perspective on the world. The law of supply and demand may not have the validity of the first or second laws of thermodynamics, but it does express strong tendencies that exist in almost all societies, especially societies with any kind of a market orientation. The concept of economic man may be incredibly shallow as a description of human personality, but it is a useful abstraction for understanding most modernizing countries or as an objective to be achieved in less successfully modernizing countries.

This does not mean that if people actually were "economic men" modernization would be successful. In fact, we believe the opposite and agree with the historian, Christopher Dawson, and with the later remarks of Alexander Solzhenitsyn, that much of modern society works well because it still has a number of virtues and qualities inherited from the medieval period. To the extent that these virtues and qualities disappear certain essential social cements and lubricants become dangerously absent.

In a society where the basic human relationships are taken care of by more or less traditional means, the additional activities stimulated and modified by economic considerations of the sort described by the abstract model of an economic man can be extremely useful in analysis, in policymaking, and in practice. One should not decry conventional wisdom just because it is conventional or just because it recognizes realities that some perceive as unpleasant.

THE ISSUE OF CULTURISM AND NEO-CULTURISM

There is great concern in the world with racism, sexism, excessive nationalism, and other "isms" that are believed to create undesirable, if not immoral, attitudes. We define culturism as the belief that culture is rather sticky and difficult to change in any basic fashion, although it can often be modified. Culturism assumes that various cultures differ not only in their aesthetic tastes, customs, values, and traditions, but also in their abilities to cope with various kinds of problems and situations. Specifically, cultures differ in their capacities for modernization either in their indigenous setting or in various foreign settings. We believe that this ability to modernize often depends upon time and place. Sometimes what are relatively minor changes from the viewpoint of the basic culture can make huge differences. (It is as a result of such relatively small changes that neo-Confucian cultures are now probably more adept at modernization than Western cultures.)

We think of ourselves as culturists or perhaps neo-culturists. The prefix neo- is appropriate because we believe in the basic adaptability of cultures as well as their tendency to resist basic changes, and we believe that under modern conditions it is going to be increasingly easy for almost every culture to modernize.

We do not think of cultures as genetically determined. We would he very surprised if the existence of any significant genetic element in determining the variations among most, and perhaps among all, cultures is established. We do not, however, deny the theoretical possibility of such an element. In principle there is no reason why some psychological dispositions might not be genetic. But we know of no persuasive evidence for the existence of genetically determined cultural differences.

Our point is simple. Different cultures socialize children differently. Even with a relatively unitary culture, child rearing practices vary over time, place, and class. These child rearing practices and the other existing institutions strongly affect the performance of the culture. Because it is easy to visualize the political and ideological abuse of such a belief as neo-culturism, there is a tendency to deny or ignore important cultural differences that significantly affect the behavior of individuals and nations. We argue that it is difficult if not impossible to understand the kinds of issues we are discussing unless one is a neo-culturist. We are not cultural determinists, but we do believe in the strong influence of culture.

We are also cultural relativists. At least for most cultures, we believe that the notion of one culture as generally superior to another culture has no particular meaning except from a specific perspective and by specific criteria that often depend on time and place as much as on the cultures being compared. We do not argue that all cultures are equally good but only that all cultures have good and bad points, especially if judged from their own perspectives and often if judged from other perspectives as well.

This doctrine could be dangerous. Many believe it translates easily into racism, excessive nationalism, or other unpleasant attitudes. We believe that under current conditions most of this concern is excessive. Such attitudes are not caused by a distortion of neoculturist doctrines but vice versa. The nationalism, racism, or other attitude already exists, and then "observations" about different cultures are used to rationalize them. [. . .]

We are aware that excessive emphasis on this kind of doctrine may lead to problems, even if it doesn't turn into racism or nationalism. It might but normally does not lead to a feeling of inferiority by other cultures. Most people have a remarkable ability to live with these kinds of differences and function well unless the demonstration and discussion is more flagrant and invidious than seems likely to occur.

The converse, however, is less true. It is likely, for example, that members of neo-Confucian cultures will get a sense of superiority, whether cultural, racial, or nationalistic. We do not think it is bad for Westerners or others to understand and accept our cultural arguments. We do believe that Japanese society, South Korean society, and to a lesser extent other neo-Confucian minorities around the world may become arrogant and self-satisfied in ways that would be unpleasant if not dangerous. Some Confucian societies have a long history of cultural arrogance, self-confidence, and self-respect. When limited, this is extremely constructive and healthy, but it is easily carried to an excess that includes contempt for other cultures or practices. We noted in recent travels in these neo-Confucian societies they have begun to accept their "cultural superiority" with great ease. Indeed, many want to carry it a bit further than we feel is either useful or justifiable.

Such feelings of superiority have existed at one time or another in almost all groups, cultures, and nations, including the French, the English, the Germans, the Japanese, and the Americans. (An American congressman early in the twentieth century said, "Someday Shanghai will arrive at the cultural level of Cincinnati"; Napoleon called the British "a nation of shopkeepers.") It seems to us there is a very good chance of a revival of contempt for the West and particularly for the Americans. [. . .]

In many ways Western cultures appear decadent—at least from any traditionalist perspective. Young people appear, superficially, to be less patriotic than their parents and grandparents and also distinctly less willing to make sacrifices for the public interest or even their own careers (except as part of a trendy fashion such as environmentalism). They are distinctly less willing to accept military training or any kind of onerous task or discipline, no matter how valid or important the local or national need. There is extreme hedonism, self-indulgence, decadence, and vice. [. . .] In this respect, the current Western campaign in favor of human rights may backfire badly because in many Confucian societies it looks like a campaign for selfish, self-indulgent, and reckless individualism and egoism. [. . .]

HIGH MORALE, COMMITMENT, GOOD CULTURE, AND GOOD MANAGEMENT IN DEVELOPING NATIONS

We have already pointed out that businessmen, government leaders, and cadre of almost every country where rapid economic development has occurred have been characterized by an impressive degree of commitment and unity of purpose. This was as true in Holland and England in the eighteenth century as it is today in Japan, South Korea, and Taiwan. Evident in such seemingly trivial matters as sobriety of behavior and dress, these attitudes can, in both the socialist and capitalist worlds, be more important than material resources and technical aid.

If resources are copious, impressive visible changes in the physical aspects of a developing country can easily be created: new roads, dams, skyscrapers, telephone systems, airports, modern factories, and so on. Such activities are not only useful in themselves but can help to create an atmosphere conducive to development. However, if overemphasized or done inefficiently or incompetently, they can hurt. Such undue emphasis can lead to counter-reformation by traditionalists, to waste, or to excessive inflation. Simply creating opportunities for participation in the modernization process and demonstrating that things are happening is important but insufficient and can be counterproductive. People must eventually want to take advantage of these things and have the motivation needed to sustain commitment and effort. And the effort should itself be economically productive and self-sustaining or be a basis for eventual economically productive and self-sustaining activities. Premature attempts by poor countries to leap into ultramodern activities because of a desire to gain the appearances of modernity are usually wrong.

Showy projects such as four-lane highways and modern aircraft for national airlines may emphasize the wrong symbols. They furnish good jobs and useful facilities for elites and are admired and used by them, but most developing countries have a much greater need for dirt roads from the farms to the village and secondary highways from the villages to the cities. One of the problems with many governments is that they furnish the kind of public goods they and their friends want and not what the general public needs and wants.

Joseph Schumpeter has pointed out that it is much easier, politically to "sell the socialist case" than the capitalist, despite the obvious superiority of capitalism for most developing nations, at least until now. Actually, it is not easier to sell unity and commitment in a socialist society to the average person but usually only to politicized elites and young idealists. Effective unity and commitment are more likely to arise from useful economic activities which the people or community concerned own, manage, and gain from than when they work for a state-owned and state-directed organization, do not gain much directly for their labors, but are told that the nation has gained. Propagandists, ideologists, and intellectuals generally find the socialist terminology and the socialist arguments more compelling, whether or not the people concerned are actually benefiting from development or even feel they are benefiting. This can lead to genuine confusion.

A striking example occurred in India. India did well economically during the emergency (from 1975 to 1977). The upper 60 percent of the population were rising relatively rapidly; however, the bottom 40 percent were standing still or losing slightly. The average progress was rapid— and was widely if not completely shared. However, many socialist or welfare-oriented Indians (especially, it seemed to many observers, the affluent ones with good jobs), found it difficult to justify such a situation. These people argued that development should be judged even in the short run, according to its effects on the bottom 40 percent of the population. While one may question this position, its rhetorical acceptability is clear.

Many of these people were doing very effective work and helping India to modernize, but the official rhetoric was socialist. And one big advantage of socialism over capitalism is clearly a matter of rhetoric and argumentation rather than performance. It simply appears too self-serving when an individual who has profited greatly from the system says, "My labors also improve the country as a whole." In a socialist system, where all are presumably working directly for the common good, the fact that the elites in most Third World socialist countries are uncommonly well rewarded is overlooked. Some perceptive and witty scholar has observed, "Those countries devoted to freedom have done more for equality than those devoted to equality have done for freedom or equality."

Capitalism should be defended by intellectuals who are not gaining so much from the system as well as by businessmen. But businessmen should still play a larger part in the ideological battle than they have. While it may be too simple to say that if businessmen do not defend their own interests nobody will, this remark is still cogent. But businessmen should not claim to be totally altruistic. Nothing annoys many Americans more than a glossy ad in a popular magazine claiming that oil company XYZ is going to the farthest reaches of the earth to find oil for them. This is true but misleading. The company should say instead: "Our business takes us to the farthest reaches of the earth, and this is good for both you and us." While many American and foreign businessmen are as altruistic as anybody, they are not excessively so. Indeed, Adam Smith, an admirer of business, once observed that when two businessmen get together, even for social reasons, they tend to start plotting restraint of trade.

It is important for people to believe in, admire, and respect "the system" even if they are not completely satisfied with it. They should sense that good things are happening and that one is not selling out by committing oneself personally to the system. If a truly viable change that is pervasive, orderly, survivable, and persistent is to be attained, most of the people in a nation must become "involved." It is not necessary that everyone understand the development process, but many must accept some of the often unpleasant realities associated with development. This kind of acceptance and understanding usually occurs after takeoff, when the good results are visible to all—or when the nation is under a clear and present danger.

[. . .] One of the real difficulties that many developing nations labor under today is that they have no clear and present danger which they must face up to. While being developed is still desirable even if there is no clear and present danger to surmount, it is difficult for idealistic young upper-middle class people to believe this if they happen to be under a barrage of propaganda challenging the concept of development that is being carried out in their country. This is a particularly important problem with young people who are being educated outside their nation and find that their nation's government is severely criticized for one reason or another by various groups in the school or country in which they are being educated.

At least initially, development is often carried forward by relatively small groups, but they at least must be committed to their task. This is often a necessary precondition for a more pervasive national approach. Such spearhead groups are normally at least as motivated by private gain as by the public interest. It is important to have the two largely overlap—and to understand that they overlap—even if the group motivated by private gain could hardly care less.

This process is increasingly difficult in the modern world because so many of the signals emanating from the developed world tend to be misleading, counterproductive, and even destructive, often to some of the very elites who should be the vanguard—e.g., the offspring of the middle and upper classes. These signals often confuse, obscure, and even block the messages that the development authorities should be trying to get across. More than anything else, these negative signals highlight the need for the kind of consciously thought through and carefully implemented process of education, information, and indoctrination we suggest below.

We are not saying that people everywhere are obligated to support all the choices and tactics adopted by their leaders; quite the contrary. It is often constructive to have a genuinely free and open discussion of these issues, but less so to have a barrage of propaganda undermining morale and commitment. Furthermore, the current tendency for elites in the developed world to send the wrong messages to the less-developed world is often as much a matter of self-indulgent propaganda as the result of serious thought and discussion. Since the personal and community commitment to modernization is still very fragile (if it exists at all) in many areas in the world, anything that weakens this commitment can be terribly counterproductive for the future of the people concerned.

We especially deplore the activities of self-appointed missionaries who want modernizing nations to return to their supposedly noble state of innocence and ignorance. Among these missionaries are many outsiders who want to prevent important economic development projects in order to "protect" the environment. In reality, most developing nations are long on environment and extremely short on economic development. In many cases, these nations are taking "appropriate" precautions to minimize the environmental impact of the disputed projects. (The quotation marks are intended to emphasize that the word appropriate includes full weight being given to economic needs.) While outsiders can play an important role in making people aware of environmental issues, excessive zeal and self-righteousness can be destructive and, we would argue, often willfully and callously so.

The literature of development contains at least three important counterproductive—or at least problem-creating—views. First is the traditionalist who, in Reinhard Bendix's phrase, "fears a loss of harmony among men." People correctly fear a loss of traditional sources of meaning and purpose; of the familiar and comfortable; of status and power; of religious, ethical, and aesthetic values. This viewpoint is created, in part, by a protective reaction against a second group of concepts—that development should "break with the old" and create wholly new individuals and societies. Sometimes these are conceived of as faithful imitations of the early European development process and sometimes as similar to the "creation of a new man" in Maoist China.

The third group of views more or less assumes that the postindustrial world—or its equivalent—is already here. Some of these variations of small-is-beautiful and limits-to-growth thinking that hold that traditional industrialization is a mistake, others just want to "knock off" or have less hassle. These approaches can be labeled "excessively pro-traditional," "tabula rasa," and "preemptive postindustrial." In our view, they all are misleading, irrelevant, or counterproductive. A modernizing society should build as much as possible on its old traditions but be willing to modify or reject many aspects of the past.

The medium-term goal should be increased affluence and technological capability. The long-term goal should be the postindustrial society in one form or another. We believe the latter can be achieved within a century or two by almost all cultures and societies, but not in a decade or two. We also believe that there are "many mountains leading to heaven" (the postindustrial society goal) and many roads up each mountain. Not only must a mountain be chosen, but also a road must be found that avoids molehills, wandering in the foothills, and other dead ends. And there must be some degree of unity and commitment about the particular mountain and road that are chosen. Two reasons for trying to build on the old as much as possible are that it makes it much easier to create this unity and commitment, and that it reduces the hostility of the traditionalists.

ON THE IMPORTANCE OF A "GOOD" CULTURE AND "GOOD" MANAGEMENT

Some readers may feel that our general culturism and our use of such phrases as "the Atlantic Protestant culture area" involve not only unwarranted generalizations, but also reveal some sinister habits of mind, perhaps even crypto-racism. Many may be even more annoyed at the pervasive idea that culture and national character have often been crucial for economic development. We have also made many remarks about the importance of good leadership and good management.

We are indeed convinced that the world environment for development is still so felicitous that any country that enjoys adequate leadership or management should be able to develop rather rapidly, if it can get access to the modern world. This should be possible unless the cultural background itself prevents "good" leadership or management from emerging. We also believe that worldwide economic and technological trends will make it easier for most countries to exploit their assets and to alleviate their weaknesses. Even if there are grave cultural or other deficiencies, it should become increasingly easy to cope with these deficiencies—unless unwise policies or side effects of the less beneficial aspects of the new environment for development either exacerbate the problems or otherwise make solutions more difficult.

The experience of the United States can serve as a prototype for some aspects of this concept. Wave after wave of immigrant groups came in at the bottom, moved up, and were then replaced by later waves. While there are some hard core poor groups among United States blacks, almost half the black population can be judged to be lower-middle or middle class, and another sixth or so to be relatively well off. Most blacks are now well above the poverty line; they think of themselves as middle class and are thought of in this way by their neighbors. (An American with a regular job is normally considered to be middle class rather than working class in attitudes and life style.) Furthermore, less than half of the poor in the United States are now black. Although extensive poverty exists among female-headed families, black females as a whole now earn as much as white females with similar education. Puerto Ricans and Mexican-Americans, while hard hit by the recent recession, are responding to a large degree to economic opportunities like the traditional immigrant groups. Poverty in the United States is now mostly associated with old age and sickness, voluntary intermittent employment, withdrawal from the system, some kind of pathology or special circumstances, or extreme isolation. Within a century something similar should be true of the world as a whole; to a startling degree, it holds today in mature economies.

Another analogy can be made with recent trends in the United States. At present the United States is in the midst of a rapid reversal of roles between the Northeast and the South and the Southwest. Traditionally, before World War II, the Northeast was the technologically advanced, dynamic, industrializing, rapidly growing region; the South was the most lethargic. Since the war these two roles have been basically reversed. The Northeast has grown about 2.5 percent per year and the South and Southwest about 5 percent a year. This is often called the sunbelt shift, but this is only partly correct. First and foremost, while there is much movement of people, there is little or no movement of industry. Rather, the new industries that are starting in the United States are overwhelmingly started in the South and Southwest, partly because of the availability of a relatively hardworking and dedicated workforce. This includes such places as Alabama and Mississippi that are scarcely thought of as part of the normal sunbelt (vacation-oriented) areas.

The continued existence of traditional American values seems to be as important as climate. We believe that the subculture of the South and, to some degree, the Southwest, which was once thought of as relatively inimical to industrial development, is now far superior in this respect to the subculture of the northeastern United States. This position can be maintained even if full allowance is made for the additional problems of the Northeast in having aging cities and the impact of the automobile in making it much easier for living and developing in open areas of the South and Southwest.

Something much like this is also occurring worldwide, where the currently affluent countries are playing the role of the Northeast and the middle income countries the role of the South and Southwest.

ON POVERTY AND MORAL IMPERATIVES

We believe that the developed world everywhere has a moral responsibility to help the poor of this world to become reasonably well off (or at least what we have called "middle income"—neither affluent nor poor).

We do not believe that the developed world bears any overwhelming moral imperative to decrease gaps, the large differences in the average incomes of nations. It is probably desirable to do so, but only as a relatively low-priority objective. We see extreme poverty as an evil that should be decreased and perhaps eliminated as soon as possible. We do not take anywhere near as strong a moral position of achieving relative affluence, except as it helps reduce absolute poverty. We view reducing inequality as the least important moral objective, if it is a moral objective at all.

Unfortunately, we do not have three words for degree of poverty—say poverty1, poverty2, and poverty3. Poverty1 could refer to extreme material deprivation; poverty2 to the psychological deprivation that many feel who have relatively adequate access to material goods but possess fewer amenities than their neighbors; and poverty3 how very affluent observers believe that lower income people should feel, even if they do not. Thus, everybody is aware that many people in the United States with an income below $5,000 per year for a family of four are officially judged to be poor by the government, although in many parts of the world this income would place them firmly in the middle or upper-middle class. Indeed, many families in New York City received in services and cash the equivalent of about $10,000 in 1978 from public assistance and welfare authorities. All three variants of the word "poverty" may be legitimate and useful, but the last two are very different from the kind of desperate material poverty we normally mean when we refer to poverty in this book—i.e., poverty1. [. . .]

11

‒‒‒‒‒ ᪣᪡᪣᪡ ‒‒‒‒‒

The Alienated-Affluent
Society

W e can take what we now know about past and current American
styles of life together with some current trends—and our knowledge of these is far from complete—and add what we believe or find plausible about the socialization of the child, the development of character,
character changes in later life, ways in which social structure and culture
change, and so forth, and on this basis try to assess the consequences of
some simple, basic trends. These include relatively easy affluence, new
technology, absence of absorbing international challenges, and considerable but not disastrous population growth. We must ask, in effect, how
these trends might furnish or constrain possibilities for change. [. . .]

The first salient factor seems likely to be a vastly increased availability
of goods and such services as transportation and communication. A second is a likely increase in leisure and a concomitant reduction of the pressures of work. A third is the likelihood of important technological changes
in such areas as psychopharmacology, with possible radical consequences
for culture and styles of life. Perhaps the most important is a likely absence of stark "life and death" economic and national security issues.

How can we assess the impact of these changes even on a current situation which itself is imperfectly understood? One of the greatest problems
of all psychological and sociological speculation has to do with the dialectical quality of the processes involved. It is difficult to know whether

[Herman Kahn and Anthony J. Wiener, *The Year 2000: A Framework for Speculation on the
Next Thirty-three Years* (New York: Macmillan, 1967).]

to extrapolate trends or to postulate reactions against the same trends. For example, if work will occupy fewer hours of the average person's life, it is plausible to speculate that for this reason work will become less important. On the other hand, it is at least equally plausible that the change in the role of work may cause work as an issue to come to new prominence. The values surrounding work, which in the developed areas have evolved over centuries, may emerge into a new flux and once again become controversial sources of problems within a society and for many individuals. The ideologies that surround work and give it justification and value, in individual and social terms, may become strengthened in support of what remains of work; on the other hand, they may increasingly come into doubt and become the objects of reaction and rebellion. Indeed both trends may materialize simultaneously in different parts of society and may cause conflicts within many individuals. Clearly one can write many scenarios here, with many different branching points. These quandaries must be resolved ultimately by at least partly intuitive and subjective judgments; the most one can claim for such speculations is that no alternative possibility seems much more likely.

ECONOMIC PLAUSIBILITY AND POSTINDUSTRIAL LEISURE

Let us assume, then, with expanded gross national product, greatly increased per capita income, the workweek drastically reduced, retirement earlier (but active life-span longer), and vacations longer, that leisure time and recreation and the values surrounding these acquire a new emphasis. Some substantial percentage of the population is not working at all. There has been a great movement toward the welfare state, especially in the areas of medical care, housing, and subsidies for what previously would have been thought of as poor sectors of the population. [. . .]

It seems not implausible that one-half the people would work in more or less normal fashion, and that one-fifth of the people would work longer hours than normal, either for income or for compulsive or altruistic reasons. Because of the excess contribution of this group, it may be possible to maintain something close to a high GNP, even though some 20 to 30 percent of the normal labor force contribute little or no labor. The underproducers might be, in effect, hobbyists working a few days a month, or a few months a year, to acquire the income to pursue their hobbies. One can also assume that "normal" frictional unemployment will be somewhat higher than usual, and that there will also be something which might be considered "semi-frictional" unemployment (that is, people who have lost jobs but are taking some time looking for another by using their vacations, or who have unusually high or unrealistic standards of what their jobs should be or who are just lying around living on savings.) There could also be a group, assuming the above conditions, who reject any sort of gainful employment on the ground of principle or preference. And finally, there should be people who are more willing to be on relief than not, if only because they have personal or family problems that make it unwise for them to work if they can survive without; or there may be some who are simply and cynically "on the dole." The above suggests that in place of the current 20 percent poor, we may have a similar number, but differently situated, who do not participate normally in the vocational life of the nation.

Consider now the problem of the annual number of hours of work. There could easily be either a four- or five-day week [. . .] It is difficult to guess what patterns will be assumed. It should be noted that if any of the four-day week patterns were adopted the "normal" worker could spend less than 50 percent of his days on his vocation (but only seven to seven and one-half hours per day), less than 50 percent of his days on an avocation (possibly working somewhat longer than seven and one-half hours per day), and then still have one or two days off a week for just relaxing. In other words, it would be possible to pursue an avocation as intensely as a vocation and still have a good deal of time for "third-order" pursuits. As we pointed out, such patterns can be consistent with continued economic growth at reasonably high rates.

SUCCESS BREEDS FAILURE: AFFLUENCE AND THE COLLAPSE OF BOURGEOIS VALUES

John Maynard Keynes addressed himself to this dilemma in one of the earliest and still one of the best short discussions of some of the issues raised by the accumulation of wealth through investment. As he put it,

> . . . the economic problem, the struggle for subsistence, always has been hitherto the primary, most pressing problem of the human race. If the economic problem is solved, mankind will be deprived of its traditional purpose. Will this be of a benefit? If one believes at all in the real values of life, the prospect at least opens up the possibility of benefit. Yet I think with dread of the readjustment of the habits and instincts of the ordinary man, bred into him for countless generations, which he may be asked to discard within a few decades. . . . Thus for the first time since his creation man will be faced with his real, his permanent problem—how to use his freedom from pressing economic cares, how to occupy his leisure, which science and compound interest will have won for him, to live wisely and agreeably and well.

There are those who would argue that with increased freedom from necessity men will be freed for more generous, public-spirited, and humane enterprises. It is a commonplace of the American consensus that it is poverty and ignorance that breed such evils as Communism, revolutions, bigotry, and race hatred. Yet we know better than to expect that the absence of poverty and ignorance will result in a triumph of virtue or even of the benign. On the contrary, it is equally plausible that a decrease in the constraints formerly imposed by harsher aspects of reality will result in large numbers of "spoiled children." At the minimum many may become uninterested in the administration and politics of a society that hands out "goodies" with unfailing and seemingly effortless regularity.

One may choose almost at will from among available hypotheses that may seem to apply to the situation, and one reaches contrary conclusions depending upon the choice that is made; this indeterminacy is perhaps a measure of the inadequacy of contemporary social thought as a basis for generalization, relative to the complexity of human phenomena.

For example, one may take the [. . .] frustration-aggression hypothesis and conclude that aggressiveness will be greatly tranquilized in a society that provides much less external and realistic frustration. This is opposed to the more complex and more psychoanalytically oriented point of view of Freud who points to the role that frustrations imposed by external reality may play in shoring up the defenses of the character structure—defenses that are crucial strengths and that were acquired through learning, with difficulty, as an infant to defer gratification and to mediate among conflicting energies of instinctual impulses, conscience, and the opportunities and dangers of the real world. Research might show, if research could be done on such a subject, that many an infantile and narcissistic personality has matured only when faced with the necessity of earning a living—others only when faced with the necessity for facing up to some personal challenge, such as military service or participation in family responsibility. (The well-known finding that suicide rates drop sharply during wars and economic depressions is subject to diverse interpretation, but it may suggest that such external challenges can serve crucial integrative or compensatory functions for some personalities, and perhaps, less dramatically, for many others.) This is not to say that equally effective or perhaps superior external challenges could not be found to substitute for the working role—or wartime experience—as a maturing or reality-focusing influence. If they are not found, however, while the economy and international and other threats make fewer demands, the decline of the values of work and national service may have some destructive effect.

Thus, there may be a great increase in selfishness, a great decline of interest in government and society as a whole, and a rise in the more childish forms of individualism and in the more antisocial forms of concern for self and perhaps immediate family. Thus, paradoxically, the technological, highly productive society, by demanding less of the individual, may decrease his economic frustrations but increase his aggressions against the society. Certainly here would be fertile soil for what has come to be known as alienation.

The word alienation has been used in many different senses, some of them well defined and some in the context of systems of explanation and prescription for the ailment. The young Karl Marx, for example, followed Ludwig Feuerbach (and to some extent anticipated Freud's *Civilization and its Discontents*) in the belief that alienation resulted from civilized man's "unnatural" repression of his instinctual, especially sexual, nature. Later, however, Marx concluded that alienation resulted from the worker's relationship to labor that had to be done for the profit of another; the cure was to have the worker "own" the means of production; thus alienation could be reduced by shortening the working day, and "the worker therefore feels himself at home only during his leisure."

The alienation that we speculate may result from affluence could have little or nothing to do with whether the society is capitalist or socialist. In either case, the control of the decision-making apparatus would be perceived as beyond the reach of and in fact of little interest for the average person. Thus, whatever the economic system, the politics (and even the culture) of plenty could become one not of contentment but of cynicism, emotional distance, and hostility. More and more the good life would be defined in Epicurean or materialistic, rather than Stoic, or bourgeois terms. The enhancement of private values combined with the increased sense of futility about public values would also entail a kind of despair about the long-run future of the whole society. More and more people would act on the aphorism currently attributed to a leader of the new student left: "If you've booked passage on the Titanic, there's no reason to travel steerage."

Thus the classical American middle-class, work-oriented, advancement-oriented, achievement-oriented attitudes might be rejected for the following reasons:

1. Given an income per worker [. . .] of well over ten thousand dollars in today's dollars, it may become comparatively easy for intelligent Americans to earn ten to twenty thousand dollars a year without investing very intense energies in their jobs—in effect they will be able to "coast" at that level.

2. It may become comparatively easy for an American to obtain several thousand dollars a year from friends and relatives or other sources, and to subsist without undergoing any real hardship, other than deprivation of luxuries.

3. Welfare services and public facilities will generally probably put a fairly high "floor" under living standards, even in terms of luxuries such as parks, beaches, museums, and so on.

4. With money plentiful, its subjective "marginal utility" would probably tend to diminish, and there would probably be a greatly increased emphasis on things that "money cannot buy." Economic and social pressures to conform may diminish as the affluent society feels increasingly that it can "afford" many kinds of slackness and deviation from the virtues that were needed in earlier times to build an industrial society.

5. If the "Puritan ethic" becomes superfluous for the functioning of the economy, the conscience-dominated character type associated with it would also tend to disappear. Parents would no longer be strongly motivated to inculcate traits such as diligence, punctuality, willingness to postpone or forego satisfaction, and similar virtues no longer relevant to the socioeconomic realities in which children are growing up.

6. Yet the need to "justify" the new patterns may remain, and to the extent that there is any residual guilt about the abandonment of the nineteenth- and early twentieth-century values, there would be exaggerated feelings against vocational success and achievement.

Many intellectuals and contributors to popular culture would help to make the case against "bourgeois," "managerial," "bureaucratic," "industrial," "Puritanical," and "preaffluent" values. There would then be considerable cultural support for feelings ranging from indifference to outright contempt for any sort of success or achievement that has economic relevance.

Other factors would augment these effects. For example, presumably [. . .] much more will be known about mood-affecting drugs, and these drugs will probably be used by many as a means of escape from daily life. At the same time, the young, those without responsibility in the social system, will be increasingly alienated by a society that conspicuously fails to meet what it judges to be minimal standards of social justice and purpose (standards which look impossibly utopian to decision-makers). Ideological movements would form to rationalize and justify rebellion and renunciation of old "obsolete" values by youth from all classes and strata of society. Less articulate but equally rebellious young people would contribute to a great rise in crime and delinquency. Other symptoms of social pathology, such as mental illness, neurosis, divorce, suicide, and the like would also probably increase. Traditional religious doctrines might either continue to lose force or continue to be reinterpreted, revised, and secularized so as to pose few obstacles to the current general way of life.

On the other hand, the resources of society for dealing with these problems, perhaps in a (suffocating?) paternalistic way, would also have been greatly augmented. Before discussing the differences that might be made by social responses to these problems, let us see how they might affect various social groups.

OTHER FACTORS IN ALIENATION

In discussing alienation, attention ought also to be given to other aspects of cultural change that may contribute to ego disintegration and feelings of disorientation. Here we meet the difficult problem of diagnosing the malaise of our times. [. . .] In any case, it seems plausible that the "end of ideology" and an inevitable disenchantment with the ideals and expectations of American democracy and free enterprise, coupled with a continued decline in the influence of traditional religion and the absence of any acceptable mass ideologies, have and will continue to contribute to a common spiritual and political rootlessness. As secularization, rationalization, and innovation continue to change the culture in the direction of sensate and bourgeois norms, the influence of traditional Weltanschauungen seems more likely to continue to wane than to undergo any resurgence [. . .].

Furthermore, some things have happened or are happening that change man's relation to his universe in ways that may be unsettling for many people. For example, the inventions of nuclear weapons and intercontinental delivery systems have probably made human life permanently more precarious, and have introduced into international relations a new level of potential horror that is difficult even to imagine with any precision. At the minimum they provide any who wish for it a good excuse for aimless drifting or horrified resentment; in addition, they are ample reasons for both realistic concern and widespread neurotic anxiety and despair.

Technological change itself may contribute to feelings of estrangement from the new physical world and also from a society strongly affected by continual innovation and disruption. There is a long tradition in American letters of hostility to the machine, and, at least since World War II, an increasing perception that the social consequences of science and technology are, at best, mixed blessings. Machines that perform some functions of the human mind far better than humans can are likely to be even more resented, in spite of their economic benefits, than machines that do the same for human muscles. The human place in the world may be most seriously disturbed by new medical technology. New drugs will raise sharply the questions, what is a real human feeling, and what is a genuine personality? Plastic replacements for hearts and other vital organs raise in new and more difficult form the old problem of defining life and death, and add a new difficulty to the old question, what is a human being?

The exploration of space already under way may also have a somewhat disturbing impact on the imaginations of many people. It is well known, for example, that many schizophrenics are preoccupied with fantasies of space exploration (as well as fantasies involving the immense destructive potential of the H-bomb). Phenomena such as weightlessness, dependence for existence on a wholly artificial and technologically sustained environment, and isolation from familiar objects and humankind may have obvious impact on some minds and more subtle impact on a great many. The unconscious is, as Freud has reminded us, an inveterate punster, and it may not be accidental that phrases such as way out, far gone, out of it, and out of this world are currently used to mean strange or bizarre; and that, moreover, phrases such as way out, dropout, flip-out, freak-out, turned on, tuned in, out of my head, and cool are supposed to refer to desirable conditions. Perhaps the most important alienating influence will be a purely negative thing—the absence of the traditional challenge of work, community approval, and national needs.

HUMANISM AND THE VALUE OF TIME

It is possible to suppose that something else might happen. For example, John Adams, our second President, once suggested that: "my sons ought to study mathematics and philosophy, geography, natural history and naval architecture, in order to give their children a right to study painting, poetry, music, architecture, statuary, tapestry and porcelain. . . ."

The passage is peculiarly American; almost no (correspondingly upper-class) European would use the word "right." The most he would have said would be that his sons ought to emphasize mathematics, philosophy, geography, and so on, in order that their sons could emphasize painting, poetry, music, and the like. He would feel that some interest in painting, poetry, and music was proper and unremarkable. On the other hand for most Americans a man who is deeply preoccupied with porcelain, or any of the fine arts, may still be, even in this less Philistine age, a bit suspect—whether as effeminate or as simply not sufficiently serious and practical. Adams's statement is characteristically American, in that it gives an overwhelming priority to the needs of national security and statesmanship and asserts that no one has a right to devote his attention to "finer things" for their own sake, until these needs have been adequately met. A contemporary parallel is the American upper-middle class view of the proper relation between work and play. Typically, an American businessman or professional man apologizes for taking a vacation by explaining it is only "in order to recharge his batteries"; he justifies rest or play mostly in terms of returning to do a better job. The European by contrast seems to enjoy his vacation as a pleasure in its own right, and does not hesitate to work for the express purpose of being able to afford to play in better style.

We have already suggested that in the postindustrial society that we are describing, in continental Europe the middle and upper classes could, in effect, return to or adopt the manner of the "gentleman." Many Europeans, of course, argue that things are now going the other way, that under the impact of a mass-consumption, materialistic culture the humanistic values that have been so characteristic in Europe are rapidly eroding or disappearing. Results—minor or widespread—may become apparent in forms such as political disruption, disturbed families, and personal tragedies—or in the pursuit of some "humanistic" values that many would think of as frivolous or even irrational.

Humanistic values are, of course, a question of definition. While some may judge certain ideologies that invoke humanistic language as better described as sentimental, self-indulgent, or rationalizations of quite irrational feelings of rebelliousness and selfishness, others will accept the ideology. (While this is, of course, more or less a value question, facts and analysis have some relevance to it.)

Consider this question of humanistic versus irrational or indulgent behavior. In 1926 the British economist Arthur Redford said, in describing the adjustment of British yeomen to industrialization: "In the course of a generation or two it becomes quite 'natural' . . . for a fixed number of hours each day, regulating their exertions constantly . . . there may be some temporary restlessness among the 'hands,' but the routine soon reestablishes itself as part of the ordinary discipline of life." While this may be a rather callous observation, "progress" and other conditions predominantly made the adjustment a necessary one.

In the post-affluent world [. . .] we will not likely, and presumably should not, be willing to ask people to make sacrifices of this order. However, new issues will arise. Consider the following two statements put forth by Berkeley students on signs they were carrying while picketing and later on a BBC television broadcast:

> I am a human being; please do not fold, spindle, or mutilate.
> Life here is a living hell.

One can only agree with the first, assuming we understand precisely in what way the students believe they are not treated as well as IBM cards. Thus it was widely believed, especially in the 1930s and 1940s, by people who thought they were "psychologically sophisticated," that any kind of discipline for children causes undesirable repression, inhibits creativity, and creates neuroses; that almost completely permissive upbringing is necessary for a parent not to "fold, spindle, or mutilate." Today psychoanalysts are emphasizing that a reasonable level of benevolent but firm discipline is very much needed by a child, and that excessive permissiveness is more likely to result in a child marred by guilty willfulness, irresponsibility, and inadequacy.

Of course, the students would argue that they do not mean anything so extreme, but just that they ought to be treated better than items processed by machines. One can only sympathize with their lack of ability to communicate with a seemingly unfeeling, bureaucratic administration choosing to enforce computer decisions. But to argue that the idiosyncrasies of a computer that allows ten minutes between classes which require fifteen minutes to reach, or that assigns art classes to basements and engineering classes to top-floor rooms with windows, creates difficulties for students, is rather different from arguing that life is a "living hell." The most that students could reasonably say was that the administration made life unnecessarily complicated and frustrating, and had occasionally overstepped its proper bounds. Yet they chose to state (and no doubt felt) these issues in moralistic, politicized, ideological, and emotionally extreme terms. Similarly, increasing numbers of Americans are likely not only to reject currently held work-oriented, achievement-oriented, advancement-oriented attitudes, but are likely to adopt the kind of "spoiled child" attitudes that seem to have characterized at least some of the Berkeley protesters.

WHAT IS A STABLE STATE FOR THE
ALIENATED-AFFLUENT SOCIETY?

Nevertheless, such a society—affluent, humanistic, leisure-oriented, and partly alienated—might be quite stable. It might, in fact, bear some resemblance to some aspects of Greek society (though of course Greek society did not develop primarily because of affluence). We can imagine a situation in which, say, 70 or 80 percent of people become gentlemen and put a great deal of effort into various types of self-development, though not necessarily the activities which some futurists find most important for a humanistic culture. But one could imagine, for example, a very serious emphasis on sports, on competitive "partner" games (chess, bridge), on music, art, languages, or serious travel, or on the study of science, philosophy, and so on. The crucial point here is that a large majority of the population may feel it important to develop skills, activities, arts, and knowledge to meet very high minimum absolute standards, and a large minority more or less compete to be an elite of elites. One issue is whether or not people who are not well rounded in a number of areas simultaneously, more or less as a gentleman should be, will be considered seriously inferior, or whether it will be sufficient for a person to fulfill himself even if he wishes to do it very narrowly. In both cases, however, there are likely to be at least subtle social pressures for such self-development. In the absence of such social pressures, then, we would still expect much of the same kind of activity but now more in the range of 20 or 30 percent of the population than 70 or 80 percent.

Thus there is a very large difference between merely having community acceptance of the right for an individual to spend a lot of time and money on improving himself in this way, and community "demand" that he do so in order to be considered a reasonable or full member of the community, or an educated man. It is hard to believe that in the long run we are not going to get something on the order of the latter in the affluent, postindustrial society. That is, people who are behaving in the new modes will simply look down on those who are not. Indeed there are now such pressures on families in middle-class communities, where there is great emphasis on giving the children dancing lessons, music lessons, and fostering nonutilitarian skills which improve their ability to enjoy themselves and, most important, to be more socially desirable. In other words, middle-class children in the United States are now being treated in a manner not too dissimilar from the way aristocrats treated their children some years ago, except that there is little emphasis on being hard and tough, having a sense of noblesse oblige, and there are somewhat less demanding standards of performance. But while contemporary American parents are in many ways very soft on children, and certainly demand much less in the way of help with chores or housework than they did several generations ago, when it comes to socially important achievements in school, dancing, music, athletics, and so on, they tend to be rather startlingly demanding. While it is true that in many cases the children enjoy these activities and do not resent having their schedules so filled, there are many cases in which they do, in fact, feel overburdened by their demanding routine and still feel real pressures to maintain it.

SOCIAL RESPONSE TO NEW DIFFICULTIES

The most serious issue raised by these speculations (in addition to their validity, of course) is whether they are not just modern manifestations of traditional "aberrant" behavior, or whether they represent a reasonable adjustment or transition state to new traditions and mores. There is also the question of to what degree society will be self-correcting and self-adjusting. Doubtless, however, there will be much room and need for improved social policies. Just as it seems likely that societies have learned to handle routine economic problems sufficiently well to avoid serious depressions, it may be that we have begun to understand social and psychological problems well enough to avoid the partial passivity and failure implicit in these speculations. While few would now believe that the mere multiplication of productive powers is likely to bring mankind into utopia, or into anything resembling it, it would be ironic (but not unprecedented) if this multiplication of resources were to create problems too serious for the solutions that those very resources should make feasible. Efforts will doubtlessly be needed to invent and implement ways of coping with the new and unfamiliar problems that will certainly arise. [. . .]

III

THE CHALLENGE OF THE FUTURE: FUTUROLOGY, METHODOLOGY, AND POLICY RESEARCH

12

⸺◦◦◦⸺

The Objectives of Future-Oriented Policy Research

W hat can policy research do to help avoid undesired results of decisions? Obviously a good deal less can be done than an engineer or
doctor is often able to do about problems within his technical expertise.
But research can be helpful if carried out with a proper sense of limitations. One can attempt to accomplish one or more of the following objectives: (1) To stimulate and stretch the imagination and improve the perspective; (2) To clarify, define, name, expound, and argue major issues; (3)
To design and study alternative policy "packages" and contexts; (4) To
create propaedeutic and heuristic expositions, methodologies, paradigms,
and frameworks;[1] (5) To improve intellectual communication and cooperation, particularly by the use of historical analogies, scenarios, metaphors,
analytic models, precise concepts, and suitable language; (6) To increase
the ability to identify new patterns and crises and to understand their
character and significance; (7) To furnish specific knowledge and to generate and document conclusions, recommendations, and suggestions; (8)
To clarify currently realistic policy choices, with emphasis on those that
retain efficiency and flexibility over a broad range of contingencies; (9) To
improve the "administrative" ability of decision-makers and their staffs to
react appropriately to the new and unfamiliar.

A good deal of thought has gone into framing and describing this list of
objectives. We believe it is useful and productive for the researcher to go

---

[Herman Kahn and Anthony J. Wiener, *The Year 2000: A Framework for Speculation on the
Next Thirty-three Years* (New York: Macmillan, 1967).]

through a conscious process of focusing specifically upon what he is trying to achieve. Doing this may simultaneously open up new opportunities and areas for analysis and limit ambitions in others. We also believe that trying to be explicitly and thoughtfully aware of the possible objectives can be an equally healthy exercise for the reader and can help him to achieve desirable objectives.

STIMULATE AND STRETCH THE IMAGINATION AND IMPROVE THE PERSPECTIVE

The very process of systematically arranging all the factors that have or conceivably might have a bearing on the issues being studied makes demands on the imagination. Making up such lists forces one at least briefly to make distinctions and to examine nuances that are ordinarily overlooked or disregarded and to give attention and thought to potentially important situations and influences that would normally be outside the range of consideration, possibly because they are nonobvious or improbable or, more likely, because of emotional, professional, or doctrinaire biases. The effort of imagination and intellect required to bring a range of potentially relevant factors into focus is not likely to be wasted. Even if most of them should never acquire significance for action in the real world, some very likely will. Almost invariably some small but important number of the distinctions and nuances that are missed the first time will ultimately become important. In particular, possibilities that do not seem live options today may become worthy of serious consideration overnight as a result of new developments. Surprising developments happen often enough to make worthwhile the spending of valuable time and resources in preparing for them—at least intellectually—despite intellectual, social, bureaucratic, and other difficulties.

It is often the borderline or extreme cases that open up new vistas or new fields. Also, alternatives that no one would choose, either today or tomorrow, may still illustrate important principles in a simpler and more persuasive fashion than complex examples taken from reality. To be fully aware of the shape of reality it is necessary to glance beyond its boundaries on all sides. Proper perspective requires a view of the setting. Perhaps most important, our intuitions are no longer as reliable a guide as they used to be. Many currently useful ideas seemed bizarre or ridiculous when they were first considered. The seemingly improbable or hypothetical may, on analysis, be judged to have been unfashionable, novel, or unpleasant rather than unlikely or unrealistic. Thus research that opens the mind to new concepts and possibilities, fine distinctions, and subtle nuances is essential training and education for the analyst. For this reason alone such research should not shy away from examining extreme, implausible, or unfamiliar situations.

The reader of speculations on the relatively distant future may believe there is a danger of bringing too much imagination to these problems and a risk of losing ourselves in a maze of bizarre improbabilities. Yet if we review past performance in this field, we find comparatively little evidence of harm through excessive concern with the unfashionably hypothetical, even when short-run policies are at issue. Although there has been the occasional fashionable chimera that diverted attention and resources from projects that later turned out to have been more needful, a brief consideration of unfashionable improbabilities is not open to the same objection. In any case, it has usually been lack of imagination, rather than excess of it, that caused unfortunate decisions and missed opportunities. It is just because the fashionably hypothetical may dominate current planning and discussion that it is important to emphasize the relevance of the unfashionably hypothetical. It is hoped that reality will not introduce some of its acid, but potentially very painful, operational tests.

It may also be important to have some perspective on the role and relative importance of any particular issue or problem. There are important differences here between the roles of the researcher, the policy-adviser, and the policy-maker. In many areas good work can result only from systematic, sustained perseverance, often in the face of intellectual, social, bureaucratic, or other difficulties. Often sufficient motivation for such an effort can result only from an exaggerated estimate of the importance or of the likelihood of success that leads to a dedicated or even fanatic intensity of effort. However, when it becomes time to integrate this work into the total body of policy, the subject must be restored to its proper perspective [. . .]

CLARIFY, DEFINE, NAME, EXPOUND, AND ARGUE MAJOR ISSUES

It is occasionally assumed that there is widespread and explicit agreement about (a) what issues are important, (b) what stands on them are possible or reasonable, and (c) what are the major arguments for each of these stands. In point of fact, no such second-order agreement[2] exists, except possibly within a few close-knit circles or on a few limited issues that have been in the spotlight of attention in recent years. Many other equally or more important issues remain unrecognized, undefined, and undiscussed. Such recognition and definition is of the utmost importance.

Clarification and definition of the issues also involve naming, for a choice of categories is in effect a choice of subject matter. This can lead to difficulties, for any system of categories comprehends some real distinctions and likenesses while ignoring or deemphasizing others. In the long run, problems shift and the nomenclature that is left over from an earlier focus or context makes discussion of later issues more difficult. [. . .] Appropriate words are often "used up" by acquiring a special technical meaning. Moreover, the technical terminology employed may make it difficult either to see or to discuss these new issues usefully. However, we believe in the convenience of having simple labels for relevant packages of complex issues, even though the future will likely make even the best classification and naming system more or less obsolete. This is why one important aspect of technical competence consists of the ability to learn current classificatory systems with skill and discretion and to modify or replace such systems as their relevance diminishes or vanishes.

We employ the term naming, however, in a more specialized sense here. It functions as a metaphor in calling to mind analogous categories. Thus to label a concession as a "Munich" is to categorize it usefully even though the risk is run that the term will be applied to an appeasement that successfully appeased a world-be aggressor or to a concession that in fact satisfies the dictates of current standards of international justice. Although such names can, and likely will be, misused, we would argue that they carry too much useful information to be dispensed with. Again, one aspect of technical competence will involve using such names in ways that enhance their information-bearing rather than their information-degrading consequences. Their ambiguity also serves a desirable function, for they often initiate debate in a way that clarifies issues further. Thus, just as the clarification and definition of issues involve naming in a more general sense, so this more specialized kind of naming can be used to enhance discussion of the stands that are possible and the arguments that support them.

The main object, of course, is to determine what stands on each issue are reasonable and which are the major arguments for each stand. What is important here is to take each issue seriously enough and to carry the argument deeply enough so that a further superficial examination will not uncover crucial new arguments and factors. The position taken by the participants should be informed enough to stand up under the usual analysis.

It is startling how often in meetings it occurs that the raising of a single not-too-complicated point shifts many positions. Conversely many (unshiftable) positions are revealed as simple and unconsidered, even if strong, reactions to narrow aspects of the problem. In other words, the customary arguments used are often parochial, specialized, mostly unexamined, and sometimes self-serving. This not only leads to unnecessary biases, it may even be counterproductive to the holder's interests. For example, from the viewpoint of efficient political manipulation, it is of some importance to be empathetic with the audience to be manipulated. It is a fair characterization of most reports prepared in various subdivisions of the United States government that they tend to be prepared for audiences of "friends and relatives." They have almost no chance of carrying conviction with or persuading a skeptical, not to say a hostile, audience. Yet to be useful, the exposition and argumentation must be comprehensive enough, as discussed in point four below, to appeal to the relevant "majority." Such an attempt, even if motivated by the most parochial considerations, will still result in better recommendations. From this point of view, in the past even relatively simple concepts were not fully understood until several different analysts in many different studies contributed to their clarification and definition.

FORMULATE AND STUDY ALTERNATIVE POLICY "PACKAGES" AND CONTEXTS

One important aspect of exposition and arguing policy issues is the use of proper contexts. Few measures can be evaluated in isolation. They must be evaluated in a context of other measures that are being pursued and also in terms of the criteria and contexts set by the values and assumptions held by the policy-maker (or policy-makers). In order to facilitate such systematic comparisons it is important to assemble a relatively large number of packages of specific measures, so that one relatively complete policy can be compared with another relatively complete policy. The number of packages will, of course, be very small as compared to the total that is possible. However, in a relatively well-understood area, such a small number may still provide a large enough set of examples so that almost all of the relevant people can recognize their views in one package or the other. If it is necessary to make finer distinctions, subpackages within each package can be defined or designed.

It should be clear that people with different attitudes and views may be put in the same package, since these packages are likely to be fairly general and highly aggregated. But to the extent that these issues can be discussed without going into the greater detail that would separate the adherents of the same packages, it is often worthwhile to do so. One can then at least get much of the general discussion earned through in a systematic way. Of course, eventually one must go into details that may be crucial and that will more or less eliminate this superstructure of "packages," but it seems that about 90 percent of the debates, particularly those conducted in government offices, committees, interdepartmental conferences, briefings, and so on, can be discussed at a relatively general and aggregated level. This discussion can be greatly facilitated by the previous preparation and discussion of specific packages and the creation of shared understandings or even of second-order agreement about most of the major issues raised by the comparison of such packages. A similar set of observations applies to the contexts in which these packages are evaluated and reevaluated. In practice more of the real controversy involves assumptions about overall contexts than about specific details.

In general, the systematic and careful study of the factors affecting the main issues, and the constructing of a number of policy packages in relation to varying contexts, will reveal a great number of interactions among variables, including various incongruities, inconsistencies, incompatibilities, and dissonances as well as mutual reinforcements. A realistic attempt to reconcile and balance the costs and benefits of including, modifying, or excluding important variables and ingredients should lead to an improved synthesis and balance. In particular, the formulation and study of alternatives yields insights into the objectives and assumptions that are behind each choice.

CREATE PROPAEDEUTIC AND HEURISTIC
METHODOLOGIES AND PARADIGMS

[. . .] By paradigm we mean something a bit more structured than a framework, and a bit more elaborate than a metaphor made explicit, though we mean something much less formal than an analytical model, in the sense of applied mathematics. We mean a relatively structured set of explicit assumptions, definitions, typologies, conjectures, analyses, and questions. Robert K. Merton has argued (and, with examples, has demonstrated) the great value of such paradigms for sociological analyses; his points are equally valid for analyses of problems in public policy. Paradigms, he points out, have five closely related functions:

First, paradigms have a notational function. They provide a compact parsimonious arrangement of the central concepts and their interrelations as these are utilized for description and analysis. Having one's concepts set out in sufficiently brief compass to permit their simultaneous inspection is an important aid to self-correction of one's successive interpretations, a result difficult to achieve when one's concepts are scattered and hidden in page after page of discursive exposition.

Second, the explicit statement of analytical paradigms lessens the likelihood of inadvertently importing hidden assumptions and concepts, since each new assumption and each new concept must either be logically derivable from the previous terms of the paradigm or explicitly incorporated in it. The paradigm thus supplies a pragmatic and logical guide for the avoidance of ad hoc (i.e., logically irresponsible) hypotheses.

Third, paradigms advance the cumulation of theoretical interpretation. In this connection, we can regard the paradigm as the foundation upon which the house of interpretations is built. If a new story cannot be built directly upon the paradigmatic foundations, if it cannot be derived from the foundations, than it must be considered a new wing of the total structure, and the foundations (of concepts and assumptions) must be extended to support the new wing. Moreover, each new story which can be built upon the original foundations strengthens our confidence in their substantial quality just as every new extension, precisely because it requires additional foundations, leads us to suspect the soundness of the original substructure.

Fourth, paradigms, by their very arrangement, suggest the systematic cross-tabulation of presumably significant concepts and may thus sensitize the analyst to types of empirical and theoretic problems which might otherwise be overlooked. They promote analysis rather than concrete description.

Fifth, and in this accounting, finally, paradigms make for the codification of methods of qualitative analysis in a manner approximating the logical, if not the empirical, rigor of quantitative analysis [. . .]

Quantitative procedures are expressly codified as a matter of course: they are open to inspection by all, and the assumptions and procedures can be critically scrutinized by all who care to read. In frequent contrast to this public character of codified quantitative analysis, the [. . .] analysis of qualitative data is assumed to reside in a private world inhabited exclusively by penetrating but unfathomable insights and by ineffable understandings. Indeed, discursive expositions not based upon an explicit paradigm often involve perceptive interpretations; as the cant phrase has it, they are rich in "illuminating insights." But it is not always clear just which operations with analytic concepts were involved in these insights. There consequently results an aggregate of discrete insights rather than a codified body of knowledge, subject to reproducible research.

Since all virtues can readily become vices merely by being carried to excess, the [. . .] paradigm can be abused almost as easily as it can be used. It is a temptation to mental indolence. Equipped with his paradigm, the (analyst) may shut his eyes to strategic data not expressly called for in the paradigm. He may turn the paradigm from a [. . .] field-glass into a blinder. Misuse results from absolutizing the paradigm rather than using it tentatively, as a point of departure. [. . .]

As in any field of inquiry in which concerted efforts and possibly even cumulative improvements are sought, propaedeutic and heuristic devices are urgently needed. One of the difficulties with getting enlightened and informed decision-making today is that so many people have to know so much about each other's fields. About half the time of any particular, specialized decision-maker is spent becoming familiar with allied information from complementary and supplementary specializations. It is of extreme importance, under these circumstances, to have in effect a simple "college outline" type of literature that is directly pointed to the needs of these people. Such a literature, of course, can only be produced to order; it is not produced accidentally. By "literature," we include, of course, methodologies for analysis and design.

The kind of work that has to be done on issues such as national security, international order, and the "quality of life" requires the integration, at least at a superficial level, of a large number of different disciplines. Almost anything that would help in doing this should be encouraged. We must maintain standards of depth and thoroughness, but these should not be self-defeating standards that prevent an important job from being begun. Almost necessarily, interdisciplinary workers must rely on "secondary sources," or on the advice of experts whom they have difficulty evaluating, though this problem can be much alleviated by a suitable playing of experts against each other. "Teams" of experts have important limitations; at some point a plan or solution must be achieved, and this can take place only "within a single skull" (in Clyde Kluckhohn's phrase). Thus one or more specialists must step outside their fields, or one or more nonspecialists must perform the final integration of specialties. However disagreeable such a task may prove, it is necessary and will be done better if better shared concepts and common vocabulary as well as special propaedeutic devices are developed.

IMPROVE INTELLECTUAL COMMUNICATION AND COOPERATION (PARTICULARLY BY THE USE OF HISTORICAL EXAMPLES, SCENARIOS, METAPHORS, ANALYTIC MODELS, PRECISE CONCEPTS, AND SUITABLE LANGUAGE)

One difficulty in devising pragmatic rules and heuristic hypotheses to deal with such novel situations as the proper conduct of international relations in a thermonuclear world is that we do not have a great fund even of intellectual experience to draw upon. Thus the meaningful concepts and metaphors, all of which are useful if not essential for the proper analysis and discussion of any complicated aspect of social relations, are lacking to us. Small groups that work together on these problems tend, in the absence of community experience, to develop special connotations for words and elements of precision in their terms that outsiders do not share, even though it may seem to the outsiders that the debate contains nothing that they fail to follow. The wider the relevant public and decision-making circles, the more this lack of shared experience hampers the communication process that is necessary for adequate decisions. Thus, although it is true that all truly professional groups develop a professional jargon of which outsiders are not fully cognizant, this problem is exacerbated in dealing with public issues. Moreover the jargon is not fully understood and communication is faulty even among many who consider themselves professional, except for some tightly knit small groups. One helpful device for overcoming this problem to some extent would be to create and to use artificial "case histories" and "historical examples" to supplement the paucity of real examples; but we note that there seems to be an insufficient exploitation of the examples that are already available.

INCREASE THE ABILITY TO IDENTIFY NEW PATTERNS AND CRISES AND UNDERSTAND THEIR CHARACTER AND SIGNIFICANCE

The major reason why one needs such artificial devices as a specially created "college outline" type of literature and paradigms for policy planning is the rapidity with which changes occur. If the changes were slower, the various specialists would gradually learn what is needed for them to perform their functions effectively, and the normal methods of providing textbooks, literature, and expert professionals would suffice. So the essence of our problem is that we must cope with new problems and concepts. By devoting attention to possibilities in a number of future settings it is possible to identify and study patterns and thus to become expert in the recognition of the patterns that are actually developing in the real world. Thus a series of studies like the present one can be of service in facilitating reaction to such patterns. As a result, there may be fewer wrong decisions, fewer unpleasant surprises, and fewer missed opportunities. Understanding developing patterns may not make the future our servant, but it certainly helps us to take advantage of some of its opportunities. Often recognition of a problem in time to cope with it is more of a limitation on adequate governmental action than are expenditures or levels of effort. Therefore, the early recognition of developing patterns has become of the utmost importance.

If subsequent efforts to investigate the distant future achieve some success, many of the new and unusual problems of policy planning will seem much less bizarre and will appear instead as a routine responsibility of the proper staffs. It will be less likely that we fail to guard against or fail to prepare to exploit possible developments because of overconcentration on the current pattern. To the extent the present is emphasized, it will be deliberate, and not by default. Nonetheless, the pragmatic approach typical of Americans and their government is not going to be—nor would we agree that it should be—replaced by merely technical procedures. Indeed one way to view the whole program sketched out above is as a basis for a kind of planned muddling through. It prevents the foreclosure of options that would make muddling through impossible, and enhances the consensus on basic directions and destinations that makes muddling through successful.

FURNISH SPECIFIC KNOWLEDGE AND GENERATE AND DOCUMENT CONCLUSIONS, RECOMMENDATIONS, AND SUGGESTIONS

[Our type of approach], unlike the typical policy study, contains few specific conclusions, recommendations, or suggestions. It is intended [. . .] as a framework for speculation and discussion. If we have succeeded in doing useful groundwork for the future debate, this work should result in further studies by ourselves and others that will be more productive in recommendations and suggestions.

Even so, such studies can rarely be definitive. They must necessarily limit themselves to particular aspects of a wide field and cannot be expected to be conclusive outside rather narrow limits. Furthermore, while they can make the consideration of imponderables more explicit, they can scarcely enable the decision-maker to evade his prerogatives and responsibilities by supplying him with specific solutions for various trades, compromises, and dilemmas.

It is true that on rare occasions a study will be able to make its final recommendations with great force and authority: but such recommendations will almost always be limited to a very narrow area that has been thoroughly covered by the study and in which the basic context and assumptions—at least as to objectives—are not controversial. Broader recommendations and suggestions with respect to more controversial assumptions or values cannot be expected to have as great force.

This is by no means to say that the decision-maker should disregard "narrow" studies. On the contrary, it will nearly always be of advantage to take the results of such studies into account in the process of reaching a decision. There is a great difference between an informed choice and a decision from ignorance or by default.

CLARIFY CURRENT CHOICES—HEDGING, CONTINGENCY PLANNING, AND COMPROMISING

Current choices are presumably based on the realities, objectives, and assumptions of today. Because all of these can change rapidly, it is important to understand explicitly the relationship of the choice to such realities, objectives, and assumptions, so that the choices can change when the basis on which they were made changes. It is surprisingly hard to do this, because most people—even most professional analysts—tend to forget the original reasons for their choices, and are then not willing to change their positions. It often helps to reconstruct the histories of how individuals arrived at their positions; then they know explicitly what they would be giving up if they changed their minds. But it is not enough to know and remember the reasons for one's choice. No choice is fully meaningful unless its alternatives are also understood and appreciated. It is especially important to understand the negative side of one's choice: the drawbacks and the costs associated with it. A thoroughgoing satisfaction with all aspects of one's position is often no more than an inability to see its problematic sides. Clarifying a choice involves some awareness of the fact that there was a choice and that something had to be sacrificed or compromised in committing oneself to it.

This underlies the concept of hedging and contingency design. By hedging we mean a modification of the preferred "system" that enables one to cope with "off-design" situations. Inside their own range of past experience, decision-makers usually understand the need for hedging against failure, that is, for acquiring emergency capabilities for dealing with relatively less favorable—including improbable—contingencies than those expected when the choice was made. It is less frequently remembered, but often equally important, that one should be able to take advantage of unexpected but more favorable situations if they arise. That is, one should also hedge to be in a position to exploit opportunities.

Equally important as hedging and analytically very similar to it is the process of attaining necessary accommodation with other people's values and assumptions. This is the process of putting together the relevant majority; and it has many similarities with other political processes. Forming policy is part of political give-and-take, but one of the special problems is that the give and take involves so much time that when the policy is finally set valuable opportunities may have been lost, or points of no return passed. Thus it is important to take into account other points of view in advance. Moreover proposals that do not sufficiently take into account other points of view may be rejected before they receive a "fair" hearing.

BROADEN AND IMPROVE THE BASIS FOR BOTH POLITICAL DECISION-MAKING AND ADMINISTRATIVE ACTIONS IN DEALING WITH NEW TRENDS AND CRISES

Any improvement in the technical or political debates, any improvement in communication and shared understandings, in making basic issues clearer, is likely to result in greater understanding at the upper levels of government, within intellectual elites, and among people generally. But such understanding can be more than intellectual. It can also result in participants becoming morally sensitive, morally informed, and intellectually more serious. Stimulating the study of crucial problems and drawing attention to potentially necessary decisions and acts are minimal requirements for coping successfully with the problems of the future. How much more can be done is problematical. It may be that all we can do is improve our capability to muddle through. But this in itself will be an achievement [. . .] .

NOTES

1. We use these rather pedantic words reluctantly, but they seem to be the best available to describe our objectives. By propaedeutic we mean pertaining to introductory instruction, although there is no suggestion of the oversimplified. Because creative integration of ideas must ultimately take place in a single mind, even a very sophisticated and knowledgeable policy-maker, analyst, long-range planner (or member of an interdisciplinary study group) must absorb many ideas from unfamiliar fields. Hence, propaedeutic techniques are indispensable. By "heuristic" we refer to that which serves to discover, or to stimulate investigation, or to methods of demonstration that lead an investigator to probe further. While heuristic techniques are not necessarily scholarly or rigorous, their value need not be belabored. Paradigm, a structured set of propositions, is discussed more fully below.

2. By first-order agreement we mean agreement on substance—that is, on assumptions, values, or the policy to be pursued; by second-order agreement we mean agreement on what the agreement or disagreement is about.

13

—❧—

The Agnostic Use of
Information and Concepts

One of our major "methodological" tools is the agnostic use of information and concepts. To explain this tool, we begin by contrasting
the academic and the practical styles, exaggerating the differences to
heighten the contrast. Consider professor-student interactions. Normally
professors exposit certain topics that they understand well, covering all
the issues that are relevant from their perspective. Then the professors test
the ability of students to understand and use the concepts by formulating
clear-cut questions that have verifiable answers. Enough information has
been supplied, or will be easily available using resources on campus, so
that students can answer the questions satisfactorily. To the extent that
any theoretical reasoning is used in answering the question, the theories
are also available and are known to be relevant, valid, and complete. Finally, the students are given sufficient time to find and use whatever the
information they need. Note that: Proper background has been supplied
in advance; Questions are clearly formulated; Adequate high quality information is available; Adequate high quality theories are available; Clear
distinctions exist between right and wrong answers; The time needed is
available.

None of these conditions obtains in most situations studied by the Hudson Institute (or indeed in many real life situations). Decision makers
have to make do with what they have available. This means that the questions are not precisely formulated; the answers are not verifiable; high

---

[*World Economic Development: 1979 and Beyond* (Boulder, Colo.: Westview Press, 1979).]

quality data, adequate theories, and sufficient amounts of time are not likely to be available. [. . .] In fact, the biggest issues may be "What is the question? How much time is available? What information and theories that are accessible are relevant? If these are contradictory or inconsistent, how do we deal with them?"

A similar situation is encountered when one looks at the differences between a professor's own doctoral thesis and most real world problems. In the thesis, the question or issue is almost always carefully and narrowly formulated to make it possible for the work to be original; enough time is allocated to make the work of publishable quality; and the dimensions and scope deliberately specialized to fall within one's normal field of interest or capability. In the real world, of course, the scope of the problems and quality of solution are determined by the existential context and time pressures are ignored at great peril.

It is a hopeless, even irrational illusion to expect real world business or political situations to be as neat and orderly as the problems presented in academic discussions. It is even more hopeless to expect to find high quality theorems and models that will be realistically applicable. And only rarely has all the relevant and available information been gathered. Business and political decision-makers have to come up with reasonable solutions based mostly on low quality information and theories applied in situations where the questions are imprecisely or inaccurately formulated and where no one knows ahead of time whether the answers suggested are right or the politics devised will work. Controversy will continue even after the fact because there will be different interpretations of what actually occurred and why.

Sometimes decisions come up in such a way that additional study and analysis may be possible. But even then, decisions cannot be held up indefinitely. In most cases the additional analysis will probably not be decisive, particularly if the situation is changing rapidly. Indeed, a slow-moving study will often lag far behind events. How, then, should one proceed? Presumably as people have always proceeded: by using their best judgments, intuitions, and guesses. Often the basic reasoning and methodology will be faulty if applied generally or inexpertly. Yet decision-makers often arrive at good answers to the specific problems they have to deal with.

I have some experience with this situation in an area where most laymen would not expect these kinds of problems. As a theoretical physicist I worked closely with some of the best physicists of our generation. Contrary to popular impression, these scientists did not always work rigorously, nor were they as careful as their reputations and self-confidence would indicate—even in their own fields. They often put forth hypotheses as if they were mathematical theorems of universal validity, although it was easy to show that they weren't. Nevertheless, they rarely made errors in dealing with the practical applications of these hypotheses. Even though they thought of these theorems as universally applicable, the hypotheses had generally been developed out of very special problems. The scientists intuitively applied the theorems only to areas and under conditions where, in fact, they did fit. As a result, they almost always obtained correct or at least usable results, even though they claimed more for their theories than was actually provable.

Decision-makers are often in much more precarious positions. They may have little available to them beyond experience in varied and not always relevant fields; theories that are often a synthesis of various anecdotes, metaphors, and analogues; and, sometimes, empathy with various important groups. Yet many competent, pragmatic decision-makers have done very well. Throughout much of human history, leaders have used the same basic techniques. They intuitively understood the specific issues facing them so well that they could deal with them in an empirical, pragmatic ad hoc fashion; or they used some kind of theoretical framework to produce solutions that were quite reasonable; or they creatively exploited limited but perceptive observations.

Until quite recently, no scientific survey data existed, nor did much formal theory. More often than not, the theorists in economics and sociology do not originate their "inventions." Rather, they describe events that occurred before the theories were devised. The theorists' contributions were and are less inventions than descriptions of the actions of practical people in a more or less rational and comprehensible manner. Constructs or institutions emerge or are invented by very practical people and often become quite developed before the theoreticians even notice them. In recent years this has happened with the transnational corporations as a pervasive world force, the Eurodollar market, the rapid economic emergence of Japan and the New Industrial countries, and by and large, the current stagflation.

Our more or less agnostic use of information and concepts is intended to resemble but is not identical to the traditional pre-scientific way of proceeding. First, we are genuinely agnostic about many of the themes we use; we simply do not know whether they are correct or not, or if they are, we are not sure of the extent of their validity. It is therefore important to hedge against these theories being right without relying on their being right. Second, we are often willing to use these concepts as dramatic and pedagogically useful ways to explain or illustrate certain principles or facts. In many cases, sophisticated empirical or theoretical explanations can be used to show that the concepts do apply, but these are likely to be both confusing and complex. Sometimes relatively simple arguments are more persuasive, more heuristic, and thus more useful to the reader. Also, such materials may produce interesting scenarios, basic contexts, apt metaphors, significant hypotheses, and a language that is both precise and rich.

THE CONCEPT OF THE SIX DEGREES OF BELIEF

Because we are dealing with uncertain and controversial material, we find it very important to be consciously and intellectually aware of where we and others stand on many positions and issues. It is almost impossible for us to get along using a simple true-false dichotomy or even a dichotomy of true, uncertain, and false. In a sense, we are trying, in this kind of situation, to give our own and others' subjective positions, or the likelihood that a certain proposition is true, or that a certain policy will work—and our confidence in our own beliefs or others' attitudes toward our own beliefs. Using numbers giving estimates of these subjective probabilities and degrees of confidence, or other precise estimates and ranges, would give a misleading appearance of a nonexistent precision and analytical clarity.

Our problem is like that of an individual studying the colors of a rainbow who wishes to relate these colors to other colors he notes in the environment around him. Our culture has decided to divide the rainbow into seven colors: red, orange, yellow, green, blue, violet, and indigo. All adult members of our society recognize, of course, that there are no sharp dividing lines. Not only are the boundaries indistinct or arbitrary, various shades other than those mentioned can be identified. In fact, every conceivable wave length of light between 4,000 and 7,600 angstrom units is available in the visible portion of the rainbow. But nothing would be sillier than saying we think of a certain shade such as orange as being precisely 6,400 angstrom units—or even ranging between 6,300 and 6,500. We simply do not think like that; we cannot estimate that precisely what we mean by orange or any other color. We could say orange is in the region of 6,400 angstrom units, but that would be unnecessary since the term orange exists and gives about the degree of precision we need. Furthermore, orange covers other mixtures or blends such as red and yellow that give the human eye the appearance of orange and which we wish to include in this category. We would also like our terminology not only to reflect our uncertainty about purity and wavelength, but also to have a little connotation as well as denotation—that is, to have some emotion and feeling about it.

We propose to do the same thing for degrees of belief. We argue that it is useful to distinguish at least six degrees of belief in a theory, a proposition, or a policy: atheism, agnosticism, skepticism, deism, Scotch verdict, and acceptance. For most purposes we find in these six degrees and some associated nuances a satisfactorily rich and precise vocabulary. Our usage of these words will be slightly idiosyncratic but it is close enough to the normal literary meaning so that readers who are not cognizant of the definitions that follow can still comprehend our use of these terms.

Most readers will be familiar with all but one of the above terms—Scotch verdict.[1] In criminal proceedings in Scotland, the jury need not choose only between guilty or not guilty (the only two verdicts in most Western judicial systems) but may decide on a third verdict, "not proven." This means that the case against the defendant was very persuasive and for practical purposes (i.e., lending an individual money, hiring or firing a person, etc.) most laymen would probably accept the case presented by the prosecutor, but that it has not met the legal requirement of "beyond any reasonable doubt."

Note that we have largely used language derived from religious, metaphysical, and legal discussions. This is not surprising because it is exactly in these areas where the issue of proof and degree of belief has been most thoroughly explored and discussed in much the same way that interests us.

Atheism, naturally, implies more or less total disbelief or rejection. The agnostic position is that one does not know whether to believe or not. If one has an agnostic position toward some relevant issue or data, one may wish to have contingent or complex plans that work if the alleged facts or theories are valid, but does not rely on them being so. By skeptical we mean the denotation and not the connotation of the term—that is, we are not implying a leaning toward disbelief or hostility. We use the word to mean that one is prepared to believe but has some doubts and therefore wishes more data, argumentation, or other evidence of validity. The deist position accepts that there is "something in the idea" but is not sure about specifics and degree of validity. There are some insights in the proposition being discussed but one is not prepared to endorse every item. A deist is more willing to base plans on the information than the agnostic or skeptic but is still not willing to rely on it being right.

The Scotch verdict often denotes what might be called an "almost proven" or "good enough for me" (or "good enough for our purposes") situation. It is for us probably the most important category, since in our considerations we often have information that we consider valid enough for public policy purposes or for decisions of most private individuals and yet may not quite approach rigorous academic or mathematical standards. Whether or not one is willing to go ahead on this "not proven" basis, the other side cannot argue that the position has been proven false or is unlikely to be untrue because the case is simply too plausible. This is an important aspect of the "not-proven" concept. Neither side may be able to force the other side—intellectually or morally—to accept its position, nor

can it dismiss opposing views out of hand. The intellectual support behind most of the more complex or controversial decisions made in public
policy or business is of the "not-proven" variety—good enough for the
supporting group, taken seriously by individuals and most opponents,
but not rigorously provable.[2]

One can have a different kind of support than the Scotch verdict when
decisions are made on the basis of a position accepted by some narrow
professional group, academic school, public group, or even by the broad
academic community or the general public. This could be "proven beyond a reasonable doubt" but also be more of an ideological or religious
position held by its supporters. Or it could be even more ad hoc or idiosyncratic.

Acceptance does not normally mean validity, only that the group concerned does not question it. Often it just implies being consonant with the
group's values, ideology, or even prejudices. This can apply to general academic as well as broad public acceptance of any concepts, theories, facts,
or other information. Such acceptance is often so obvious, immediate, and
widely shared that it is almost unperceived. Thus, acceptance is often too
automatic to involve serious discussion or questions. One of the reasons
for explicitly discussing many concepts is to cast doubt on some propositions that command widespread and automatic acceptance. Much public
and private business is, of course, conducted on what is sometimes called
"conventional wisdom." Of course, the conventional wisdom—widely accepted propositions—can also be valid, or at least more valid than positions held by its challengers. An important purpose of this book is to
make the reader more conscious of these intellectual and ideological underpinnings. This enterprise is not necessarily constructive. If we shake
people's faith in certain concepts or assumptions, we may erode their confidence and commitment. Confidence and commitment are very important to success. However, more often than not, this is a risk we are willing
to take.

Any attempt to base policies solely on rigorous studies and documentation is simply a recipe for inaction, not for improved policy-making. Attempts to glide over this fact can lead to endless delays while pursuing
more information, or attempts to obscure the "inadequacies in the information available" or the degree to which one is relying on uncertain information or personal judgments. Obtaining the appearance of rigor and
objectivity is a typical motive (conscious or unconscious) for devising or
using a large-scale computer model. Such a model can create (at least
sometimes) an illusion of universality and certainty. In most applications
with which we are familiar such models have been a much less useful
guide than the intuitive guesses and judgments of reasonably experienced
or knowledgeable individuals. It can be even worse to attempt to base

policy in a particular issue on evidence restricted to careful academic studies that leave out all that can be gained by the careful use of one's eyes, ears, intuition, and empathy.

We started our discussion by using the analogy of a rainbow. But every reader knows that one could not use the canonical colors of the rainbow in a simple way to describe the many characteristics of real world colors. First of all, as already noted, colors are often complex, made up of a mixture of other colors. They can vary in complexity, hue, intensity, and brightness as well as purity; the texture and finish of the surface makes a great deal of difference in their appearance; and so on.

It would be similarly simplistic for us to imply that the degrees of belief can be ordered in a simple way and described as neatly as we indicate below. We will, however, normally use a simple ordering because it will be more useful than not in most of the situations we discuss. However, we would like to be able to modify the simple question of degree by indicating that there are different kinds of attitudes even where the general category has been specified. We therefore suggest that the reader examine the following list and comments carefully.

Atheism (Disbelief)

a. Hostile Rejection: Has absolutely no interest in position, no wish to discuss it, will not use the language, and is dismayed if the proposition is put forward.
b. Tolerant Rejection: Does not believe but does not care if others believe.
c. Neutral Rejection: Often a technical or analytic rejection held without emotion or passion.
d. Empathic Rejection: Perfectly willing (or even prefers) to let other people believe; usually willing to discuss relevant issues seriously and empathically with them.
e. Metaphoric Acceptance: Not only tolerant and willing to discuss relevant issues, but willing to use the same metaphors and images.

As examples of what we mean by the above, one might easily have each of these five attitudes, respectively, toward somebody's (a) acceptance of astrology or witchcraft; (b) belief in lucky days, charms, or numbers; (c) belief that there are (or are not) 3 trillion barrels of recoverable oil to be found in the next three decades; (d) belief in a religion one did not accept, but approved of or at least did not wish to challenge; and (e) willingness to talk about God, salvation, and heaven in much the same terms the believers do, with or without constantly making one's basic atheism clear.

Agnosticism (Does Not Know)

a. Disinterested Ignorance: Could be thoughtful or considered; could be an issue that just never came up before—or at least one had not thought seriously about it and therefore had no position on it (perhaps does not even want to).

b. Cannot Be Known: Very often an individual feels that a subject is simply unknowable, at least in the absence of divine revelation or an extraordinary breakthrough in theory or data; would be perfectly willing if he knew how to do it to increase his knowledge, but might feel that it is not possible to do so at least with the time and resources available.

c. Open Mind: The person may well have a quite different attitude from the two indicated above. He wants to know and thinks he can know, but at the moment has not yet made up his mind.

Skepticism (Open to Persuasion but Has Doubts, Wants More Evidence)

a. Friendly: This is very close to the open-mind agnostic position, but leans much further toward belief.

b. Neutral: Self-explanatory.

c. Hostile Skepticism: While basically negative, takes possibility of believing seriously perhaps because of official position or context; indeed, one may have to take the position that one is open-minded and prepared to be persuaded, but really be more of an agnostic or atheist than can be admitted.

Deism

One feels that there is something to the concept but is not sure what. In religion it can go all the way from belief in a unique and supreme but unknown Being who is terribly interested in human beings to a clear concept that this Supreme Being (or Force) may exist but that we do not understand anything of its purposes or goals—if such anthropomorphic concepts apply at all. There can be a very large range in deist positions, but without any claim to many, if any, specific revelations. Deists do not accept much doctrine or dogma. We will often take a deist position, or something more, about the various historical theories discussed earlier (and later).

Scotch Verdict (Not Proven, but Most Reasonable People Will Accept)

a. Legalistic or Moral Rejection: Since the individual is not convicted one has to treat him as innocent even though many feel almost certain that he is guilty.

b. Grounds for Hedging or Great Care: The information concerned cannot be ignored even if it is not good enough for "conviction." Certain limited or hedging actions should be taken.
c. Practically Accepted: Will act largely as if issue has been decided.

In almost all cases of Scotch verdict that interest us, our attitude will be of the last type (c). We understand that we have not quite proven the case and therefore we have to be cautious and even open-minded, but will still normally proceed as if there were proof.

Acceptance

a. Proven Beyond Reasonable Doubt: This, of course, is a legal concept.
b. Professionally or Academically Acceptable: Passes the technical standards of the profession. These may not be universal, but are accepted within the group concerned. What is proven to a physicist is often not proven to a mathematician.[3]
c. Issue of Ideology or Religion: One believes because it fits into his Weltanschauung, his entire belief structure. It is easy for the individual or group concerned to believe. Perhaps he or they have had revelations.
d. General Acceptance by Community: In this case the acceptance is usually so complete and automatic that it is uncritical. It is a bit like a fish in the water; the fish may not even know it is in water until it is taken out and put in air. So the general acceptance by the community can involve a low grade of proof, even though the proposition is accepted as being correct beyond any reasonable doubt. "The earth is flat" or "the sun goes around the earth" are good examples of "beyond reasonable doubt" in some intellectual milieu.

NOTES

1. Note to our Scottish readers. We follow the customary British English and American English usages of the term Scotch. No offense is intended and partisans should feel free to refer to this important concept as the Scottish or Scots verdict if they so desire.
2. This concept of *Scotch verdict* is closely related to another concept that we have found extremely useful, the concept of *surprise-free*. We argue a scenario or prediction can be surprise-free to one group and not to another group, so therefore the concept must be related to the people who hold it. We do *not* mean by surprise-free "most probable," "most likely," or "most important" (though these adjectives often apply). We simply mean that we would not be surprised if such a

prediction turned out to be valid, or if such an event occurred. So two surprise-free projections can be inconsistent, since we would not be surprised if one *or* the other occurred. It should be noted that most of the world's business is conducted on the basis of surprise-free projections, which may or may not include a validity equal to that of the Scotch verdict. The usefulness of this terminology is that it makes explicit what one believes about the projection and makes it simpler to advance and discuss these concepts systematically in either an academic or practical discussion. This is nothing new, except for this explicitness; however, this explicitness can be very important.

3. The word *heuristic* is very interesting as it applies here. The concept is important in physics, mathematics, and some branches of sociology. The distinction is almost never made in English, humanities, language studies, and so on. In these areas, if the argument is plausible, it is usually good enough.

14

―――∞∞∞―――

Forecasting the Future: History Happens in Straight Lines and Curves

To a remarkable degree, the two most important and basic methods for conjecturing, forecasting, or studying the future are (1) relatively straightforward, simple extrapolations from current trends (but with the rate of innovation included in the "current trend"), and (2) the more or less obvious use of historical examples. Although many futurologists object to "simplistic" extrapolation, it is a matter of record that in many cases journalists and social commentators have used simple extrapolations to predict the future better than have very skilled scientists and engineers. Also, those knowledgeable in history have done better than those who confine their thinking to the present. Of course, any method may be abused, and the very simplicity of extrapolation and historical analogy lends these areas to abuse; nevertheless, they are the most basic, important, useful, and flexible tool we have.

The simplest extrapolation model is a straight-line projection in which past data fit a fairly linear function, and in which it is assumed that future data will also fit this same linear function. Normally, this is true for uncomplicated phenomena or because the analyst chooses a coordinate system that produces a straight-line curve.

It is important not to confuse these two basic models. Many phenomena of interest to futurologists appear to increase more or less exponentially for a period of time, perhaps at a varying rate of growth, but they reach a maximum growth rate and then pass through a point of inflection.

[*American Outlook*, February 1, 1999.]

From that point on, the rate of growth decreases until the curve more or less flattens out. This is the expected curve for world population or gross world product.

It is of the utmost importance to try to understand when and why these curves will turn over or flatten out. For example, in a Hudson Institute study of the Prospects for Mankind, it is argued that the expected curve for world population and gross world product will turn over mainly as a result of urbanization, affluence, literacy, new birth-control technology, the adoption of current middle-class values and style of life, and other changes in values and priorities. That is, the flattening comes from the effects of relatively free choices by billions of people who decide to have fewer children and eventually decide not to work so hard to increase their income. We do not expect that, worldwide, the curve for population and gross product growth will be strongly influenced by famine, pollution, or limitations of nonrenewable resources.

In dynamic situations, particularly in technological and economic growth rates, the crucial issue is the estimation of the rate and character of innovation. Experts often have the greatest difficulty in dealing with this. After all, if they knew how something was going to be done in the future, they would do it that way now. Indeed, often the expert does not really understand his own inability to accept the fact that such innovations will occur. He may feel, therefore, that a less expert individual who does accept this premise must be giving insufficient attention to countervailing forces or other problems.

Clearly, however, the dynamism of demographic, technological, or economic change will depend very much on the surrounding social, political, and cultural milieu, as well as on the innate characteristics of the population, technology, or economy. These sociopolitical factors are especially important in the case of population growth. For the world as a whole in the last thirty years, population growth has been relatively steady. For individual countries, few analysts have been successful in making twenty-year or thirty-year projections of population growth.

Where political and socioeconomic factors dominate a rate of change, it is very often difficult to project beforehand how rapidly these factors will be dealt with by the governing institutions. In northwestern Europe and North America, we can be reasonably confident that problems of environmental pollution and ecological damage will bring about major corrective actions rapidly; in fact, progress in these areas in the last several decades has often been remarkable. This points out that it is necessary not only to rely on past data but also to analyze and make judgments about the driving forces behind the rate of change. Often an analyst will use past data as a basic trend and analyze its causes to determine the extent to which the basic trend should be modified.

An equally difficult choice concerns the appropriate baseline on which to base an extrapolation. Consider, for example, a country that has maintained a 2 percent growth rate for a long period but has shown a 6 percent rate for the past ten years. One could choose either the previous decade or the long-term trend as the most relevant base, or the analyst could choose some average between the two. The choice would depend very much on the analyst's judgment about the underlying forces responsible for the growth rates and for the change in growth rates. The more recent data might be a special situation related to highly specific and no longer continuing causes, some other kind of aberration, a "catching up," or a fundamental change in the country's dynamism. It is usually possible to rationalize the choice of a baseline and the choice of the determining socioeconomic forces used in making a projection, and very often the rationalization turns out to be justified.

Thus it is often essential to examine the mechanisms behind the data or functions being extrapolated. In relatively complex situations, some set of interacting phenomena is being projected, and not all the interactions will play the same role in the future as they have in the past.

In examining these complex situations, two very different attitudes and types of analysts might be described, using an analogy from the stock market, as the chartists and the basics. The chartists concentrate on examining the prices on the stock exchange, and argue that the flow of stock prices, by integrating the judgments of buyers and sellers, is the best predictor of future prices. The basics, on the other hand, examine the data and institutions behind these prices, and analyze companies, the economy, and other economic, technical, political, and social factors that may affect the flow of prices. They use current price information but do not let the pattern of these transactions dominate their thinking. The chartists often reject the "extra" information and analysis, believing that such data will inundate them with too much information and thereby impede their intuitive and perhaps subconscious judgment. Instead, they may substitute the use of regression formulas, methods of extrapolation derived from statistical theory, or other special theories, to impose a pattern on the flow of economic data.

A similar difference in attitude and technique separates bettors on horse races. Some focus attention on the track record, and others concentrate on the heredity and other basic characteristics of the horse. All these attitudes and techniques are applied in futurology studies as well as in the stock market and at the racetrack, and each has its own strengths and weaknesses.

15

⸻⸺

A Methodological Framework: The Alternative World Futures Approach

"Alternative World Futures" may seem an awkward, even an offensive phrase, since it implies an abstract, perhaps a naive, approach to the tangled reality of contemporary international affairs and to their potential developments. Yet we have found no better term to describe a tool which we believe to be a modest but useful contribution to the objectives of policy research [. . .].

SOME GENERAL COMMENTS

The decision-maker who must deal with international affairs, inaugurating long-range programs or establishing other policies that will have consequences in the distant future, has the problem of coping imaginatively and realistically with future situations he can only dimly perceive. The analyst, in trying to develop a context for "serious" studies, may wish to range more widely and peer even further into the future. Historians usually are reluctant to study even the contemporary period because perspective is lacking, but the future obviously is harder yet to interpret, and any kind of perspective even more difficult to achieve.

[*The Alternative World Futures Approach* (Croton-on-Hudson, N.Y.: Hudson Institute, 1966). Also in Tugwell Franklin, ed , *Search for Alternatives: Public Policy and the Study of the Future* (Cambridge, Mass.: Witrop Publishers, 1973).]

The decision-maker or planner, though knowing his own inadequacy and the probable inadequacy of his advisors, must nevertheless make decisions and plans now which will seriously affect the success or failure of those who follow him, and which will even influence those who see the future differently or seek different future objectives. Since he can neither plan for, nor think of, everything, the planner presumably should try to look at a relevant range of possibilities, remembering the importance of examining possibilities which seem relatively unlikely but which would have very desirable—or catastrophic—consequences if they occurred. Indeed, the enhanced importance of unlikely events is a novel and most significant element in our age of technology; and to plan prudently means increasingly to extend the boundaries of plausibility. Prediction about future possibilities depends upon an understanding of the present and past, and it also involves the making of imaginative and analytical leaps as well as extrapolations. Again the analyst, being less responsible for immediate decisions than the government official, but more responsible for "stretching the imagination," should, on occasion, be more willing to consider seriously the unlikely and the bizarre, or spend more energy in re-examining and reinterpreting the old and familiar.

To appraise the future is, at the simplest level, difficult because important aspects of the future are not only unknown but unthought of. Even those aspects of the future which are relatively accessible to the imagination— more or less simple projections of present trends—may still be ignored because an individual's view of the future is necessarily conditioned by emotional and intellectual biases. In addition, the future is uncertain in a statistical or probabilistic sense. There are many possibilities, and while one can attempt to pick the "winner" of the "race," unless this choice is overwhelmingly probable it is more prudent to describe the probability distribution over the potential winners. Even then a planner is most unlikely to do as competent a job as an amateur, much less a professional, racecourse handicapper or stock or commodity speculator. The military-political analyst is not only unlikely to be less "skillful" than the handicapper or speculator, he has less reliable or objective criteria available for making and checking predictions. Not only have such criteria not been devised, they are not likely to be.

Yet the modern policy-maker or analyst cannot evade these problems. Many aspects of aid programs, alliance arrangements, weapons systems, and military-political strategies tend, in the common phrase, to be "cast in concrete" for years to come by present decisions, and the planner must begin now to develop concepts and doctrine for systems, programs and policies which will address the challenges he expects to face in the decades ahead. Systems, programs and policies should, of course, be made as flexible as possible, and be designed to enable future decision-makers to "muddle through." Yet the problem is that unless such a "muddling through" capability is thoughtfully designed—that is, unless the range of possibilities in various challenges, requirements, and opportunities is adequately foreseen—the decisions made now are likely to prove to have many undesirably inflexible consequences. One must explicitly arrange to have a sort of "lobby for the future" or else some of the claims of the future are likely to be neglected.

Nor do ordinary standards of care and prudence suffice for those responsible for such decisions or even such studies. U.S. political and military decision-makers—and analysts—not only carry the burden of American national security, but their work may greatly affect the future of the world. They can and should be held to higher standards of responsible examination and thought than any ordinary man in ordinary times; they are not likely to be excused responsibility in case of disaster on grounds that the outbreak or conditions of a crisis cannot easily—or even "reasonably"—be foreseen. The problem, however, is not entirely hopeless. While it may be impossible to predict the future in detail, it is possible to speculate usefully on many aspects of the future and even predict some. And even moderate care and prudence—hedging—can have spectacularly useful results should the unlikely occur.

To predict trends, government and industry most often refer the problem to one or more "experts." But experts typically do not offer systematic explanations of the bases of their predictions. Experience also suggests strongly that they tend: (1) to be immersed in the past—and even more in the current—professionally relevant details of the situation being projected; (2) to know the details of how professionally relevant similar situations have developed or are developing; (3) to have worked out for themselves a few useful rules of thumb in regard to the historical processes of interest to them (although these may not always be clearly stated); and (4) to have imaginatively or prosaically fused these elements of thought into some kind of (at least implicit) picture of the future. In general this is no doubt one of the most convincing approaches to social and political prediction. However, it is usually more adaptable to a smaller scale of prediction than world or other gross trends: for the grasp of empirical detail which forms half of the presumptive cases for the method is seldom sufficient to take account of events on truly extensive or long-term scales. There is also the danger of professional bias, or parochialism. Beneath the texture of such informed intuition there may be a selective professional distortion of the reception of data, the formulation of the problem, and the structuring of intuitions.

No matter how badly overall studies—as opposed to the specialist's predictions—are needed, the problems in doing them successfully are immense. Moreover, until recently there was relatively little motivation to do them. Until World War II it was virtually axiomatic in academic life and scholarship that serious knowledge about any area was obtained only by a lifetime of highly specialized research. The breadth of the area to be studied would depend upon the individual and the field, but there were pressures on a researcher not to attempt a wide field of scholarship. There were good reasons for this, the most obvious being that any attempt to go beyond intensive specialization involved the risk of falling behind in the initial specialty, risking superficiality there as well as failing to achieve more than superficiality in other areas.

An even more important inhibition against broad studies has resulted from the circumstances that until recently there has been almost no scholarly market for integrated, overall work unless the author is a recognized "authority"—or an elder statesman. There has not even been a nonscholarly market except for authors with a facility for dramatizing and popularizing this kind of work. Today, though, such "grandiose" studies are becoming more fashionable; we may soon suffer from the problem of too much demand and a subsequent vulgarization. Almost all who have attempted such broad research agree that the danger of superficiality is great even when these generalizing or synthesizing efforts are carried out with high seriousness. But, just as detailed and specialized research is worth doing even if it often proves to be of narrow or sharply limited relevance, general treatments may also be worthwhile, even if they begin in superficialities.

Extensive, "shallow" studies, in order to be useful, must often meet higher standards than intensive and narrow research. The risk of total "failure" is much less in the narrow study, since even a routine level of competence can usually guarantee some usefulness for the product—if it is sufficiently specialized. But the broad contextual study normally must be done unusually well if it is to have any usefulness at all; however, when it is done well, it is likely to be of correspondingly unusual value.

The task of creating a usable context for an overall study is probably best done iteratively. Once an overall context has been set forth for discussion, generalizations can be corrected and most of the superficiality removed. Ordinarily it is at just this point that the interdisciplinary approach can yield important and unusual dividends. Eventually the corrected context may be made into a usable and respectable framework or "paradigm."

THE BEST TOOLS VERSUS POLICY
RESEARCH METHODOLOGIES

In dealing with the problems of national security and international order, there are no adequate substitutes for such "tools" as relevant and accurate knowledge, experience, perception, judgment, insight and intuition. Yet though substitutes may be inadequate, decision-makers may nonetheless have to make use of substitutes. In some, perhaps in most, of the subjects of greatest concern to decision-makers relevant knowledge, experience, perception, judgment, insight, and intuition may be wholly or partially lacking. People may also have the mistaken belief that they possess these qualities when they do not, or they may believe that they have them in a greater degree than they in fact do.

On particular aspects of various problems there will, of course, be people who do have the qualities we have listed, and to the extent that the decision-maker can identify these people and the limits of their capabilities, he will wish to use them. But even then, for most issues that arise, for an advisor's judgments to be valuable to decision-makers and analysts it is necessary that he be able to convey explicitly and "usably" how he arrives at his conclusions. In some cases it may be more useful to the decision-maker to have erroneous counsel which nevertheless can be explicated, and therefore corrected and effectively made use of in conjunction with other conclusions and assumptions, than flat declaratory statements which may be correct in their context but which must stand or fall on their apparent merits. If one does not know how flashes of intuition fit into a chain of reasoning, in general one does not know how to make use of them, particularly under changing conditions, assumptions, or criteria—even if one has faith in the intuitions. An unquestioning faith is hard for a responsible policy-maker to achieve in dealing with great issues. In the absence of such faith, it does little good for a decision-maker to be provided with information which is in a form he cannot use. Occasionally, and usually with respect to a narrow topic, a study, rather than claiming to supplement the judgment of the decision-maker, may claim with some justice to define a policy which is as reasonable as can be obtained in an imperfect world, and the study group will argue that the best thing a decision-maker can do is simply to accept the conclusions of the study. But such situations are rare. Normally the results of policy research studies are quite inconclusive, since the techniques are so limited and the assumptions and criteria so uncertain. In these circumstances it is almost worthless to give only results. One must explain how the results depend upon assumptions, values, and calculational techniques, and even more important, how decision-makers can use these results in formulating their own policies within their own assumptions, values, and calculational techniques.

The kind of policy research we are concerned with here, then, emphasizes attempts to derive substitutes for "relevant knowledge, experience, judgment, perception, insight and intuition." It tends to rely heavily on such things as empirical research and analysis, and simple theory; metaphors and historical analogues; analytic models (involving an analyzable description of systems, devising alternative policies, and explicating criteria, objectives, or values); propaedeutic and heuristic methodologies and paradigms; scenarios, gaming, and other use of "arbitrary" specifications and stimulation.

EMPIRICAL RESEARCH AND ANALYSIS AND SIMPLE THEORY

The first, and in some ways the most important tools of the decision-maker are empirical research and analysis, and simple theory. These make up the simple attempt to examine carefully the realities of some relevant aspect of the world, and to draw immediate and direct conclusions from the examination. It is startling how often this produces unexpected information, at least in the study of rapidly changing or isolated portions of the world, since many issues or questions have for one reason or another—bureaucratic, geographical, technical, or intellectual—not been properly examined. Any careful examination may disclose facts or even central issues that are very different from what commonly is expected or asserted [. . .].

It is often possible to supplement empirical research and analysis with very simple theory which indicates trends or possibilities. Such theory is rarely rigorous but it may be stimulating or illuminating. Some simple ideas that could constitute simple theory are: The friend of an enemy is often an enemy. The ally of an enemy is almost invariably an enemy. The enemy of an enemy is often a friend, and is almost invariably at least an ad hoc ally on many issues. If the basis for an alliance changes, the alliance itself may soon be strained unless it too changes to fit the new conditions. A violent left wing revolution is likely to parallel the experience of the French, the English, or the Russian revolutions in many of its phases, rather than the U.S. experience. A hostile but submerged and suppressed emotion may easily emerge when conditions allow it to.

We will not discuss these political aphorisms or theories in any detail here, but such simple ideas can, when applied, be very stimulating, particularly when others are not applying them. There are similar ideas in the strategic field, for example: If one's offensive weapons are vulnerable, there may be serious instabilities in deterrence. If one's civilians are vulnerable, deterrence is likely to become a two-way street. When deterrence becomes a two-way street, strategic guarantees are likely to be considered less reliable. Permanent conditions are more important than results that ensue from temporary defeats and wartime disorganization, so one should not be misled by such early postwar conditions. Since technological secrets are rarely kept for more than five or ten years, it is not likely that major nations will be more than ten or fifteen years behind the United

States and the Soviet Union. And so on. While all the above seem trivially obvious today, four years ago it would have taken a bold and perceptive observer to advance them.

Closely related to research on the current situation is the derivation of simple theories from such research. Such research on historical situations or on various current aspects of a culture or society often generates simple generalizations which, in effect, summarize the descriptive data that has been supplied by such research. [. . .] The kind of theory which comes out of such study is often difficult to apply rigorously. Sometimes, as indicated in the next section, such theories are best used as metaphors rather than as strict tools for analysis; but they are more than metaphors since they are likely to be better grounded, to have more valid or useful structural analogies with the explicit situation being studied. It may be just as much a disservice to ignore the insights and extrapolations that such theorizing and generalizing can generate, as to abuse them by taking them too literally or misinterpreting them.

METAPHORS AND HISTORICAL ANALOGUES

Many studies of historical or current situations obviously can be seriously misleading if applied to a specific situation of interest today, since many or all of the conditions that apply to the example may not apply to the specific situation. Often the most that can be argued is that the historical analogy should be used metaphorically rather than analytically; that while there is no particular reason to assume that the two situations are similar as far as prediction goes, it is still useful to refer to the analogy simply because it enhances communication. If one is using such an analogy as a metaphor then there is no theory of historical inevitability or prediction being assumed or argued, but simply a facilitation of communication through the use of a vivid, rich, or concrete example. One can also argue that certain insights or perceptions hold true for new situations without arguing that the fact that they were true in old situations makes them in itself any more likely to be valid in the new situation. For example, in conjecturing about difficulties that the Soviets may have with any future foreign "Communist" or "pro-Communist" leaders, it is useful to be able to say, "He might play the role of a Tito—or a Mao—or a Sukarno—or a Castro—or an Ulbricht—or a Nkrumah—etc." There obviously are many other important roles they could play that have not yet occurred, and for which we do not have names. Thus, in many cases the range of discussion is unfortunately restricted to minor variations on that which has already occurred. One of the major tasks of this kind of research—or "presearch"—is to identify new possibilities and to give them names (perhaps by using scenarios or artificially specified contexts as described below).

The list below not only illustrates a range of phenomena covered in the use of metaphors, scenarios, and historical analogues but includes some of the most important ones for Hudson studies (a careful consideration of the list would reveal a good deal about some of our major preoccupations).[1] If space were available it would be worthwhile to give detailed descriptions of almost every one of the metaphors and their historical analogies, since if the richness of the metaphor is increased and shared with the reader, later communication is greatly improved. The "indefensible" enclave (Berlin-Goa). The extensive limited conventional war or police operation with neighboring sanctuaries (Korea-Vietnam-Algeria). The counterinsurgency war (Malaya-Algeria-Venezuela-Bolivia). The problem of the restive satellites (East Germany-Hungary-Poland-Rumania-Czechoslovakia). The problem of Communist (and democratic) heresy and revisionism. The problem of a coalition being taken over by a radical party—from salami tactics to coup (Czechoslovakia in 1948; Cuba sometime in 1959 or 1960). Aggression by a risk-taking irredentist power (China-Egypt-Indonesia). Rapallo. Revisionism (against "unfair" postwar treaties). Reichstag Fire. Munich. Pearl Harbor. Russo-German Pact. Catastrophic economic depression. "War is unthinkable" syndrome. Loss of nerve by status quo nations.

For the modern man who, even though he may be highly educated, may be relatively ignorant of history, the chief source of historical analogies and inspiration for metaphors and scenarios is likely to be the events of the last four decades. The period includes the depression, the rise of fanatic and chauvinistic movements in such relatively developed nations as Japan, Italy, and Germany and their subsequent almost hysterically aggressive careers, the demonstration of weakness by the seemingly strong and powerful status quo nations and the various events of World War II and of the Cold War. This brief span of modern history is rich in the kind of problems many believe can arise again. Some, of course, argue that we are too preoccupied with these particular problems; having once experienced a "Munich," we may be overly fearful of any negotiations with or concessions to an opponent. Having experienced Pearl Harbor, Americans may be overly preoccupied with the danger of surprise attack. The author would argue that these judgments may, in a sense, be both correct and irrelevant. Such dangers as appeasement and surprise attack require a relatively high standard of prudence in a government. While popular or even professional discussion may overestimate these dangers, the government, in terms of actual preparations, has tended to underestimate them.

But while the last four decades supply a rich store of historical examples of problems which could recur, it is no complete catalogue of possibilities. Yet it is startlingly difficult for most people, even analysts and decision-makers, to discuss seriously problems for which they cannot find analogies in these last four decades.

ANALYTICAL MODELS

The next important methodological technique is the use of various types of analytical models. The first difficulty with models is that they require a description of the systems to be analyzed which is complete enough to include all of the relevant characteristics. The classical example of how abstract and simple such a description can be is the mass point of astronomy and physics. All that one needs to know if one wishes to predict an astronomical body's motion is its total mass and the location of its center of gravity. All other details such as shape, color, texture, composition, etc., are irrelevant. But such simplicity is rarely found in the kind of study considered here. The second difficulty with models is that the description must be phrased in such a way that the analysis can, at least conceptually, be carried through. Generally this means either quantitative description or at least a fairly explicit detailing of the various components so that a chain of logical reasoning can be conducted.

One must also explicate for the model the various policies that are to be tested. Here there is often room, or need, for creativity. One often can invent new and very advantageous policy programs; one can then set forth a model which emphasizes the unfavorable aspects of the preferred policy and favors an alternative policy and still show that the recommended policy is superior; or one can provide a break-even analysis describing what assumptions or parameters one must have, or believe will obtain, in order to justify the recommended policy. But often, if unfavorable assumptions and simplifications are used, the values or advantages of the recommended policy are not so overwhelming that its preference can still be demonstrated.

In addition to the interaction of policy and model, there are questions as to the criteria, objectives or values to be used in judging alternative policies. Again it often proves very difficult to explicate all the relevant criteria, objectives or values, and the result, often enough, particularly in the simple cost-effectiveness type of analysis, is an analysis of only that part of the problem which is easily subjected to analysis, leaving it up to the "judgment" of the decision-maker to take account of the "imponderables." If this kind of analysis is done well, it may be possible for the decision-maker freely to use his judgment and modify the analysis correspondingly. But to do the analysis well is not easy, and normally the final "meta-analysis" comes down to a simplistic intuition or an expression of bias rather than a careful synthesis and balancing of the analysis with more subtle qualitative considerations.

Thus, in the problems we are considering here, the role of analytical models of the cost-effectiveness type is limited. It often is impossible to include all the important relevant aspects of a system in the model, or to devise a suitable range of alternative policies, or to explicate criteria, objectives or values in such a way that the analysis can be carried through. This does not mean that it is unimportant to do those parts of such an analysis as can be done with a model, particularly if they are done in such a way that the decision-maker can combine the results sensibly with his own judgments.

It often happens that one cannot set forth an analytical model with all the properties that are needed in order for it to be directly useful to policy research. Such models can often, though, be used metaphorically—that is, the analyst can concede that there is no necessary analogy between the findings resulting from his analytical studies of models and the real world, yet his study of analytical models may well enable him to define and deepen concepts and issues and thus enable him to develop a language in which the problem can better be discussed—in particular, important elementary issues and principles can often be discussed more clearly and intensively than if the examples were taken from the real world. One can then also use the model, if he desires, in a metaphoric fashion. Much of the current study of game theory is useful in this way (and usually only in this way). Other simple models or theories can be equally useful. Trouble can ensue if the lesson learned from such models is blindly applied to more complicated and real problems. But it is better to take the risk of misuse than to forego the attempt to develop a clear understanding of some issues or parts of the problem (e.g., it is difficult to discuss what role rationality may play in deterrence and war unless one first has some idea of what is or is not rational conduct).

PROPAEDEUTIC AND HEURISTIC
METHODOLOGIES AND PARADIGMS

We have already used these terms (if apologetically). In defining propaedeutic and heuristic, we noted that the concepts they express are so basic to the method and purpose of this paper, and to much policy research in general, that they deserve and need names; similarly for the concept of the paradigm.

For our purpose, a paradigm is an explicitly structured set of questions, assumptions, typologies, concepts, outlines, classifications, descriptions, definitions, etc., that attempts to provide for a problem or issue frameworks, patterns of relationships, and some relevant approaches or points of view. We may think of it as between a metaphor and a model, but more rigorous, more careful, more complex, more relevant than a metaphor, without attempting to be as complete or rigorous as an analytical model. However, a paradigm attempts to be as much of a model as is possible, given the limitations of information and analytical capabilities. [. . .]

The terms propaedeutic and heuristic are, however, more relevant to this essay than "paradigms." In looking at problems as complex as the ones discussed here, one is automatically involved in interdisciplinary research. Today, "interdisciplinary research" tends to be regarded with some disillusionment and skepticism, if not with hostility. The reason for this is that such research is primarily workable when the questions at issue have been clearly and well formulated. If, for example, the only question is, "How do we answer the following question?" and if there is relevant knowledge available, the problem is simply to bring this knowledge to bear, and an interdisciplinary committee of "equals" will succeed. More often, though, the problems require creative integration and synthesis, the answering of the question, "What is the question?" (i.e., "What kinds of knowledge are needed? What are the issues?"). In this kind of interdisciplinary research, integration and synthesis are widely held to be possible only, [. . .] "within a single skull." Much information must be absorbed by that one mind, accurately and rapidly. The problem is then to cram a great deal of relevant "interdisciplining" into one skull.

Similarly, in the complex decision-making problems we are addressing, the decision-maker requires access to a large number of different skills, even though his own background, and even the major issues, may be relatively specialized. Thus there is a great need for the organization and presentation of material which is propaedeutic and heuristic, and much policy research is occupied with the development, explication and exposition of methodologies and paradigms of this kind. [. . .]

Of course, experts in particular fields are likely to feel some annoyance, if not anger, at how complicated ideas must be used in seemingly simplistic ways in interdisciplinary research for planning and policy purposes. But this is a classical problem: nonexpert usages often seem to experts to caricature, vulgarize, or satirize their stock-in-trade. And experts are almost always annoyed by intruders who have an ad hoc competence in their fields while lacking the depth and background that the expert feels are essential. Though we sympathize with this feeling, it seems clear that the necessities of planning are overriding. We believe it to be an observable fact that planning requires that at least some participants step outside their specialties.[2]

The kind of work that has to be done on problems of national security and international order requires the integration of a large number of different disciplines, and almost anything that can help in achieving this should be encouraged. Nonspecialists must maintain reasonable standards of depth and thoroughness, but these standards should not be self-defeating or so high as unnecessarily to prevent an important job from being done. In any case, interdisciplinary workers must almost necessarily rely on secondary sources, or on the advice of experts whom they have difficulty evaluating, though this problem can be much alleviated by a suitable playing of experts against one another.

"Teams" of experts or staffs cannot avoid the problem of the nonexpert. At some point a plan or solution must be achieved within a single mind and communicated to other minds. However much the result is the product of collaborative efforts, it is clear that the result cannot require more than one mind to understand it. Thus, one or more specialists must step outside their fields, one or more nonspecialists must perform, and subsequently receive and comprehend, the final integration of specialties. Both the seriousness of this problem and the somewhat unreasonable irritation we have referred to will be much reduced if a better set of shared concepts and common vocabulary as well as special propaedeutic devices are developed.

Probably the most important heuristic technique and the most dangerous as well (i.e., the one most subject to abuse) is to make explicit some shared agreement and then without expending a great deal of time and resources (perhaps because it is not practical to do so) to proceed on the basis of this shared agreement. Scholars are often very uncomfortable at this procedure. Among other things, such a procedure could easily succeed in spreading more widely, confirming, or even canonizing whatever errors actually exist as a result of the biases and errors of current assumptions.

This possibility is particularly likely if the discussion is restricted to some narrow group with a more or less similar professional, institutional, or other common perspective-shared assumptions which arise out of a narrow group perspective are particularly likely to reflect narrow, invalid, or poorly interpreted experiences and analyses—and are likely to have these biases and emphases reinforced if the assumptions are explicated but not challenged. Fortunately even if the discussion takes place in a narrow and relatively homogeneous group the very act of explication is likely to increase the probability that the assumptions will be challenged or limited more carefully. In any case, in the policy-research policy-making fields, one must deal with issues on the basis of whatever data and theories are available. Where scholarly data and rigorous theories are not available—or are misleading—then shared perceptions or shared rules of thumb are all that one has. To ignore these is to condemn oneself to ineffectiveness and futility—to decision by default and inaction or to unnecessarily abstract and misleading judgments. While explicating widely held assumptions and theories may seem to be giving them too great a validity, the various dangers are probably decreased, not increased. As already suggested, uncovering and discussing shared understandings and then making explicit conclusions is especially desirable to establish limits and cautions on the process; such limits could not, or would not, be recognized in the absence of such explicit consideration of both assumptions and consequences.

Such explication is particularly important if there has been, or seems to have been, a basic change in the situation and the official rhetoric has not caught up with the change. In this case, many people know, more or less unconsciously, that the official rhetoric does not really express their actual positions so they try to trim their conclusion to make up for the bias in the official rhetoric. They are often shocked to find, when the new position is explicated, that it is often a rather widely held view rather than an idiosyncratic and special perception of the individual concerned. Furthermore, it is just because these new perceptions are not part of the official rhetoric, but nevertheless widely held, that they go unexamined and excessive interpretations or suggestions are based on them. Once the new position is explicated, people often see that they have pushed the new idea too far and the reason why others do not agree with them is not that they do not share the new point of view but that these others are simply not willing to push it so far. Thus, whether the new view is right or wrong, explicating it can be helpful by making clear the disparity between the lagging official rhetoric and the widely held new idea and thus cause both positions to be more closely examined.

SCENARIOS, GAMING, AND OTHER USE OF "ARBITRARY" SPECIFICATION AND STIMULATION

One of the most important aspects of the postwar international arena is the emphasis on deterrence. This often has meant that military programs were supposed to work without a single failure; thus there can be no realistic testing or straining of the system without having one failure too many, or risking such a catastrophe. However, deterrence does seem to work remarkably well in the sense that almost everybody judges that if both sides are competent, central wars, or even very intense crises, are relatively unlikely to arise between the Soviet Union and the United States in, say, the next decade or two. And yet the weapons exist and might be used. Even those who think that thermonuclear war is unlikely in the next hundred years; even those who believe that the invention and procurement of thousands of nuclear weapons in the middle of the twentieth century has effectively abolished, or will lead peacefully and inevitably to the abolishment of, all-out war cannot be certain. They still have need to examine the circumstances in which these weapons might be used or, possibly more important, the ways in which their existence or threat of their use might influence subwar events in an important way. One of the most important problems in this examination arises from the inherent implausibility—whether justified or deceptive—of the kinds of events which are being studied. One basic objective, therefore, is somehow to find and examine the most plausible examples of the most important cases that tend to be overlooked by the standard methods of studying these problems.

Two now common semianalytical approaches to this problem are the "scenario" and the "war (or peace) game." These are methodological devices which have become more and more common wherever efforts have been made to generate relatively plausible contexts in which the requirements of future weapons, command and control systems, war-fighting strategies, and arms control agreements may be tested or at least evaluated or discussed. While the kinds of scenarios and gaming that we will be discussing in this essay have in fact been most useful in the deterrence-crisis-nuclear war context suggested above, they also seem to be useful, though perhaps to a lesser degree, for a much larger range of contexts—in fact, for the study of international relations generally.

Such scenarios attempt to describe in more or less detail some hypothetical sequence of events. They can emphasize different aspects of "future history." Some scenarios may explore and emphasize an element of a larger problem such as a crisis or other event which could lead to war, the process of "escalation" of a small war or local violence into a larger war, the spread or contraction of a limited war, the fighting of a war, the termination of the war, or the subsequent peace. The focus of the scenario can be military events and activities, the internal dynamics of various countries, bargaining among enemies, or inter-Allied relations, and so on. The scenario is particularly suited to dealing with several aspects of a problem more or less simultaneously. By the use of a relatively extensive scenario, the analyst may be able to get a "feel" for events and for the branching points dependent upon critical choices. These branches can then be explored more or less systematically.

Some of the advantages of the scenario as an aid to thinking are:

1. They serve almost all of the objectives of policy research by calling attention, sometimes dramatically and persuasively, to the larger

range of possibilities that must be considered. They are one of the most effective tools in lessening the "carry-over" thinking that is likely even when it is clear to all that 1975 cannot be the same as 1945 or even 1960. Thus scenarios are one way to force oneself and others to plunge into the unfamiliar and rapidly changing world of the present and the future by dramatizing and illustrating the possibilities they focus on. (They may do little or nothing for the possibilities they do not focus on.)

2. They force the analyst to deal with details and dynamics which he might easily avoid treating if he restricted himself to abstract considerations. Typically, no particular set of the many possible sets of details and dynamics seems specially worth treating, so none are treated, even though a detailed investigation of even a few arbitrarily chosen cases could be most helpful.

3. They help to illuminate the interaction of psychological, social, political, and military factors, including the influence of individual political personalities upon what otherwise might be an abstract analysis, and they do so in a form which permits the comprehension of many interacting elements at once.

4. They can illustrate forcefully, sometimes in oversimplified fashion, certain principles or questions which would be ignored or lost if one insisted on taking examples only from the complex and controversial real world.

5. They may also be used to consider alternative possible outcomes of certain real past and present crises, such as Suez, Lebanon, Laos, or Berlin.

6. They can be used as artificial "case histories" and "historical anecdotes" either to make up to some degree for the paucity of actual examples as discussed earlier, or as "existence theorems" or examples to test or demonstrate the technical feasibility or plausibility of some possible sequence of events.

However, even if used as an existence theorem, specific scenarios, war games or other artificial devices normally cannot and should not be used to "prove" anything. They are literary and pedagogical tools rather than instruments of rigorous analysis, are useful to stimulate, illustrate, and teach, to provide both preciseness and richness to communication, and to check details. [. . .]

The use of scenarios has been criticized as being both "paranoid" and "schizophrenic." In the first case, the criticism is sometimes that only the paranoid personality, unjustifiably distrustful and suspicious, could conceive of the kind of plots and hostilities that characterize many scenarios.

This criticism seems largely misguided. The analyst is, of course, interested in ingenious or unpleasant means others might contrive to injure or to destroy his country; he is also interested in what they might not do. To the extent that the criticism of paranoia is justified, it pertains more to the implausibility of a particular scenario than to the methodology in itself.

A second criticism may be more to the point. It is that scenarios may be so divorced from reality as to be not only useless but misleading, and therefore dangerous. However, one must remember that the scenario ought not to be used as a predictive device. The analyst is dealing with the unknown and to some degree unknowable future. In many specific cases it is hard to see how critics can be so certain there is a sure divorce from a reality which does not yet exist and may yet surprise them. Imagination has always been one of the principal means for dealing in various ways with the future, and the scenario is simply one of many devices useful in stimulating and disciplining the imagination. To the extent that particular scenarios genuinely are divorced from reality, this seems more a fault of particular scenarios than of the methodology.

NOTES

1. In particular it should be clear that we are as interested in what can go wrong as in what may go well, and almost every item in the list illustrates an important way in which history can paraphrase itself more or less unpleasantly. This is in some ways a reasonable bias, but the list probably gives an exaggerated picture. Unfortunately, for many of the "constructive" things to be considered we do not have simple metaphors or historical analogues. This is one of the things which makes their serious discussion and study difficult. But this last gap in our language can in part be filled by specially written scenarios and contexts.

2. A personal note may help to clarify some of the resistance that is felt toward people who work outside their own specialties. I was trained as an applied mathematician and physicist, and occasionally I have explained certain ideas in either applied mathematics or physics to people trained in other fields. Later, I have heard these explanations used by these people in their own lectures or briefings. I usually had no specific objection to what they said, but felt slightly frustrated and annoyed. When a speaker on a platform discusses a subject, there should be an iceberg effect—he should be giving only about ⅛ of what he knows. But these speakers were inverse icebergs. They were telling approximately ⅞ or more of what they knew about that particular subject. Even though the speaker often apologized for lecturing outside his field, I still felt, quite unreasonably, that some degree of fraud was being perpetrated on the audience. For one thing, I knew that at that point the speaker could not answer "deep" questions. There was the not-uncommon feeling that anyone who speaks publicly or writes on a subject ought to be able to answer such questions, whether or not they are asked, and even

though, strictly speaking, they would be irrelevant to the point he was making. But it was also that I could not help being annoyed at the subtle differences in style—almost like having the wrong accent, or wearing the wrong clothes—by which the nonexpert gives himself away even when he is making correct statements. Such reactions are both to be expected and suppressed (or sublimated). They should not be permitted to interfere with work that needs to be done.

16

---oeeo---

The Method of Classes
of Variables

We are attempting to examine, look at, and discuss the future. We are not, of course, trying to pick the winner of a horse race, only to describe most of the important horses that are running—important perhaps because the probability of winning is high or because the payoff for winning is so spectacular, or for an appropriate combination of probability and intrinsic importance. We would also like to give some "feel" or orientation as to the reasonable odds on various horses.

In trying to examine the variables which might affect important issues of the future or even determine them to some degree, we find it convenient to divide them into six categories as indicated below:

1. *Relatively Stable*: Climate, gross topography, language, religion, "national character, institutions and style," many frontiers, etc.
2. *Slowly (Exponentially or Linearly?) Changing*: Natural resources, demography, capital resources, skill and training, technology, GNP, welfare policies, etc.
3. *"Predictable"*: Typical scenarios, prime movers, overriding problems, etc.
4. *Constrained*: More political changes, alliances, business activity, defense budget, morale, military posture, military skill, etc.

[*The Alternative World Futures Approach* (Croton-on-Hudson, N.Y.: Hudson Institute, 1966). Also in Tugwell Franklin, ed., *Search for Alternatives: Public Policy and the Study of the Future* (Cambridge, Mass.: Witrop Publishers, 1973).]

5. *Accidental*: Some outcomes of war or revolution, many natural calamities, some kinds of personalities, some kinds of foreign pressures and intervention, some kinds of other events.
6. *Incalculable*: Excessively complex or sensitive or involving in an important way, unknown or unanalyzed mechanisms of causes.

To the extent that one feels the future is more or less predictable, one tends to emphasize the importance of the first categories—particularly the first four. To the extent that one feels the future is unpredictable, one tends to emphasize the latter categories—particularly the fifth and sixth. We, of course, will adopt the position that many important aspects of the future are predictable—particularly if "other things are equal"—that many important aspects are not, and that the effect of the predictable things may be quite different from what we think because of the effects of the unpredictable variables—yet that it still may be worthwhile to try to "predict" that which can be predicted, or at least to describe the possibilities and turning points. Indeed, it is the purpose of policy to plan for that which is more or less predictable and hedge against that which is uncertain, both to be able to exploit favorable events and to guard against the consequences of unfavorable ones.

The first class of variables, the *Relatively Stable*, are by definition slow to change, though they may change faster than is usually believed. Thus the climate of an area can certainly change within a matter of centuries, perhaps even within decades. Topography also can change. In fact, some soil specialists have argued that it has usually taken about a thousand years for a typical civilization to wear out the fertility of the soil. There now exist relatively efficient possibilities for deliberate topographical engineering, so this rate might in the future be slowed down indefinitely, or even speeded up for specific purposes. Language is also always evolving and, in particular, may become "corrupted." In any case there is an enormous difference in the speaking style of Americans today and pre–World War I. Similarly, religion, or at least its social content and influence, may change quite rapidly, though the forms tend to change slowly. But the change can still be revolutionary even though the form is not explicitly affected to a great degree.

[. . .] National character, institutions and style change remarkably slowly even in the modern world, and [. . .] in many areas one can often see traits today that are directly traceable to characteristics formed a hundred or even a thousand years earlier. Frontiers too seem today remarkably stable. Latin America has several simmering disputes, but none that seem likely to boil; Western Europe (except for the German frontiers) looks remarkably stable, and so on. The crucial point about these relatively stable variables, however, is that while they can indeed change, for many of our predictions, particularly those dealing with a decade or so ahead, the change in these variables is likely to be small or negligible. This is so obvious that we often do not realize that we are assuming they are constant when we are making predictions. So we need not only to make the point that this is a reasonable assumption, but also that it is an assumption that could be wrong.

The second class of variables, the *Slowly (Exponentially or Linearly) Changing*, are the kind most usually studied when one is "predicting." One can often do amazingly well on these variables, at least in the short or medium run, and occasionally even in the long run. While these variables change, the change tends both to be slow and proportional to what already exists, so that if one knows what the variable is and the rate of change, extrapolation is possible. If the rate of change is more or less a constant percentage (or if one can meaningfully use an average rate), we call this an exponential variable—and it is then, of course, quite predictable. Such variables are national resources, demographic composition of the population, capital resources, skilled training, technological capability, gross national product; and to a lesser extent many welfare and tax policies, tend to change in this way. [. . .]

Other of these variables have relatively constant or characteristic rates and thus allow for relatively precise predictions—at least as long as the basic structural relations do not change. Such simple extrapolations, in the form of "envelope curves" may turn out to be startlingly accurate, often more accurate than more complicated and seemingly more sophisticated predictions done by experts, and there are good reasons why this should be expected.

A good example of a prediction based on the first two classes of variables is de Tocqueville's famous anticipation (in 1835) of the Cold War and bipolar world. There are at the present time two great nations in the world, which started from different points, but seem to tend toward the same end. I allude to the Russians and the Americans. Both of them have grown up unnoticed; and while the attention of mankind was directed elsewhere, they have suddenly placed themselves in the front rank among the nations, and the world learned their existence and their greatness at almost the same time. [. . .]

Next are what we call *"predictable"* variables. These are of special significance not because they are necessarily the most important but because they are reasonably predictable and usually overlooked so that competent policy research can play an important role in dealing with them—i.e., this is an area in which one can often "do something," even if nothing often is done unless attention is directed, perhaps by a policy research organization, to the issue. Naturally we will concentrate, to an extent, on this category of variables.

But what do we mean by "predictable"? For one thing, we can discuss situations in which certain variables can be described by typical scenarios or sequences. We need not claim that the described pattern will inevitably be followed, simply that it may be followed and the possibility should be allowed for.

Thus, any of the "simple" theories given earlier are examples of rather good "predictive rules" that are often suggestive of what may happen, although none of them are inevitable. We can rephrase them to show how they can be used to raise questions. (a) Political Rules: The friend of an enemy is . . . ; The ally of an enemy is . . . ; The enemy of an enemy is . . . ; If the basis for an alliance changes . . . ; A submerged hostile emotion may emerge when . . . (b) Economic Rules: Since bourgeoisation accompanies a creative industrialization . . . ; If an economic trend is anticipated . . . (c) Strategic Rules: If one's offensive weapons are vulnerable . . . ; If one's civilians are vulnerable . . . ; When deterrence becomes a two-way street . . . ; "Permanent" conditions are more important than defeats and wartime disorganization, so . . . ; Since technological secrets are rarely kept more than five or ten years . . .

A most important example of a simple prediction which is often underestimated (or overestimated) is that decision-makers die and others take their place. Thus as of the end of 1968, consider the ages of the following statesmen: Chiang Kai-shek 82; Salazar 79; de Gaulle 78; Franco 76; Tito 76; Ho Chi Minh 76; Jomo Kenyatta 75; Mao Tse-tung 75; Ulbricht 75. The typical underestimation of the significance of this factor is to ignore the fact that these decision-makers will be replaced. The typical overestimation comes in believing that such changes will necessarily produce immediate and dramatic differences. They sometimes do, but more usually they mean, at most, the start or acceleration of a developing or continuing process.

An important example of a typical scenario or prototype is discussed by Crane Brinton in his book, *Anatomy of Revolution*, discussing one possible sequence for a progressive revolution: (1) Ancien régime morale, etc.; (2) The rule of the moderates; (3) The revolt of the extremists; (4) The appeal to the conservatives; (5) The accession of the extremists; (6) Reigns of terror and virtue; (7) Thermidor; (8) Long-term changes. It is startling how useful the above categories are in discussing the possibilities for a progressive revolution.

Another important example of a "predictable" effect occurs when a single dominating variable is crucially important—when there is what can be called a prime mover. Examples of prime movers might include the well-known Japanese desire for prestige and status; the role the ownership of the means of production plays in Marxian theory; the pervading (and oppressive) influence of the United States on Latin American radical movements and their search for self-definition; some of the effects of modernization on traditional societies; the so-called Americanization that occurs in a high-consumption twentieth-century society; and so on. Similarly, if there is some overriding problem, such as defense from an imminent threat (early NATO), or dealing with a near-universal war guilt (postwar Germany), or internal war against a well-entrenched government (almost any postwar subversive movement), and so on, then typically there are only a small number of solutions possible and one of these will be identified and used, producing many similarities or analogies to historical events. This does not mean that there are no special or specific characteristics that are important, but only that there are some aspects in many situations which are relatively general and which can be identified.

The fourth group of variables are called *"constrained,"* since although they are to some extent predictable, they depend more on details than do the generalizations mentioned above. Factors such as political changes, alliances, business activity, defense budget, morale, military posture, military skill, etc., operate within reasonably precise and usually known constraints—at least within reasonable limits. Barring a revolution, a government can be just so radical or conservative. Under modern conditions the defense budget can be as low as 1 percent of GNP or as high as 50 percent, most likely oscillating between 5 percent and 15 percent, and so on. There are only a limited number or range of possibilities and they can be strong or weak, good or bad, high or low, etc.

The fifth category of factors is the *accidental* ones. In many cases the outcome of a war or revolution seems almost probabilistic. For example, the Germans might have won World War I in a few weeks just as Schlieffen had hoped, and the whole history of our times would then have been different. In particular, the disillusionment experienced by—and with—Europe's society in the interwar years might not have occurred, and such commonplace beliefs as that "war is unthinkable," "war never pays," and "war does not decide anything," would quite possibly never have become commonplace. Indeed, war, in the 1920s and 1930s, might have been seen as advantageous and useful. Similarly, Hitler came very close to winning World War II. One can argue that if Mussolini had never attacked Greece, or if the Yugoslavs had not resisted Hitler's attack, or if the 1941 winter in the Soviet Union had not been so severe, Hitler might have won at least the war against Russia. (Most members of the general staffs of the British, French, German, American and Russian armies seemed to have felt that Hitler had the war "won" at the end of the first summer campaign in Russia.) If Germany had won either of these two wars, de Tocqueville's famous prediction most likely would not have become true in our day. Yet the old factors which de Tocqueville had identified did operate in the way he had expected, coming to fruition in 1945. Predictable and relatively analyzable factors can be very important so long as they are not interfered with by what we here call accidental events. Finally, it is, of course, important to note that even if there were no accidents or intrinsic uncertainties, in the probabilistic sense all events still could not necessarily be predicted. Even without getting into the free will argument we note that human societies are complicated beyond the power of scientific generalization. The atomic nucleus or the genetic code are both much less complicated than social and historical action and interaction; both are only now beginning to be understood. We may still be in the nineteenth or much earlier centuries with regard to any "science" of public policy. Thus while we may not be prevented from breeding cattle or discovering and using radium, we do need to be heavily empirical and intuitive about many or most policy issues.

17

⚯

Ways to Go Wrong

L et us consider some of the mechanisms responsible for undesirable (by contemporary values) results in social processes. There seem to be at least ten important—though sometimes overlapping—"pitfalls." (1) Criteria too narrow; (2) Decisions at inappropriate point in the structure (for the end in view or consequences actually caused); (3) Inadequate thought; (4) Bad luck: unknown issues; (5) Bad luck: unlikely events; (6) Changes in actors; (7) Inappropriate models; (8) Inappropriate values; (9) Over- or underdiscounting of uncertainty or the future; (10) The best may be the enemy of the good (and sometimes vice versa). While the above are almost self-explanatory, some comment may be useful.

CRITERIA TOO NARROW

Criteria for decisions are often too narrow because the decision-makers are parochial, partisan, or self-interested, or simply not accustomed to considering the new criteria that are becoming relevant. These new criteria are disregarded simply because they are new; they were not considered in the past so it is not reasonable that they should be considered now. [. . .]

[Herman Kahn and Anthony J. Wiener, *The Year 2000: A Framework for Speculation on the Next Thirty-three Years* (New York: Macmillan, 1967).]

Because of new technologies, new wealth, new conditions of domestic life and of international relations, unprecedented criteria and issues are coming up for national decision. But in the usual bureaucratic situation an executive is expected to be concerned with his own immediate responsibilities and not to worry unduly about others except for purposes of "political" bargaining or compromise. The only man who has nominal responsibility for the "overall" problem is chief executive, who has little time to spend on anything except already "felt" pressures; and his competence obviously is limited. Furthermore, executives often do not make the crucial design decisions or even have much effective influence on them; they tend to make choices among already designed systems. As a result the principles of contingency design are often neglected, or the choices and compromises that are formulated may be far from optimal.

Thus, the national executive viewpoint may be narrow simply because there is no group whose professional and continuous job it is to worry about the appropriate issue. We have seen more than one instance in which a new issue is identified, all the officials to whom it is pointed out agree that it is significant, and it remains neglected simply because no one in the bureaucratic structure has a "mission" that would permit him to take cognizance of the new problem. Similarly it often happens that although there are offices in many parts of the government that are responsible for various parts of a problem, there is no one who has responsibility for the problem as a whole, for fitting the traditionally recognized part into a newly glimpsed total system—except of course the Chief Executive, for whom the problem may be at too high or low a level of abstraction or too low in priority in comparison to more pressing (and possibly less important) demands on his attention. It is one of the most important objectives of a policy-oriented research organization to function as a "lobby for the future": that is, to make a deliberate attempt to take a broad and long-range view of problems, and to try to create intellectual pressures on behalf of considerations outside the institutionalized criteria, particularly those considerations relevant to the long-run future or to the larger community, as in the case of issues such as international security. Policy studies should seek to discover important issues that are not currently recognized and should try to see that they are not unduly neglected in favor of more obvious, more pressing, or better institutionalized considerations.

DECISIONS AT INAPPROPRIATE POINT IN STRUCTURE

The above discussion inevitably raises the question of who determines the "good of society." This question is further obscured by the ways in which preferences are modified and decisions changed by the decision-making process. In its simplest form this is evident in the so-called Committee Paradox, in which the result of group voting—depending on the agenda—can be different from the result any member of the group would have preferred.[1]

A closely related common error is to mistake a prescription for macro-behavior as one that will affect micro-behavior, or vice versa. For example, a park and a police force are, most people will agree, good things. This does not mean that people will contribute toward them, unless they are public-spirited, for each individual is better off, on a strictly individual utilitarian calculus, if other people will contribute and he does not have to. Since decisions of all individuals are presumably independent, no individual has reason to expect that his behavior will affect that of any significant number of other people, if the community is large. (This is one reason why such goals are best implemented by collective rather than individual action.) The converse of this may also occur. If the price of wheat is dropping, a farmer may want to maintain his income by increasing his production. But the same factors that impelled him to this decision will impel others to the same decision, reducing the price of wheat still further. If it drops only a little they may still gain from their added effort, but if it drops below the marginal planting costs, they will have lost as a result of their extra efforts.

There are many other instances in which decisions that are rational for members of a group lead to results that are undesirable from the point of view of the whole group. If there is tension between two nations, they would both—considered together—usually be better off to avoid an arms race or a war; but in view of the uncertainties one nation might rationally decide that its best course is to enter the arms race, or even to fight pre-emptively; the other might then find it better to respond in kind than not.

From the individual point of view, voting may be judged to be not worth the effort, as there is no reason to believe that a tie vote will occur. During the water shortage in New York City, it was not "cost-effective" from the point of an individual for him to conserve water, as the amount he saved spread over nine million people would have been infinitesimal. In this case not only would his use of water not influence any one else, but the more people behaved as he did, the more pressure would be placed psychologically (if not rationally) upon others to save water. Yet if each followed the utilitarian rule for the individual, catastrophe might result. Thus naive utilitarianism can do considerable social damage; and moral rules are required under a variety of circumstances.

A mistake related to those in the paragraphs above is to mistake agreement on goals with agreement on means of achieving them, or to mistake agreement on a specific set of means with agreement on goals. Thus the fact (if it is a fact) that two states favor disarmament does not mean that they can agree on the rates and categories of disarmament. Many kinds of instabilities and hidden advantages or disadvantages can inhere in any specific means of implementation; no means may be substantially neutral with respect to the interests of the parties in the interim. If these asymmetries are great enough, they may foreclose agreement even though the destination is mutually agreed. Conversely, as was true during World War II, nations may be able to agree on means, for example, the defeat of Nazi Germany, while disagreeing about their destination, that is, the regime for Europe and the world in the postwar period. Sometimes these disagreements on destinations are obscured in a way that is functional for agreement on present means, say, the war effort, but dysfunctional for the future goals, because of the excessive fear of "rocking the boat" or lack of attention to "less important issues."

INADEQUATE THOUGHT

Failures of perspective in decision-making can be due to aspects of the social utility paradox, but more often result from simple mistakes caused by inadequate thought. It is, for example, common enough that unnecessarily poor analyses are made. Obviously some analyses are done badly because they cannot be done well. But often sufficient information simply is not gathered, or there is a culpable failure in understanding theory. Both errors are avoidable if sufficient thought and time are devoted to the problem. Or there may be insufficient attention paid to hedging against complexities and contingencies. It is usually possible to make a plan that will work well if things go according to specially selected assumptions but that fails disastrously if certain not-unlikely variations from the assumptions take place. It is the purpose of such techniques as systems analysis to make designs that are relatively insensitive to changes in assumptions. For a remarkable number of cases this can be done, given sufficient intelligence, care, and interest. While of course there are problems for which no reasonable "contingency design" is possible, there are still a great many plans that simply have not been thought through because custom, doctrine, or disastrous experience have not created any pressure to do so.

Most administrators dislike debating or thinking about fundamentals, even when vague, implicit, and half-formulated views obviously are governing choices, and when some searching debate is clearly desirable. Administrators resist even more "unnecessary" discussions that may become unpleasant or divisive. They tend to resist still more the very basic or very speculative thinking that may be essential to raising issues about the future, in part because of a well-grounded feeling that such thinking and discussing are usually unproductive and expose those who make the attempt to criticism, bureaucratic animosity, or ridicule. Yet it is often necessary to be courageous—or seemingly irresponsible—in suggesting and defending far-fetched issues in argument, if unprecedented but crucial considerations are to be discovered and appreciated. It is necessary to spend some time and energy in a process that frequently leads nowhere for the sake of the instances in which something new is learned.

And even when something new is learned, it is difficult to get "responsible" people to take the results seriously or to face up to thinking the issues through and then to providing relatively clear guidance or to making decisions. Again part of the reason is a lack of confidence based on experience of failure with similar issues. The result is a tendency to make important decisions almost arbitrarily, as if there were no way to judge whether any one decision was better than any other. A surprising number of government committees will make important decisions on fundamental matters with less attention than each individual would give to buying a suit.

BAD LUCK: UNKNOWN ISSUES

Sometimes, of course, certain information is simply not available. Then, in a sense, no mistake is made: the decision-maker did not understand the problem even though he thought he did and perhaps had every right to think he did; it is simply bad luck that there were aspects of the problem that could not be assessed. There are undoubtedly situations in which the theory or empirical data are insufficient not only to supply the information needed, but even to alert the planner to the fact that important information is missing. The recognition of this possibility is one of the reasons one must be both humble and skeptical about relying too heavily on either new "logical" analyses or old intuitions in unprecedented situations. It is one reason why decision-makers lack confidence in their ability to raise and settle basic issues; it is also a main justification for contingency design and for trying to defer irrevocable or firm choices by preserving flexibility as long as possible. Flexibility is not always good; firm and irrevocable policies may be better if the policies are correct, and sometimes almost any policy pursued firmly is better than no policy. More often wrong policies pursued firmly undercut good results that more flexibility would have saved. Unfortunately, no single rule of thumb is sufficiently good, and judgment will have to be exercised on each case of assumed importance.

BAD LUCK: UNLIKELY EVENTS

Sometimes the best-laid plans gang agley for "statistical" reasons. That is, a proper judgment may be made on the basis of the probabilities as they are known, but the improbable occurs; either conditions are met that are far worse than anyone could have anticipated, or some bizarre combination of accidents—each one of which was unlikely in itself but could have been handled—takes place, and "swamps" the system. The most dramatic possibility for bad luck today would be an accidental or inadvertent nuclear war caused by some extremely unlikely, but not absolutely impossible, combination of technological and human errors or failures. Good planning is designed to decrease not only the likelihood of bad luck but also the consequences if it occurs, since the "extremely improbable" is not the same as the impossible.

CHANGES IN ACTORS

Miscarriages of policy decisions can result from a lack of continuity in the effective actors or pressure groups. In a typical situation one group initiates, another formulates, a third sets up the program, while a fourth actually carries it through. It is this fourth group (or possibly still another group) that furnishes the continuous pressure and determines what the program actually accomplishes. In many cases, this turns out to be quite different from what all the previous groups wanted and intended.

INAPPROPRIATE MODELS

One kind of inappropriate model is simply technically wrong; someone has made a mistake. For example, many people feel that the unrest in underdeveloped societies results primarily from their poverty. They conclude that foreign aid can decrease the amount of unrest in these countries. Yet one thing that seems very clear by now is that the process of development is disrupting and usually increases violence and unrest. Social change is disruptive and partly destructive, causing many breakdowns and strains in existing systems and creating new systems that clash with the old.

Another kind—the inappropriate analogy—appears, for example, in international relations. Many Americans feel that every step toward integration or union among nation-states is a good thing and amounts to a step toward democratic world government or world community. Many naive enthusiasms for NATO, North Atlantic unity, and European integration stem from an American model of the constitutional convention as the appropriate solution for fundamental problems among states. This model makes it possible to ignore many issues, among them the simple reality that increasing the integration of a bloc such as NATO is not necessarily a step toward integration of the world community and may, in fact, tend to create cleavage in the world community—and be valuable, if it is valuable, for quite different reasons. This inappropriate model is closely related to the mistake discussed in number two above: what is a decision for integration at one point in the structure may, on occasion, result in unintended (or intended on the part of some of the participants) disintegration at another level.

Another common error in models is to mirror-image. One knows one's self and motives, and one imputes these motives to others. Mistaken mirror images play important roles in foreign policy, in ethnic issues, and in confrontations between classes. Most important of all mistakes arise out of attempts to treat complex and intractable issues by overly abstract or simple models. This is often done in foreign affairs as well as in middle-class judgments on the poor. No matter how much energy or effort one puts into an analysis or the execution of a policy, if the efforts are guided by a badly formulated model they can be ineffective and even counterproductive.

INAPPROPRIATE VALUES

Some of our misgivings about the future may simply be due to the fact that our values are inappropriate to the future. Within broad limits the future's values should belong to the future. It is quite possible that our apprehensions about alienations and affluence [. . .], admittedly based upon certain current middle-class and democratic American values, may seem entirely misplaced by the next century. We, of course, do not think so; but this may be our limitation.

Almost any decision-maker will find many aspects of subsequent events undesirable. The medieval church doubtless would have more strongly resisted the Renaissance if it had understood that the Renaissance would lead to the secularization of European society. Kings would have fought the rise of the bourgeoisie sooner and more strongly if they had understood that eventually the bourgeoisie would not only support them against the nobles but would eventually take over their role.

Our values may be inappropriate in still another, less easily recognized, way. We may think that we prize a certain aspect of the current system and regard it as an end in itself when in fact it would be better understood as a means to an end. It is common—and very often of great importance—for people to treat means as values, as ends in themselves, since to consider means as merely instrumental is to subject them to questioning. Yet when conditions change, the failure to reconsider the relation of old means to continuing ends can result not only in misdirected efforts but in behavior that becomes destructive to other, more important goals.

OVER- OR UNDERDISCOUNTING OF
UNCERTAINTY OR THE FUTURE

Probably the most important reason apparently reasonable decisions lead in the long run to undesirable results is that, by and large, it is so difficult to discount uncertain and/or distant difficulties appropriately—neither too much nor too little. For example, it is difficult to imagine a Virginia planter's wanting to stop the slave trade in 1620—or in 1800—because in 1861 there might be civil war. Of course, this might have been reasonable and realistic of him; the future is a region of great uncertainty; and it is the present in which we live and have the power to act. Yet two kinds of mistakes can be made: those who focus pragmatically on case-by-case decisions may take the long run too little into account, while those who are most concerned with adherence to principles, now and forever (and these principles may be radical or conservative), may fail to deal adequately with problems as they arise in the present.

Of course, the planter in our example might have wanted to stop the slave trade on moral rather than prudential grounds; and events would have shown him right in consequential as well as in absolute terms. One problem of the secular humanist's relativistic "ethic of consequences"—in which the consequences, including both means and ends of each decision, taken together, are weighed against the total consequences of the alternatives—is that it depends so much on fallible assessments of consequences. It could be argued that human judgment on such matters is so typically bad that an absolute morality, which prohibits certain means no matter how comparatively attractive the "total consequences" of means and ends may appear, actually leads to better results, even in consequential terms. On many kinds of issues we find this argument persuasive; and we would find the argument persuasive on many additional issues, if social conditions were not changing so rapidly as to require continual reexamination of means as ends change, lest the means become too much ends in themselves. Under twentieth-century conditions of flux, however, there seems to be more to lose by routinely deciding major policy questions on the basis of received doctrine or principle than by making such decisions on the basis of fallible assessments of the likely results of one choice compared to another.

THE BEST MAY BE THE ENEMY OF THE GOOD
(AND SOMETIMES VICE VERSA)

Desirability and feasibility may be separable for analytic purposes, but when it comes to making choices, they are intimately related. By trying for a great deal one ordinarily increases the risk of failure; by attempting too little one may ensure that at best one does not get very much. On the one hand, if a goal is very desirable it may be possible to arouse a great deal of enthusiasm for it, and its feasibility may be greater than one would have thought; on the other hand a goal that seems within reach looks more attractive than one that is hard to get.

Obviously there can be no general rule for making such choices; they often turn on subtle, difficult-to-evaluate factors. On the whole, our own judgment is indicated in the title above: limited objectives usually do not preclude further incremental progress, but excessive or utopian objectives often prevent even limited gains from being obtained. If there is any general idea in this field that we would generally reject, it is the radical or "dialectical" notion that to make things better one should first make them worse, since only then will people understand that something must be done. On this dubious basis Communists resisted meliorating the lot of workers during the depression, since to do so would postpone the revolution; similarly there are those who oppose intellectuals giving constructive advice to the military, political, or economic "establishment," since to cause improvements in policies is merely to cloak the "power structure" in a "veneer" of rationality. While this principle that it is desirable to refuse to improve matters, or to make them worse, no doubt works sometimes, more often it simply makes or leaves things worse than they need be.

NOTE

1. Because many readers will be familiar with this basic difficulty in determining social utilities, we will simply make reference to the following discussions: (1) Kenneth Arrow, *Social Choice and Individual Values* (New York: Wiley, 1951); (2) Leonard James Savage, *The Foundations of Statistics* (New York: Wiley, 1954), p. 207 ff.; (3) Herman Kahn, *On Thermonuclear War* (Princeton, N.J.: Princeton University Press, 1960), pp. 119–26. Daniel Bell has also called attention to the impossibility of a perfect social calculus in his "Notes on the Post-Industrial Society (II)," *The Public Interest*, no. 7, Spring 1967.

18

───❦───

Technological Innovation: Mistakes of Omission and Commission

It is often suggested that adequate technology assessment (TA) studies should be required for any technical innovation before proceeding with commercial applications—that the burden of proof be placed on the people who want the innovation. It sounds reasonable to say that it is up to the innovator to prove that his innovation is safe, but there are some difficulties in this position. If as a general matter high standards of justification were set and enforced, many important projects would not get off the ground. Full and definitive TA studies of complex projects and phenomena are often simply not feasible. We have never seen an a priori analysis that would justify the conclusion: "Let's go ahead with the project; we understand the innovation and all of its first-, second- and third-order effects quite well. There can be no excessive danger or difficulties."

Indeed, many times the people looking for second-, third-, and even fourth-order effects have often seriously erred about the first; in any case, they usually cannot establish the others with any certainty. For example, most of the limits-to-growth studies discussed in earlier chapters have many first-order facts wrong—a revealing sample of how difficult the problem is.

None of the above is meant as an argument against doing TA studies. On the contrary, in many cases much will be learned from such studies. But one cannot expect them to be complete and reliable, and placing too

[Herman Kahn, Leon Martel, and William M. Brown, *The Next 200 Years: A Scenario for America and the World* (New York: Morrow, 1976).]

great a requirement on innovators doing such studies can simply be an expensive way of doing less; it entails all the problems and disutilities of excessive caution and of slowing down innovation in a poorly designed— and often capricious—manner. The two basic kinds of innovative mistakes are those of commission and of omission. The first is illustrated by the case of DDT and by the cyclamate episode. In 1969, the U.S. Food and Drug Administration banned cyclamates (a widely used substitute for sugar in diet food and soft drinks) because rats that were fed heavy doses during most of their lives developed bladder cancer. It has now been revealed, however, that the original research that led to this finding did not permit any firm conclusions to be drawn about cyclamates since they were tested in combination with other chemicals. In addition, subsequent studies have failed to corroborate the original findings. Not only may this abrupt and premature ban have deprived numerous persons suffering from diabetes and hypertension of a medical benefit, but it also cost the food and soft drink industries an estimated $120 million. In this case the mistake of commission swamped the potential cost of a mistake of omission. In choosing between avoiding a clear danger by doing something and avoiding a less clear—though potentially much greater—danger by deciding not to do something, society usually does prefer the former.

The mistake of omission can be illustrated by considering what might happen today if a firm tried to get aspirin accepted as a new product. It is known that even a small amount of aspirin can create stomach or intestinal bleeding, and in some persons larger amounts can cause ulcers or other serious side effects. Furthermore, we still know very little about how aspirin operates. Thus one could argue rather persuasively that if a pharmaceutical company tried to introduce aspirin now it would fail to pass the standards. And yet, because of its effectiveness as a cure or palliative for so many ailments, it is probably one of the most useful drugs available. Indeed, there is now a good deal of argument that the FDA is causing more harm by excessively slowing down the introduction of new remedies than it would if the rules were relaxed a bit.

As another example, let us assume that the U.S. authorities had made a TA study of the automobile in 1890. Assume also that this study came up with an accurate estimate that its use would result eventually in more than 50,000 people a year being killed and maybe a million injured. It seems clear that if this study had been persuasive, the automobile would never have been approved. Of course, some now say that it never should have been. But we would argue that society is clearly willing to live with this cost, large and horrible as it is. In Bermuda, which restricts drivers to 20 miles an hour, there are almost no fatal accidents except with cyclists. On Army bases, which restrict speed to 15 miles an hour, fatal accidents are unknown. Similar speed limits could be introduced in the United

States if they were wanted, but the majority of Americans apparently prefer 50,000 deaths a year to such drastic restrictions on their driving speeds. In fact, the recent nationwide reduction to a maximum speed of 55 miles an hour to save gasoline clearly is saving thousands of lives a year, but there is little pressure to go further in this direction.

Another problem with technology assessments is that even a good TA would not have made a satisfactory prediction of the impact of the automobile—that is, on the one hand predicting the accident rate and related first-order difficulties, and on the other what society would be willing to accept. And it is even less likely that the TA would have foreseen accurately many of the secondary impacts of the automobile on society (just to take a small example, recall the influence of the automobile on social and sex mores in the 1920s and 1930s, or the role of the U.S. automobile industry in helping to win World War II).

This is precisely the question that concerns us: Every technology assessment study depends on having reasonable data, theory, and criteria available, and all are unreliable and quite limited in practice. Perhaps one hundred or two hundred years from now man will both analyze and control his future much better than at present; thus it seems plausible that there may be fewer problems of misunderstood or inappropriate innovation two centuries from now. And especially if man has become dispersed throughout the solar system in independently survivable colonies, there would be a much smaller possibility of doomsday. Moreover, if such a disaster were to occur on earth, it probably would be through politics or bureaucratic mistakes associated with war, rather than inexorable or accidental physical processes leading to total catastrophe. It is easy and even tempting to many people simply to ignore the costs and moral issues associated with mistakes of omission. Indeed, most people might prefer being responsible for a mistake of omission than one of commission, even if the latter were much smaller. This is particularly true, as we have pointed out, if one has been raised in an upper-middle class environment and has achieved a comfortable status. But most of the world is not satisfied with the economic status quo. It is important for these people to move forward; they are willing to accept great costs if necessary and to take great risks as well in order to improve their economic status. They want aspirins and automobiles, whatever uncertainties and terrible costs may be associated with them. On the other hand, the major pressures to retard economic development and technological progress in many parts of the world are for safety—safety from the environment, safety from the possibility of outside intervention, safety from internal political unrest, and safety from accidental disturbance of natural balances in the forces of nature.

Some years ago, after nuclear testing began in the Pacific, the debate arose about the acceptability of subjecting people to the threat that these tests could cause bone cancer or leukemia. The main question was whether this possibility was sufficiently large to justify suspending further testing. Almost everybody at that time accepted the assumption that every megaton of fission yield would probably cause 1,000 new cases of bone cancer or leukemia worldwide. Because this increase might not actually be detectable in the incidence of these diseases, many people argued that the harm was negligible. Others argued that no one would test the bomb with even one person on the island if it meant killing this person. What then gave us the right to continue testing just because the deaths would be anonymous? It would appear that people are more willing to accept deaths which are not traceable to specific causes, but only when they cannot clearly identify the victims ahead of time—and thereby possibly prevent those deaths.

It is simply a truism that most activities in our society have a finite chance of resulting in some death. For example, it was once the rule of thumb that, on the average, every $1 million worth of construction resulted in the death of one worker; this appalling ratio has decreased dramatically until now it must be something like one worker per $100 million in construction. But obviously this expectation does not stop us from putting up buildings, even of the most frivolous kind. The same principle is involved in an example cited earlier—society's unwillingness to lower the death rate in traffic accidents by reducing speed limits. It is not a sufficient answer that in the case of the automobile one voluntarily accepts the risks to which he is subjected. There are many people who would like to curb the automobile but who nevertheless run the same risk of accident as those who oppose curbs. In our view, there is nothing intrinsically immoral about society subjecting its citizens to this risk when a majority have evidently concluded that the benefits outweigh the risks and the risk is of a more or less customary sort.

Another important issue arises when the damages are spread out over time—an issue that was long misunderstood partly because of a misleading theory of the English biologist John Haldane. According to his theory, any negative genetic mutation was bad, but minor mutations could ultimately cause more damage than lethal mutations. The argument went as follows: Assume a fixed population. Assume that a parent with a defective gene passes it to one of his children. Thus every defective gene, if it does not result in premature death, is transmitted to an individual in the next generation. If the gene is lethal, it results in immediate death in the next generation and the matter is finished; there is no further inheritance. If the gene is not lethal but has a tendency to cause colds, then this gene can be passed on for many, many generations until eventually it will cause a cold in the bearer at a time when catching a cold tips the scales against the bearer and causes him to die. Then, of course, the gene would no longer be passed along in the future. Notice what happened here. The lethal gene caused an immediate death and was finished. But not only did the less lethal gene also cause death eventually and with mathematical certainty, but along the way it resulted in much damage, giving many people colds over many generations. Therefore, according to Haldane's theory, if anything, the nonlethal mutated gene caused more damage than the lethal mutation. This is certainly mathematically correct, but it ignores such issues as time-discounting and rate of occurrence, both of which should be added to the analysis when the damage is spread over many generations. It is difficult for most people to understand this concept because they often interpret it to mean that the damage is more tolerable because it is our grandchildren, not we, who will bear it; an inference which appears to be the height of irresponsibility. As a result, many scientists have come to the improper conclusion that damage spread out over time is just as bad as damage which occurs in one generation.

But consider the following counterexamples: Imagine that society must choose between four situations: (1) 100 percent of the next generation would be killed; (2) 10 percent of the next 10 generations would be killed; (3) 1 percent of the next 100 generations would be killed; and (4) a tenth of a percent of the next 1,000 generations would be killed. In the first case, one has an end of history—everybody is dead. In the last case, great damage occurs, yet it is scarcely apparent because it is spread out over such a long period of time and among so many people. Clearly the first choice is intolerable; the fourth, while tragic and nasty, could certainly be better tolerated under most circumstances—indeed, in many situations similar to the fourth case, it would not be possible to measure the damage or prove that it existed. Any analysis of the difference between the first and fourth situations must take account of this spread over time, even though the total number of people killed is exactly the same.

This example is applicable to many of the environmental problems we should consider, such as the disposal of radioactive wastes and various toxic chemicals, both of which entail the remote possibility of an accident to some unknown group of people in the distant future. It also applies to many of the issues involving genetic damage of one sort or another, in which the injury may be shared by many generations or be inflicted on future generations.

One last point in this connection is almost frivolous and we would hesitate to mention it if it did not come up so often. If there is a constant probability of some random event occurring, then no matter how small the probability, sooner or later the event will occur. This is an accurate but insignificant observation because the underlying assumptions and conditions practically never happen. It is similar to noting that exponential growth will not continue indefinitely because of the finite character of the earth, solar system or galaxy. Since we know that in reality exponential processes cannot be sustained, the question is simply what causes such curves to turn over, when this is likely to occur, and what happens when they do? Similarly, what about the argument that mankind must be disaster-prone because so many of its activities carry with them some small probability of causing catastrophes? One reply is that conditions are changing with extraordinary rapidity and the problems associated with present activities may have little or no validity in the long term. In fact, this may be particularly true of such things as genetic damage caused by radiation or chemical pollution—or by pollution generally. It seems quite probable that, within a century or so, man will be able to prevent such damage, and that calculations of accumulated damage ten to one hundred generations from now will probably turn out to be irrelevant. In fact, it is a major theme of our argument that most predictions of damage hundreds of years from now tend to be incorrect because they ignore the curative possibilities inherent in technological and economic progress. Of course, this reasoning would not apply to a world in which technological and economic progress were halted, but we do not consider that a likely possibility.

IV

THE TASK AHEAD: OBSERVATIONS, RECOMMENDATIONS, AND PARTING POLEMICS

19

∽∽∽

The Normative Perspective and the Ideology of Tomorrow

Some readers may have asked themselves: "Do the authors think this potential development is good or bad?" Other readers may feel that our judgments of the desirability of future events were all too explicit, especially if they were offended by our perceptions or manner of presenting them. [. . .] However, we have tried to take a "value-free" perspective, indulging in attempts to achieve what Marxists sneeringly call "bourgeois objectivity."

Two different perspectives can be used in future studies; these sometimes overlap and are hard to distinguish, but in most policy research projects, we can draw a line between them. The two perspectives can be labeled descriptive (or predictive) and normative. In the descriptive perspective, we try to understand what the future situation will be for the purpose of adapting to it—possibly taking into account various uncertainties in facts, theories, and values by hedging our policies. If we do this hedging, we would talk about a preferred system rather than an optimal system. A preferred system is one where a good deal of attention is paid to reliability, toughness, flexibility, and various compromises so that favorable events can be exploited if they occur and unfavorable events can be avoided or their consequences mitigated. However, descriptive forecasting is basically passive, merely attempting to record what the world will be like so that we may react to it.

[Herman Kahn and B. Bruce-Briggs, *Things to Come: Thinking about the Seventies and Eighties* (New York: Macmillan, 1972).]

The normative perspective emphasizes changing the future in a desired fashion, making more likely the good and/or less likely the bad. Like descriptive forecasting, it often employs a preferred system. In other words, normative forecasting means the setting of reasonable goals—what things should be like, what we should strive for, how we should shape the world. When an individual says, "In seven years I will be sales manager," he is making a normative forecast, which may be quite wrong. But he has some influence upon the outcome of that forecast; insofar as he strives toward that goal he will achieve the forecast situation, thus creating what is commonly called the "self-fulfilling prophecy." From the point of view of descriptive forecasting, this is cheating—our ambitious young man can directly affect the outcome. However, although descriptive forecasting may be useful in many fields where the outcome cannot be affected by choices today, decision-makers are primarily concerned with normative forecasting.

In practice, it is not possible to separate the two types completely. There are obvious constraints and limits on the ambition of any individual or institution that must be descriptively forecast before any normative forecast can be made. When working on individual projects for agencies or organizations we put our primary emphasis on the "normative" approach, trying to delineate what options are open to decision-makers and what can be the implications of their decisions; but when addressing a more general audience, as in this book, we emphasize the "descriptive" face of futurology, although normative aspects are certainly present.

It may be impossible to completely separate descriptive from normative futurology; nevertheless, we feel it is extremely important and rewarding to make a serious attempt. Unfortunately, the field of future studies is thick with normative forecasting masquerading as descriptive. Many prognostications of many distinguished American thinkers are statements of what the author wants to happen, not necessarily, what he thinks will happen, and frequently they are a bald pitch for some express policy or program. If done openly and honestly this is a perfectly valid method of political advocacy, with many honorable precedents but it tells us very little about what the future will be, except insofar as it is influenced by the ideas and desires of important men today. Similarly, a great deal of impetus behind the prophecy that humanist left values will quickly spread throughout our society is based upon the hope for their diffusion held by people sympathetic to those values. We cannot live without dreams, but we should not permit our fantasies to substitute for the real and concrete future.

But no matter how objective one may try to be (and some of us try very hard) most views of the future are almost necessarily founded upon some ideological preconceptions about the nature of man, the place of man in the universe, the inevitability or desirability of progress, national or class bias, or even ordinary optimism or pessimism. For example, in our attempts to elucidate even relatively simple and straightforward policy issues, we have been struck by the fundamental importance of the persistence of an ancient dispute between the Augustinian and Pelagian views of man. The dichotomy results from a theological squabble of the fifth century. The African bishop Augustine, author of the macro-history *The City of God*, vigorously accused the British theologian Pelagius of the heresy of believing that man could achieve salvation through his own efforts; that is, man was basically the master of his fate and through his unaided efforts could be good. St. Augustine took the opposing view, which came to be the orthodox Christian point of view, that man was fundamentally sinful and could achieve salvation only through God's Grace. In the modern world, Augustinians tend to be conservatives. The liberal tradition (including Marxism) is Pelagian. To the best of our knowledge, neither of these positions can be proved. To some extent, one position or the other is taken on faith.

The disputes over the relative importance of heredity versus environment in determining intelligence and performance in school reflect these two perspectives. If you are Pelagian, believing that man can achieve self-improvement, then you cannot accept data which purport to prove that there are hereditary differences between ethnic groups. There must be another explanation. Conversely, an Augustinian cannot accept the view that any secular program is going to change people's fundamental weaknesses. Attempts to do so must necessarily fail. Whether we are Augustinians or Pelagians strongly affects our view of the future. The Augustinian cannot admit that things are going to get much better in this world and certainly they are not going to be improved by the efforts of professors, governments, or policy analysts. And the Pelagian must necessarily believe that the future will be affected by such changes.

The same issues are raised by less fundamental presuppositions. A person who accepts the radical critique of industrial society as corrupt, dehumanizing, and self-destructive might not accept projections of its steady improvement; in fact, he could even reject unimpeachable historical data showing past improvement. The Marxist, of course, has a detailed scenario of the future worked out, and will shut his eyes to alternatives. Happily, such extreme positions are rare. But less striking differences have their effects on future perceptions. [. . .]

We should not be surprised by the reflection of present ideology in future studies because the reflection of present ideology on past studies is well known. And when we are talking about the future, we are talking about history, not just the past but the totality of man living in time. Previously, ideologies could be defined in terms of their views of the past.

[We] used the following classification of macro-historical Perspectives on Change: (1) Static, traditional, and/or repetitive; (2) Progressive: the multifold trend, progress, revolution of rising expectations, utopian, chiliastic, culminating point; (3) Decay: not competitive, "hubris," lost golden age, nostalgia, conservatism; (4) Cyclic: rise and fall, growth and decay, fluctuation, "regular" ebb and flow; (5) Patternless, unpredictable, and incomprehensible; (6) Typical (empirical) patterns: the multifold trend, irregular ebb and flow, empirical and analytic trend analysis, typical or phenomenological scenarios; (7) Eclectic and syncretic: the multifold trend, other trend analyses, other typical patterns, metaphors and analogies, some current speculations on decline and/or rebirth.

But the study and the belief in the relevance of past history may be fading. Modern industrial society may not have the same need of the past; we are increasingly rooted in innovation and change, not in authority and stability. Perhaps so. Perhaps the present interest in futurology portends the substitution of the future for the past in the center of our historical consciousness, of our perception of our place in time. Each of the macro-historical perspectives above is reflected in future studies. Of course, those who see history as static are not much interested in the field—if the world is unchanging there is no point in thinking about the future—it will be the same as today.

We still have many people in the world who see progress as inevitable. These include orthodox Marxists and classic liberals. Technological utopians, prophesying sweeping changes in the quality of life and even of man, are rampant in the futures field. Good nineteenth-century ideas of progress are very strong in American technical and middle management milieus, as well as among dynamic bourgeois elements in Japan and other rapidly growing economies. [. . .] But many modern intellectuals are losing their faith in material progress, seeing the future not as shining cities of man, but as nightmares of overpopulation, pollution, nuclear war, and/or programmed Skinnerite tyranny. And it may be that the reactionary analysis of modern culture as necessarily declining is spreading to one-time liberals. Growing crime, cynicism, drugs, and pornography cast the old liberalism in doubt. Some intellectuals have cultivated their despair to the degree of seeing all human affairs as pattern-less, incoherent, and without meaning, holding with the poet Robert Lowell that "the world is absolutely out of control and is not going to be saved by reason or unreason."

Nevertheless, most contemporary Cassandras do not believe in the prospect of irreparable decay. Even those who mournfully forecast, "decline and fall" or ecological disaster do so for didactic purposes. They wish to provoke us into taking steps to prevent the impending disaster. Almost all of these people share with most modern men, including ourselves, a view of the future as following typical patterns, resembling the contemporary view of scientific "laws," and as an eclectic and syncretic combination of all the perspectives. Even if there is an equation of history, as some who would model the future hope, man and even an individual man is an important term in that equation. Vary him and you change the outcome. We believe it is possible to alter the future normatively. In any event we can react to the future positively, even if mankind faces the worst possible "worst-case" scenarios—of thermonuclear holocaust, ecological catastrophe, or the Vandals without (or within) the gates—in any case such horrors should not materialize before 1985, we believe and hope.

20

---⊶⊷---

Transitional Problems

In the transition to postindustrial society, a vast group of intellectuals will be created as the need for expertise increases (and for self-serving reasons as well). These intellectuals may suffer from the most intense anomie of all social groups. In becoming a mass profession, they open themselves to sharper criticism as a group because their average standards necessarily decline, their contacts with outsiders wither, they become less self-conscious as a stratum but more actively self-serving, and they make clear their belief that they should wield social power. As this group's social status declines and its numbers rise, various segments will be organized, sometimes as an agency of government or other social institutions. Thus a key new form of social conflict becomes institutionalized. At the same time society faces a momentous political and social choice regarding the degree to which scholarship will be fragmented and autonomous or unified and harnessed to the tasks of other institutions. If one considers the acceptance of the zero economic growth thesis currently put forward by some groups, together with a willingness to organize and harness scholarship, one can imagine a trend over several centuries toward an essentially Confucian meritocratic social order dominated by self-serving and self-justifying—even if also communal and paternalistic—university-trained mandarins and bureaucracies.

[Herman Kahn, Leon Martel, and William M. Brown, *The Next 200 Years: A Scenario for America and the World* (New York: Morrow, 1976).]

We should also note that, just as the auspicious trends carrying us from feudal to industrial to postindustrial society have generated various new and pressing problems, so some of the projected auspicious trends of postindustrial society will certainly generate their own forms of dissatisfaction. For instance, some writers allege that a leisure revolution is likely leisure of postindustrial society, but it is at least imaginable that substantial proportions of the population will eventually work a three-day week and not "moonlight" during their four non-working days. If so, the intense boredom that afflicted the aristocracy of the eighteenth and nineteenth centuries could return with a vengeance—but probably less as a mass phenomenon than as one which afflicts various self-conscious elites [. . .].

Thus it could be said that to a great extent the problems of modern society, and particularly those affecting the quality of life, derive not from major social failures but from major social successes; for as we have seen, the most pervasive problems can result from the successful transition to postindustrial societies. This is why the discussion of quality of life takes for granted the successful performance of traditional governmental functions and the maintenance of high per capita income. Quality of life now usually refers to a set of problems that are overwhelmingly the consequences of success: anomie resulting from successful promotion of social mobility; blue-collar "blues" resulting from the successful transition out of the class structure and struggles of early industrial society; pollution resulting from successful rapid growth; perverse outbreaks of the martial spirit as a result of a generally peaceful world and the imposition of peaceful values; and intense concern with recreation and leisure issues because so many have nothing more important to be intensely concerned about. Other "failures of success" are listed in the following table. It seems to us that recognition of the fact that today's problems arise, not from centuries of human failure and rapaciousness but as the result of extraordinary and multiple successes in attaining the goals mankind has cherished most is bound to have a positive and healthy effect on social morale.

We referred to the quaternary activities which we assume will be most prevalent and important in a mature postindustrial society, but did not give a very clear or specific picture of postindustrial life. We were, in fact, deliberately vague and eclectic because we simply do not know what the United States or other nations will look like in 2176, even if trends do develop as we have projected. We do have some ideas of what may happen in the near term, though, and more important, we have strong fears concerning that near term and the emerging transition to a postindustrial society.

Consider, for example, certain South Pacific islands which, to many outsiders, seemed to be almost a Garden of Eden; in this idyllic economy,

Some Failures of Success

We have . . .

1. Affluence
2. Continuous economic growth, technological improvements
3. Mass consumption
4. Economic security, little real poverty
5. Physical safety, good health, longevity
6. Government "for the people"
7. The belief that human beings and human life are sacred and the only absolute
8. Rationalism and the elimination of superstition
9. Meritocracy
10. An open, classless society

. . . But we also have

1. No need to wait for possessions or most of what we desire, hence relatively little need for self-discipline. As a result people are at the same time overly concerned with satisfying their material wants and satiated, bored and petulant when they do and furious if they do not receive what they want immediately.
2. Impossible demands made on the government: Steady growth uninterrupted by business cycles is required as a matter of course, unrealistically high growth rates are demanded; all groups in society must grow economically at the same rate so that no one is left behind. Improvements in technology encourage unrealistic expectations elsewhere.
3. Aesthetic and commercial standards are determined by the tastes of the masses.
4. Emphasis on relative poverty, hence a desire for radical egalitarianism.
5. A neurotic concern with avoiding pain and death. Alternatively, the lack of genuine danger and risks leads to the creation of artificial and often meaningless risks for the sake of thrills.
6. No realization that there are goals higher than the welfare of the people—e.g., the glory of God, national honor, great projects and achievements.
7. The belief that nothing is more important than human life, hence that nothing is worth dying (or killing) for. Loss of aristocratic and uplifting ideals and of various distinctions between superior and inferior performance and individuals.
8. The loss of tradition, patriotism, faith—everything which cannot be justified by reason cannot be justified.

(continued)

Some Failures of Success (*continued*)

9. No sudden rises to power. Everyone must show his worth by working his way up the bureaucracy—and by bureaucratic and meritocratic techniques. Explanation and rationalization become more important than achievement and success. Further, by the time they get to the top, people have lost much spirit. Hence fewer young, idiosyncratic hotheads at the top to shake things up. Also, no respect for experience which does not constantly prove its worth by meritocratic and bureaucratic criteria.

---

many of the necessities of life—perhaps all—came virtually free. On such islands, anthropologists invariably found elaborate structures of taboos, totems and rituals. But what outwardly was an earthly paradise was, in some ways, internally a psychological hell, at least by current standards. One is tempted to argue, perhaps too quickly, that there is something in the human psyche which requires that the absence of objective external pressures be balanced by internal psychological structures and goals. Whether we accept this simple formulation or not, it may be a clue to one major set of issues. Actually, we argue that some cultures adapt more easily to affluence and safety than others. Indeed, we would hazard a guess that the "Atlantic Protestant culture" is one that has relative difficulty in adapting to wealth and safety, while the French and Chinese cultures do so more easily.

John Maynard Keynes, in his famous essay "Economic Possibilities for Our Grandchildren," provides us with some interesting insights into this problem:

> I draw the conclusion that, assuming no important wars and no important increase in population, the economic problem may be solved, or be at least within sight of solution, within a hundred years. This means that the economic problem is not—if we look into the future—the permanent problem of the human race . . . I see us free, therefore, to return to some of the most sure and certain principles of religion and traditional virtue—that avarice is a vice, that the exaction of usury is a misdemeanor, and the love of money is detestable, that those walk most truly in the paths of virtue and sane wisdom who take least thought for the morrow. We shall once more value ends above means and prefer the good to the useful. We shall honor those who can teach us how to pluck the hour and the day virtuously and well. The delightful people who are capable of taking direct enjoyment in things, the lilies of the field who toil not, neither do they spin. But beware! The time for all this is not yet. For at least another hundred years we must pretend to ourselves and to everyone that fair is foul and foul is fair; for foul is useful and fair is not.

Avarice and usury and precaution must be our gods for a little longer still. For only they can lead us out of the tunnel of economic necessity into daylight. (*Essays in Persuasion*, 1973, pp. 365–66, 371–72)

Keynes's perceptions may be somewhat romantic—We do not feel that the future belongs to the kind of "flower children" he describes, who in effect (in our terms) "drop out" of contact with most external reality—but we do believe that there will be strong trends in the direction he indicates. And we would like to endorse—in fact, emphasize strongly—the thought of his last paragraph.

[. . .]

HOW LIKELY ARE DEMOCRACY AND WORLD GOVERNMENT?

Considering the difficulty of discussing changing values and lifestyles, what can be predicted about the political systems that will govern in the next two hundred years? This is as difficult to project confidently as is the issue of lifestyles and values. Moreover, politics will both influence and be influenced by lifestyles. For whatever it is worth, we offer some conjectures.

Many countries will be relatively or at least nominally democratic, though some democracies will probably be more authoritarian than truly parliamentary. The reason is not the universal superiority of either the democratic or authoritarian types of government; rather, it is that an affluent, technological world almost has to be—at least initially—somewhat cosmopolitan, secular, pacifistic, relativistic, and perhaps hedonistic.

In deeply religious communities there is a strong tendency for the government to be conducted by a theocracy which in effect speaks to God or mediates His wishes. Heroic cultures are often governed by a great leader, an aristocracy or an oligarchy of talent, wealth or military skill. But secular-humanist cultures are not willing to legitimize any of these types of government. Their method of making a government legitimate is by social contract and the manifest consent of the governed, or by a mandate of history which clearly yields acceptable results to the governed (by their criteria).

This need for legitimization by explicit real, or pro forma, elections applies to both real and pseudo-democracies (such as many of today's "people's republics"), to relatively paternalistic, authoritarian governments (as in Latin America and Southeast Asia), or to a dictatorship more or less maintained by naked force (as frequently found in Africa and to a lesser extent in Latin America). In this respect, authoritarian should not be confused with totalitarian or dictatorial governments. In authoritarian states, there is a comparatively high level of legality and usually some lip service to parliamentary representation, including a need for something like genuine elections—if only in a validating and public relations role. Particularly if man is to experience a century of relative peace, and no great inflations or depressions, we can plausibly, but not certainly, assume that even more governments will be democratic than at present.

It should be noted that in the last two hundred to three hundred years stable democratic government developed primarily in what we describe as the Atlantic Protestant cultural area and Switzerland. In all other parts of the world, democracy still seems to be relatively fragile. Clearly, though, it has also attained strength in Israel, France, West Germany, and Japan; and to a lesser degree in Italy, Colombia, Venezuela, Singapore, Hong Kong, Costa Rica, Malaysia, and perhaps Mexico and the Philippines. But it should be noted that there are almost no other authentic democracies in the other approximately 125 nations of the world. Thus one cannot think of democracy as a movement that clearly dominates other forms of government, particularly if democracy is put under serious strains or if the people and leaders cannot act with a modicum of democratic self-restraint and a firm and informed sense of political and financial responsibility. It is also likely that there will be many functional organizations which will deal with the various international issues that will arise in the twenty-first century. Many of the most effective organizations will probably be of an ad hoc nature, but some of them will be part of larger international organizations such as the United Nations.

Many people believe that as more functions are undertaken by international organizations, there will be an almost inevitable growth toward world federal government. But unless the functions are performed with superb efficiency and effectiveness, this kind of evolution by peaceful development rarely proceeds very far without involving considerable violence. It is clear that the requirements of preserving peace and the problems of arms control, the environment and economic relations, as well as many law and order issues, all create great pressures toward peaceful evolution to world federal government. Yet we remain skeptical. One reason for skepticism arises from thinking about the likely answer of the Japanese, Soviets, Europeans, and North Americans to the following questions: (1) Are you willing to turn your lives and interests, and those of your families and communities, over to a government based upon the principle of one man, one vote—that is, to a government dominated by the Chinese and the Indians? (2) Would you be willing to turn your lives and interests over to a government based upon the principle of one state, one vote—that is, to a government largely controlled by the small Latin American, Asian, and African nation-states? Clearly, the answer to these two questions will be a very strong negative, as would also be the reply to a suggestion for a bicameral legislature with two branches organized according to the above two principles. We can imagine a world legislature based upon one dollar, one vote (dominated by the United States and Japan)—or on other realistic, if inadequate, measures of actual power and influence. But it is more difficult to imagine such a government emerging peacefully, or being very strong if it did evolve peacefully. There are many ways to create a political consensus; but none of these methods makes it easy to imagine a real world government evolving by purely peaceful means.

21

---∞∞∞---

The Expert and
Educated Incapacity

The basic notion is that, since World War II, there seems to be an amazingly high correlation [. . .] between having a better education, or at least more education, and a certain lack of reality testing and common sense. This problem is striking, particularly for younger people in many upper-middle class milieus and many New Class people.

Some readers may assume that these observations simply represent a more or less vulgar accusation of "book learning," a phrase which was commonly heard in the United States before World War II, but is now rare. I do not deny the similarity. However, I argue that while the problem existed at that time, it has now become totally pervasive. We noted in the discussion of the agnostic use of information and concepts the sixth level of belief called "general acceptance"—beliefs that are so pervasive, quick, and automatic that people tend not to realize that there could be any controversy about such issues. To the extent that the older concept of book learning is akin to educated incapacity, we argue that the problem so pervades the groups affected that they literally do not know there is an issue. For example, they either do not realize how different the "school situation" is from the "real world," or they argue for what they call "relevance" in the school situation. (By relevance they often mean something quite irrelevant to most real needs: e.g., a focus on such issues as nuclear war, ecology and environment, poverty, racism, and so on. While important,

---

[*World Economic Development: 1979 and Beyond* (Boulder, Colo.: Westview Press, 1979).]

these issues are not likely to be at the center of the day-to-day problems and lives of most people.) [. . .]

Educated incapacity often refers to an acquired or learned inability to understand or even perceive a problem, much less a solution. The original phrase, "trained incapacity," comes from the economist Thorstein Veblen, who used it to refer, among other things, to the inability of those with engineering or sociology training to understand certain issues which they would have been able to understand if they had not had this training. The training is essential to gain the skill and society wants these people to have the skills, so I am not objecting to the training. But the training does come at some costs by narrowing the perspectives of the individuals concerned.

I also often use the phrase to describe the limitations of the expert—or even of just the "well educated." The more expert—or at least the more educated—a person is, the less likely that person is to see a solution when it is not within the framework in which he or she was taught to think. When a possibility comes up that is ruled out by the accepted framework, an expert—or well-educated individual—is often less likely to see it than an amateur without the confining framework. For example, one naturally prefers to consult a trained doctor than an untrained person about matters of health. But if a new cure happens to be developed that is at variance with accepted concepts, the medical profession is often the last to accept it. This problem has always existed in all professions, but it tends to be accentuated under modern conditions.

Large organizations have the tendency to proliferate new forms of expertise and specialists who are drawn largely from a very special social and cultural milieu. Bureaucracies in our technological society depend heavily upon members of the New Class—or at least recruits from graduates of universities that emphasize liberal and progressive ideologies and viewpoints, almost to the exclusion of hard or tough perspectives. Even the practice of business seems to be in danger of becoming a professional specialty. I would guess that the more prestigious the business school and the more academically difficult the training, the more likely that the graduate will be both ideologically oriented and a narrow technician, rather than a decision-maker in contact with the pressures and insights of the real world.

Educated incapacity in the United States today seems to derive from the general educational and intellectual milieu rather than from a specific education. This milieu is found in clearest form at leading universities in the United States—particularly in the departments of psychology, sociology, and history, and to a degree in the humanities generally. Individuals raised in this milieu often have difficulty with relatively simple degrees of reality testing—e.g., about the attitudes of the lower-middle classes, national security issues, national prestige, welfare, and race. This is not to say that other groups might not be equally biased and illusioned—only that their illusions are generally reflected in more traditional ways.

Educated incapacity is becoming a worldwide problem; in many ways, the postindustrial culture is likely both to cause and to further this "malady," though all cultures have relatively general and deeply held educated incapacities. (In addition, we are all more or less the prisoners of our individual perspectives.)

For example, we have often found in examining projects for less developed countries that the perspective imposed by North American viewpoints or North American perspectives can be very misleading. We therefore developed a concept for what might be called "appropriate technology," though at the time (early 1960s) we used the term "sideways in technology" or sometimes "sideways to technology." The idea was to use whatever technology was actually appropriate to the special conditions involved. In most cases we found appropriate options by approaching the situation from one or more of the following perspectives: (1) By increasing the size, scope, or intensity of some typical activity of the developed world; (2) By decreasing the size, scope, or intensity of such activity; (3) By seeking socially and politically acceptable devices; (4) By changing some primary characteristics of the local area—e.g., through topographical engineering; (5) By scanning leverage devices or projects to establish a list of modifiable options; (6) By looking for high leverage projects in general; (7) By scanning exploitable resources to establish new requirements and possibilities; (8) Through new fixes; (9) Through overlooked items; (10) By exploiting any differences in perspective, requirements, or the performance of individuals and materials; (11) By looking for high visibility projects; (12) By finding, increasing, or modifying available talent and then modifying techniques or technologies to fit it.

ON MAKING NECESSARY DISTINCTIONS

A person has to be reasonably bright to understand the difficulty in drawing a sharp line between day and night. There is a twilight zone, a zone of uncertainty which makes the reality of artificial division between day and night difficult to define precisely. The normal way a sophisticated person handles this kind of problem is to make additional distinctions. He or she defines a certain range of conditions as being twilight or grey. While the person now has a similar problem at the new boundaries, the dramatic character of the problem has been sharply alleviated; the boundary between day and twilight or night and twilight is less significant.

This phenomenon began to be critical in the United States somewhat before the early 1960s. In the late 1950s, at one end of the political spectrum were [those], who could not distinguish between advocates of relatively moderately progressive or internationalist-minded people and "card-carrying Communists." On the equally far-out left were people who could not distinguish between the Taft-Hartley Labor Relations Act and Soviet slave labor camps, or who felt that authoritarian practices in the United States were such that they overlapped appreciably with those in the Soviet Union. They sometimes based their belief on the correct observation that Soviet authoritarianism was not as total as some advocates held. Many of these same people later believed that the role of the United States in world affairs was such that it had replaced that of Germany in the late 1930s and early 1940s. Thus, the United States intervention in Vietnam was often compared with the Nazis' genocidal policy toward the Jews—a wildly inappropriate analogy.

The Vietnamese war was not the only public issue that had a particularly low level of discussion in the 1960s. The "Middle America" issues were of the greatest importance in the United States, yet all were largely misunderstood in literate and educated circles here and in most of the rest of the world. [. . .] These were among the most important problems bothering the so-called Middle American, the middle class or lower-middle class "square" American. These Americans knew what each of these issues meant to them; they understood what was bothering them and could express their concerns in practical terms. But almost without exception, liberal and progressive press columnists, writers in scholarly journals, academicians, TV commentators, and even politicians and government officials, misunderstood the nature of these grievances and the nature of the issues. I am not saying that if they had understood they would all necessarily have agreed with Middle Americans. But I think many would have, and I am certain that almost all would have been more sympathetic.

I believe that if one read the influential American newspapers, consulted the most distinguished academicians, or watched the better TV programs, one would have been completely misinformed as to the nature of these issues and their likely impact and effect. In fact, the ignorance of upper-middle class progressive Americans was almost as complete as that of the European and Japanese press.

[. . .]

COPING WITH EDUCATED INCAPACITY

How, then, do we deal with the problem of educated incapacity? Most important is to find individuals with good judgment. This seems to be begging the question, because one next asks how to measure or even recognize good judgment. There are many ways, none of which is infallible. One method is simply to look at the record and see if the person has shown good judgment in the past. A better method is to see if an individual has clearly shown bad judgment, which is often easy to discern. One can often observe that someone is either overemphasizing the wrong information and perspectives, or worrying about trivia, or simply not understanding a problem. It is desirable in analysis to allow many different perspectives to be used—often including views sometimes thought of as fanatic, crackpot, or basically unskilled or uneducated—all to help increase insight, but not necessarily to prepare conclusions and recommendations.

An ounce of an interesting or proper perspective is often worth many pounds of brains or analysis in gaining insight. In particular, a hostile insight is often a very good way to find defects in a proposal. One simply gives a proposal to people who will be very hostile to it, and asks for comments. Political liberals and antimilitarists are very good at detecting "plots" and incompetence in corporations and the military, while political conservatives are often good at spotting flaws in social service and welfare programs.

Similarly, the friendly insight is often a good way to discover the good parts of a proposal. This is exactly the perspective of adversary proceedings in American courts. One hires two partisan lawyers; the investigation conducted by each lawyer is likely to be more thorough than if the state hired a "neutral" investigator. This technique of adversary proceedings can often be used in a research organization. [. . .] It can help enormously in uncovering seemingly obvious points and issues which most members of an ordinary team or study group might not notice.

PERSONAL NOTE: THE UNITED STATES HUNTING CULTURE AND THE RAISING OF CHILDREN

This personal note draws on one of many available examples that illustrate how ignorant and even bigoted many members of the American upper-middle class intellectual elite are about the family customs of American rural and lower income groups. It also makes an even more important point about how to raise children. The hunting culture within which these rural and lower income families rear their children is not the bloody, sado-masochistic pastime of latent homosexuals that so many in the elite take it to be, but rather a good way to live and an excellent setting for raising children. The example also illustrates some of the ambiguities that accompany affluence.

This personal note and the discussion on educated incapacity suggest that we simply are not raising the kind of elites that will provide the leadership American society and the other technologically advanced societies need to successfully cope with the future. We seem to be systematically "spoiling the children" or making them into impractical, unrealistically idealistic persons. There is a pronounced tendency in the American upper-middle class to raise its offspring on a steady diet of illusions and theory and to have them interact only with children similar to themselves. As a result, many of these children cannot distinguish book-learning from practical experience and are totally unaware of the importance of the latter or developing good judgment.

Both personal notes discuss some complex, subtle, and badly understood issues that are the technical province of psychology, sociology, and other behavioral sciences but that bear directly on the problems and prospects for economic development and social stability. I do not claim to understand these issues completely, nor do I know of anyone who has achieved such understanding, but I am convinced that they are critical. I believe, for example, that educated incapacity may well be the single most important problem facing the developed world.

During the middle and late 1960s and to a lesser extent the early 1970s, I customarily gave two or three talks a year at seminars or forums at Berkeley, Brandeis, Columbia, Harvard, Princeton, or Yale. These talks gave me contact with young people and faculty at leading universities during a most interesting and challenging time.

I almost always started my discussion by asking some questions. One common question was, "How many of you have three guns of your own?" About 30 percent of the audience usually did. I then asked those who did not have guns at home why they thought the others owned so many weapons. Most of the non-gun-owners were absolutely perplexed. They looked at the gun-owners in total bewilderment. What in the world would anybody be doing with three guns? How could it be that they were not an isolated minority of one or two, but a significant proportion of the group. Their answers ran from a confused "to protect yourself" to "for defense against attacks by blacks."

I would then proceed. "How many of the gun-owners were given a .22 rifle at the age of twelve?" Generally from 90 to 100 percent received one on their twelfth birthday. "How many of you got a shotgun at the age of fourteen, give or take a year?" The overwhelming majority. "How many got a .30-caliber rifle at sixteen, give or take a year?" Again an overwhelming majority. Back to the non-gun-owners, "What's going on?" Again, they did not know. They did not realize that they lived in a hunting culture, that these were in effect rites of passage, and that even some students at a seminar in an elite university could have been raised in such a culture. Then I would ask, "What happens to a twelve-year-old young man if he and every other twelve-year-old in town is given a .22?" I had deliberately given them a hint by saying "young man" rather than "child." In almost all cultures the age of twelve or thirteen is taken as the onset of manhood. This is the age of the Bar Mitzvah, the Confirmation, the recitation of the Koran, and so on. (The reason these young adults were not allowed to vote until they were eighteen or twenty-one is that the authorities concerned believe that voting should be restricted to mature adults, not that they were too young to assume adult responsibilities.)

A boy who is given a .22 rifle becomes a young man almost overnight, he will not be allowed to play around with a .22 because he can kill somebody or injure them severely, particularly if every other young man in town has a .22. In small-town rural America, where this culture is strongest, everybody will insist that these young people take care in handling firearms. It is similar to a custom that used to be prevalent in much of France. If a young child misbehaved, every adult present would admonish him whether or not the adult was related to the young child. People in our hunting culture areas feel free to admonish any young person who appears to be careless with a gun. If he points the gun at somebody, even in horseplay, he will be severely criticized, even punished. It is obvious that firearms are a serious matter and simply should not be used as toys. In fact, the firearms accident rate for these young people is very low.

Young persons who are given guns go through an immediate maturing experience because they are thereby given a genuine and significant responsibility. A relative or family friend teaches them how to use the gun, how to get along and survive in the wilderness, how to make a camp or break it, and so on. Since they are older and more responsible at the age of fourteen, they are given a weapon that is even more lethal. By the time they are sixteen, boys in this culture are permitted to own a .30-caliber weapon, which is extremely dangerous if used carelessly or malevolently. This hunting culture gives young men a sense of meaningful identification with his pioneer ancestors, with traditional American history, and a chance to participate with other young men in activities which are both pleasant and maturing.

Upper-middle class urban Americans generally regard this hunting culture as perverse or perverted. The liberal press frequently treats the gun as a kind of violent pornography. At one point the head of the New York Board of Education succeeded in having all rifle clubs banned from the school system. Why? "The gun is a phallic symbol, it ejaculates." One can imagine the reaction of a typical American who hears this kind of remark on television.

I believe that it is terribly important to give young people (whom we call "children" in our culture) adult responsibilities early in life—to give them experiences that are enlarging and maturing. It is a serious mistake to have them always carefully supervised and treated in ways that keep them from growing into mature adults who accept serious responsibilities arid bear the result on their own shoulders. The whole concept of a child is rather recent in our culture, and the notion of adolescence is even more recent. Previously, children were considered to be young adults.

Henry V was his father's general at the age of fourteen, and at fifteen was in complete command of the campaign against Wales. Romeo and Juliet were fourteen and twelve, respectively; one rather suspects that Shakespeare's dialogue reflects their language reasonably accurately. At the age of sixteen Alexander Hamilton was master of a ship that took a voyage from New York to the Caribbean and back through an area infested with pirates; he asserted authority as master of the ship, and accomplished some very sharp—and very successful—trading in Cuba. At the age of nineteen George Washington was in charge of a party surveying Virginia, and a year or two later was in sole charge of an assault on a French fort.

In a presentation I used to make to university seminars, I often asked the upper-middle class students if they had ever had to wait a year for something reasonable. I explained my concept of "something reasonable" as follows. If you were a young American in a middle class family and you wanted a bike at the age of six, that is unreasonable; if you wanted one at age ten, then that is reasonable. If you want a car at the age of fourteen, that's unreasonable in most parts of the country; if you want one at nineteen or twenty, that is usually quite reasonable. If you want a trip to Paris at the age of sixteen, that is unreasonable; if you want to go at twenty-one—particularly if you have earned the money or if somebody gives it to you—that is usually reasonable. Now, obviously, if you want a yacht or to change your parents or even to change your height or sex, that is almost never reasonable.

After searching through their entire lives, most of these young people were unable to identify a single situation when they had had to wait more than a year for something reasonable. One explanation has to do with the social customs surrounding birthdays and Christmas—particularly in upper-middle class families, to some degree in middle class families as well, and to a lesser degree among the rich. Twice a year the two parents get together and say, "What can we buy that little bastard that he or she doesn't already have?" And of course, whatever the parents do not buy, the grandparents do. As a result the unfortunate child is over-indulged—is given presents one, two, or three years ahead of any "reasonable" desires. The child never goes through the experience of understanding that life is not fair, that one does not always get what one is entitled to. Every upper-middle class American will recognize the foregoing as a common experience. In an incredibly large number of American families today, both Christmas and birthdays involve a veritable orgy of gift-giving; the children really get drunk with gifts.

We would argue that the lower-middle class American family is often somewhat more restrained, particularly if it feels it cannot afford such orgies; however, it often follows the upper-middle class example. Many wealthy families, however, are desperately afraid of spoiling their children. Very often at Christmas and New Year's these children get a small number of durable toys, and their closets are not filled with fancy clothes.

This is not to say that the rich raise their children well in America. They probably do not, but on this particular issue they perhaps err less than the American upper-middle class. These youngsters miss the most important lessons that a young person can learn: everybody should have the experience of wanting something badly for a long time, perhaps working and striving for it, and then sometimes getting it and sometimes not. That is a terribly important experience for a mature individual to have behind him that many young children in the United States simply do not receive.

The children of the academically oriented upper-middle class are even worse off. [. . .] Very often these young people literally have no contact with the real world that affects their thinking greatly, nor do any of their friends. Their only experiences are a warm family life, a protected social life, and a paternalistic school system. Everything is neat and tidy in all these environments; everything has a beginning, a middle, and an end. Problems are always resolved (as in an hour long television program—which may also reinforce this particular attitude—everything is complete and finished during the program). By contrast, a hunting ethic, where responsibility, self-reliance, and mature behavior are necessary is a very reasonable social milieu for child rearing. The fact that this way of raising children is strongly criticized by many upper-middle Americans shows more about their ignorance of their own country than about their supposedly superior values and sensitivities.

22

⸙

Current Western
Cultural Trends

[T]he] Atlantic Protestant culture area is prone to what we call educated incapacity, mixed with much wishful and illusionary thinking. We have argued that many citizens of these countries tend to make
overly sanguine, if not naive, assumptions about the practical possibilities
for good or even competent government in many areas of the world.
Other Europeans are less optimistic and also less Pelagian (in this case the
two go together) than most citizens of the Atlantic Protestant culture area.
But even they are less realistic (and less Augustinian) than they used to
be. We have also pointed to tendencies in Western culture toward anarchy,
terrorism, and nihilism—in effect, toward a breakdown of society. No
wonder William Butler Yeats's chilling vision "The Second Coming"
seems increasingly apt:

> Turning and turning in the widening gyre
> The falcon cannot hear the falconer;
> Things fall apart; the center cannot hold;
> Mere anarchy is loosed upon the world.
> The blood-dimmed tide is loosed, and everywhere
> The ceremony of innocence is drowned;
> The best lack all conviction, while the worst
> Are full of passionate intensity.
> Surely some revelation is at hand;
> Surely the Second Coming is at hand.

[*World Economic Development: 1979 and Beyond* (Boulder, Colo.: Westview Press, 1979).]

The darkness drops again; but now I know
That twenty centuries of stony sleep
Were vexed to a nightmare by a rocking cradle,
And what rough beast, its hour come round at last,
Slouches toward Bethlehem to be born.

While Yeats's warning comes from the right, the feeling that such fears are justified now encompasses the whole ideological spectrum.

This problem does not arise from any actual experience of economic, technological, or safety failure of our society (though there is much discussion of the possibility of such failures), but instead from a deep-seated cultural failure. Can anything be done about this? We believe so.

Perhaps the single most important thing that could be done would be to substitute reasonably accurate positive images of the future for the depressing images that now prevail, especially in the Advanced Capitalist nations. It is hard to find a leading school or university in these countries that did not at one time or another favor limiting economic growth [. . .]. While some of these emphases may be desirable, many upper-middle class elites in the affluent countries are pursuing them with irrational intensity. We believe that other approaches to these problems would be much more constructive and might make an enormous difference in the future of our society. Some of the suggestions we put forth are practical; others are overtly polemical and intended to stimulate the imagination.

The growth of terrorist movements in many places is no accident. Indeed, it is an almost inevitable result of excessive Pelagianism combined with specific historical events. From our perspective it is especially noteworthy that terrorist movements in almost every Western country draw mainly from young upper-middle class people or at least from university students. It is a movement associated with excessive and naive expectations. [. . .] We think of many of these young terrorists more as spoiled brats than as young idealists who have had their expectations frustrated—although both perceptions have some validity. In any case, there is an inadequate super-ego; the children have not been properly socialized, and there has been a lack of leadership by responsible, mature adults. [. . .]

The effect of almost two decades of these widespread, systematic, and effective attacks on our culture should not be underestimated. The adversary culture and the counterculture have taken their toll. However, the consequences of the anti-growth movement may be even more serious. The children of our privileged classes are led to believe that in our society the rich get richer and the poor get poorer, and that this crime is perpetrated by exploiting the defenseless, plundering the planet of precious resources, polluting the environment, and sometimes by poisoning the food with dangerous additives. The whole is compounded by business indulging in rapacious, unethical, and even illegal behavior as a matter of course. They are taught, furthermore, that this process is leading, perhaps inexorably, to disaster. From this point of view the emphasis by many American businessmen on teaching America that "profit is not a dirty word" is almost laughable. They are being accused of murder, poisoning, genocide, debauching the public, despoiling the environment, and robbing the poor and the grandchildren!

It is, for example, almost never mentioned in any school course I have seen on food that, except for lung cancer, the age-specific incidence of cancer has gone down. (Cancer of the lung is presumably caused by smoking, which does seem to be a genuine problem.) The reason that deaths by cancer have gone up is less because of an increase in carcinogens in food and the environment, and more because of increased longevity; people are no longer dying at younger ages of other diseases. Carcinogens may have increased in food and the environment but not sufficiently to negate the increasingly positive qualities of the overall physical and social environment.

At one time, the United States was probably the worst offender in indoctrinating its upper-middle class young against its own society. One reason was the impact of the Vietnam War. But even about such issues as world starvation, pollution, and limiting growth, some completely indefensible programs are promoted. For example, the World Council of Churches once conducted a systematic campaign urging that Americans eat less meat in order to provide more grain for the starving people of India. As it happens, plenty of grain was then (and remains) available at about $250 a ton—not at about $100 per ton. If a few Americans eat less meat, this price is not affected significantly, so the campaign would not increase the grain supply for Indians. The issue was purely financial. The Indians needed about 10 million tons of grain, and the question was who was going to pay for it. When the World Council of Churches was repeatedly confronted with this fact, they finally changed their campaign: eat less meat to show your moral solidarity with Indians; then take the money you save and send it to the Indians so they can buy more grain. This is a difficult way to raise money in the United States for any cause. Obviously the purpose of the exercise had nothing to do with the Indians. It had to do with trying to make Americans feel guilty for living well.

An even more dramatic technique for doing this is the following example much used in American schools. The United States has about 6 percent (approximately one-sixteenth) of the world's population. The metaphor used to describe the world is that sixteen men are in a raft. One (the American) has ten barrels of water; the others are dying of thirst. The American intends to take a public bath in each barrel, one per day. The American believes he owns the water because he earned it, but the others think he stole it. Since he is a decent fellow, he gives the others a cup of water a day. His policy is obviously stupid, counterproductive, and immoral—stupid because the American will soon run out of water for himself; counterproductive because he is almost guaranteeing a revolt in which the water will forcibly be taken away from him; the immorality needs no comment.

This picture has nothing to do with reality. As we have already pointed out, about 25 percent of the world is affluent today; another 45 percent is middle income; and only 30 percent can be considered poor. Furthermore, the outstanding supplier of "water" (i.e., grain) to the world is the United States, and much of it is supplied at concessionary prices. Finally, the issue is not one of the "ethics of a lifeboat," where water is not available at any price, but the exact opposite: grain is plentiful everywhere at a reasonable price. The issue is almost purely a question of why the thirty percent have not jumped on the development train, despite the many opportunities available during La Deuxième Belle Epoque. They may need help, and some help by outside private and public organizations and individuals should be supplied. But basically the solution lies in increased productivity by the countries concerned.

WHAT DO WE REALLY BELIEVE?

We stated that we do not believe there is any validity in the simple limits-to-growth position that claims that we are running out of many critical resources or that we cannot deal satisfactorily with current pollution problems. Such language as "energy-scarce world," a special emphasis on "renewable resources," or the belief that the high-consumption society is immoral because it uses up resources that will be needed by "the grandchildren" are all notions that can be dismissed—at least as worldwide problems, if not always locally. We remain willing to examine evidence that suggests these concepts are relevant, but so far we have found none. Much of our argument holds up even if there were such physical limits to growth. However, the notion of adequate long-run availability of resources (at least to a modern technological society that is also moderately well-managed) is basic to most of our considerations. [. . .]

Under current conditions, extraordinarily important social limits to growth are emerging in every affluent capitalist economy and, unless dealt with reasonably, are likely to develop rapidly and perhaps even too rapidly. Without suggesting that these limits are necessarily undesirable in the long run, we argued that their premature emergence is counterproductive. We think of them as cultural contradictions of economic growth. The social-limits-to-growth movement has also become a problem in the developing world. This movement causes confusing signals to be communicated to elites in the developing countries, to attendees at international conferences, to students from the developing world enrolled at universities in developed nations, and to various progressive and liberal groups. The elites as a result are often unsure whether economic progress is being promoted as a goal to be sought after, an evil to be avoided, or a weakness that one lives with but controls.

23

—∞∞∞—

Futurology and the Future of Economic Development

SOME USES OF SCENARIOS AND IMAGES OF THE FUTURE

Our basic thesis is that the medium and long-range prospects for successful economic development for all nations from the desperately poor to the most affluent are much brighter than commonly perceived, and that probably the single most important way to improve the prospects further would be for this to become widely recognized. We realize that changing world opinion is extremely difficult, and we hardly expect that our argument by itself will have much impact. We hope that it will inspire studies and progress that cumulatively may have an impact. The suggestions we make below are for programs that we think of as possibilities for refocusing the discussion of economic development.

First, we recommend developing various long-range scenarios to replace the essentially negative, pessimistic view based on such dubious concepts as physical limits to growth, the widening income gap, the eroding quality of life, and the like. We think that individual countries or major world organizations looking at economic development regionally or worldwide could construct scenarios of what they can realistically expect to achieve in the next twenty-five, fifty, and one hundred years. These scenarios could center around specific targets of improvements in living standards that can be easily measured. Such targets might include: better health leading to the elimination of protein deficiency and to the increase

[*World Economic Development: 1979 and Beyond* (Boulder, Colo.: Westview Press, 1979).]

of life expectancy; the elimination of illiteracy; education at all levels; improving housing conditions; increasing the number of households with electricity or telephones; making modern goods and services available; and so forth. Other purposes could include: providing a sense of inspiration and vision; encouraging greater efforts; giving a useful perspective for setting realistic goals; and explaining to the population, especially indigenous intellectuals and elites, that modernization can be achieved by virtually any nation but only over many years with sacrifices and hard work.

Many people find writing, reading, revising, or suggesting scenarios stimulating and enjoyable. It is generally easy, if it is considered advisable, to involve many people in some stages of the process. In most countries, many people at almost every level would voluntarily participate in producing scenarios with modest official support or encouragement. Most of those who feel uncomfortable with the exploration of images of the future need not participate, nor is there any need for a serious organizational commitment to the results unless there is a decision to promulgate some of them systematically.

One useful possibility for developing scenarios is from the vantage point of a mythical historian in the year 2000 or 2025, looking back over the events of the preceding twenty-five or fifty years. This is not only a dramatic device, but it also places many discussions into a perspective that can be much more objective and creative than one that focuses on current issues from today's perspective, with all the anxieties, hopes and politics normally involved in such a discussion. The mythical historian of 2025 could round out his story by attempting a scenario projecting the next fifty or one hundred years. If a country wished to exploit such scenarios and related images of the future, it could begin with an official or unofficial conference discussing and elaborating them. [. . .] At this conference, many medium-run and long-run possibilities for development could be described and elaborated dramatically and informatively. If desired, a much broader public than those present could be reached through the media and subsequent publications or presentations.

One result might be a variety of useful materials such as books, pamphlets, films for schools and educational television (and perhaps for wider distribution), illustrated wall charts, and video tapes of part of the proceedings. Some of the materials might be created during the meeting and some through a follow-up. Other information programs and various independent and semi-independent products might be stimulated by the conference or its ancillary activities. Second, the proposals are intended to depoliticize discussions and to separate political issues from development issues by focusing on the importance of increasing GNP and GNP per capita rather than on worldwide north-south issues or internal income distribution. The double standard used for comparing non-Communist and Communist nations; the various forums that have given worldwide prominence to outspoken critics of the developed world from the developed nations (such as the Non-Aligned nations and the Group of 77); and the terminology used (north-south problems, widening gap, neocolonialism) all politicize and distort the real issues. Individual nations would counter these by developing their own growth scenarios or ideologies and advertising their long-range visions. These could be used to make the point at international meetings that while left or right wing demagogues are still blaming their nations' problems on everything but their own incompetence, other countries are successfully accomplishing the Great Transition. [. . .]

Another way to make this point would be to create new organizations that would refocus world attention. [. . .] It might also be possible to create an organization of New Industrial States (NIS) made up of the NISs and other rapidly growing middle income countries that are on the verge of becoming fully industrialized. Such an organization might become an openly pro-growth lobby comprising the world's most dynamic countries. It might also be tied in with the OECD. The OECD could set target dates for anticipated entry of new countries. Becoming a member of the OECD or NIS club could be seen as a symbol that successful development had been achieved and could draw attention to the fact that economic development is no longer an exclusive club of former Western great powers and early starters. Hopefully, this might change the oversimplified rich-versus-poor view of the world to a more constructive image of a complicated and mutually beneficial interdependent world economy. It would emphasize that development is a step-by-step process. As poor countries take off and enter the transitional stage, transitional countries are entering the fully industrialized stage. Third, our suggestions are intended to give greater attention to the more successful developing countries by drawing attention to their accomplishments. One way of doing this would be to have an international school for economic development in some NIS countries that would give visiting students a sense of what can be done as well as practical insights into how to do it.

A BOURGEOIS (INDUSTRIAL) GROWTH-ORIENTED IDEOLOGY BASED ON FUTUROLOGY

The development of the classic industrialized Western world has frequently been linked to the ideology called the Protestant Ethic, encompassing a belief in the virtue of hard work and a willingness to defer the material rewards of that work. As the West has grown progressively richer, this ethic has weakened considerably, first among the intellectual elite and more recently throughout the population. The phenomenon heralded a decade ago as the end of ideology is now seen more appropriately as a loss of faith in the old ideology.

The late 1960s brought with them a need for a new or renewed faith. This need has been met for many Americans by a movement toward traditional doctrinaire, dogmatic evangelical sects and away from the increasingly transcendental mainstream Protestant religion. Other parts of the population found some fulfillment in such disparate phenomena as the new youth culture, a return to religious enthusiasm, various Eastern and mystical or magical sects, the proliferation of groups militantly pursuing self-expression in ethnic, spiritual, or psychological terms, and often in the Fourteen New Emphases generally.

We have argued that humanity will soon be entering a new state of development—the postindustrial society. We believe that the transition to this stage is likely to cause serious stresses and that it is very important to have some kind of overall concept to help organize thinking, program action, furnish a supportive moral and political philosophy, and provide a framework for the creation and analysis of programs. Such a concept would also provide, where justified, high morale to better cope with what might be called the current failure of nerve among upper-middle class elites in much of the free world [. . .].

We believe all this can be done by taking a reasonable perspective on how we got where we are today, and where we may likely be in the year 2000, particularly if sensible programs are adopted. We are suggesting that a new kind of ideology is needed that we tentatively label a Year 2000 Ideology. As ideologies go, this one is relatively weak, but it can meet all our needs. An ideology emphasizes certain values and attitudes, it contains a theory of the past, present, and future (all theories generally have emotionally held normative elements). It provides a rationale, spur, and guide to action and a theory of success and justice (i.e., high morale). In sum, it provides a context and content for overall policies, for applications, for coordination of criteria and expectations, and for meaning and purpose in life. In effect, the ideology should promise some combination of God, gold, and glory (or, if you will, honor, glory, and riches).

Some of the reasons why an ideology of development based on futurology could help with rational planning for a peaceful and affluent world in the future—in particular by setting achievable goals and avoiding unnecessary conflict are obvious: It will put population growth, GNP growth, impact of R&D cultural changes, and other long-term and compound interest issues in perspective and will enable realistic criteria to be set. Also it should: energize elite groups—in part to set example, persuade late beneficiaries to "wait," relieve "ancient regime morale" stigma from current programs and institutions, enlist alienated and frustrated groups, and energize whole society.

Many persons suggest that we need much more intense or serious ideology that can bring such benefits as: disciplined and dedicated cadres; legitimacy and appeal; mass movement (or mass acquiescence); recruiting; external allies and sympathizers; "wave of the future" charisma. We argue that this is not needed. For one thing, intense ideologies also frequently bring many disadvantages, including: foreign axes to grind; extremist programs; excessive use of terror; crackpot theories; crackpot administration; excessive attention to foreign intervention and proselytizing; excessive wastage of tangible and intangible assets and resources. Intense ideologies are also much more difficult to manufacture and to control. We argue that once it is accepted and believed, the area under discussion and the world in its various parts can be placed on a more or less reasonable course. The crucial issues then become to avoid derailment and catastrophe and to improve current programs. This entails a sound, moderate, businesslike approach to development programs and reasonably high morale, assurance, and commitment.

We believe this perspective can be made persuasive. It may then be possible to take a very different attitude toward a number of currently perceived problems from those of many neo-Malthusians and catastrophists—provisional or otherwise. (A catastrophist believes that current trends and events inevitably lead to some kind of catastrophe. Provisional catastrophies agree but add, "as long as we continue current policies, but if we change policies [presumably according to their recommendation], this is not necessarily so.")

It then becomes possible to envisage and set in motion an era of great human improvement in material standards of living and hopefully in other ways as well. [The future-oriented ideology] provides a justification for such an approach. It offers a conception of how successful this approach might be and where we might be able to go. No doubt the projections will turn out to be inaccurate in important details, and perhaps even in certain basics, but it is still likely that its fundamental direction and programs will be useful and will promote humane adjustment to material change and growth. This is very different from the attitude typified by the following from Robert Heilbroner: "Development will fall into the hands of dedicated revolutionary groups. Mild men will not ride the tigers of development, neither will mild political or economic systems contain or impel it" (*The Great Ascent*, 1963, pp. 134–35).

The Heilbroner view argues that rapid development can only be brought about by violent revolutions and by elites willing to incarcerate, or kill if necessary, a relatively high percent of the population to achieve their goals. We believe that many of the strains that tend toward crisis or violence can be alleviated without great cost to material and spiritual progress and that a milieu can be created that supports and enhances movements and institutions of human justice and progress. For this reason, it is most important to give many groups, nations, and people a stake in a future that is to be achieved by peaceful means and not by violence and disruption. It may well be necessary—or at least desirable—in many situations to turn to authoritarian methods, perhaps even for a time to some violence and repression, but none of this need be as severe as Heilbroner indicates, and in many cases it need only be temporary. We think of the future-oriented ideology as more or less a Western capitalist ideology that is made trans-ideological by our approach. However, it can easily be fitted into almost any culture. The socialist countries can participate in much the same way without significant conflict with the capitalist societies so long as they give up the concept of mass warfare and armed conflict with the West, at least by not letting these concepts dominate day-to-day programs.

Giving people a sense of their stake in the future emphasizes the importance of developing a valid vision of the future. It is critical because peoples' visions of the future, although often unarticulated, dominate their responses to current issues. Giving people a new vision of the future depends on two things. First, there must be an intellectual understanding of the issues that is technically sound, psychologically relevant, and dramatically imaginative. Second, there must be organized efforts to get people to accept or use the new vision of the future communicated to scholars, opinion leaders, and directly to the public.

24

---⊗⊗⊗---

The Task Ahead

We would like to have been able to be completely optimistic, to present a view of the future which argues that while struggle, dedication and intelligence may be required, mankind will resolve all of its problems if only a reasonable effort is made—and even that man's dream of an egalitarian utopia on earth may soon come close to realization. Unfortunately, no such assurances have ever been possible; nor are they now. In particular, we believe that large income gaps between nations could persist for centuries, even though there will be some tendency to narrow. Moreover, our discussion of the long-term environment had to be so uncertain and inconclusive that it may have left many readers with considerably lowered morale after our predominantly optimistic presentation of such issues as growth, energy, food and resources in the previous chapters. Our own attitude is certainly basically positive—and we do not believe that the persistence of income gaps is necessarily either tragic or immoral—but our picture of one aspect of current reality does make us apprehensive. We are not among those who are pleased or take any satisfaction in finding out that great tragedy, even doomsday, is indeed possible—or at least not to be ruled out—and that various degrees of catastrophe are still possible even in the face of man's best efforts. Such possibilities have always been present, but now they seem to arise as much from man's activities—that is, from what we

---

[Herman Kahn, Leon Martel, and William M. Brown, *The Next 200 Years: A Scenario for America and the World* (New York: Morrow, 1976).]

call the Faustian bargain—as from nature. On the other hand, it is clear that our basic image of the future emerges as bright, and since this image is based on careful analysis and projection—and takes as full account of negative possibilities as we can—it should go far to reassure those who are excessively apprehensive.

It is also equally clear that we would perform an enormous disservice to all, including the poor, by raising expectations or defining what is a relatively normal, healthy, and near-permanent condition as a serious moral problem which has to be solved. What most people everywhere want is visible, even rapid improvement in their economic status and living standards, and not a closing of the gap. They would love to double their income in fifteen to twenty years (thus going from poor to middle class), and they are generally shocked to hear that this is indeed a possible and practical goal (which it is in most poor countries)—or would be with reasonable government policies.

THE FIRST TASK: A REALISTIC IMAGE OF THE FUTURE

Projecting a persuasive image of a desirable and practical future is extremely important to high morale, to dynamism, to consensus and in general to help the wheels of society turn smoothly. But we also want to emphasize that we are only interested in improving morale after we are ourselves convinced of the truth of our message. To us, the virtue of the image of the future presented here is not that it may prove useful (though we are highly pleased that this may be so), but rather that our forecast of the future may prove accurate, or at least about the most plausible image one can develop now. If we could not realistically justify an optimistic image, we would be quite willing to portray a negative one, arguing that it is our business to call the shots as we see them. Furthermore, such a negative image, if persuasive and realistic, might help elites to mobilize to face real problems (as opposed to unrealistic negative images, which tend to raise false issues, create unnecessary controversy, and divert resources and attention from practical solutions). Actually, we believe that it is almost always easier, except in the direst emergencies, to mobilize society around a positive rather than a negative image. It is also our view that if the negative image is largely inaccurate and morale-eroding as well, it could be destructive if widely disseminated. This might be especially true if it dominates the educational curriculum—as indeed the limits-to-growth view has in a surprisingly large portion of the Atlantic Protestant culture and Japan.

It is also worth noting that it is not true, as many people contend, that what might be called the "max-min strategy" would require taking a limits-to-growth perspective. In such a strategy one examines the worst that can reasonably be expected to happen with each policy and then picks the policy that limits one's risks—that is, of all the policies available, the one with the least damaging of the possible outcomes. We would argue that, in reality, almost the opposite may be true. It is not our postindustrial perspective which would force enormous repression on individual countries and which would consciously continue, in a dangerous way, absolute world poverty. Indeed, it is the limits-to-growth position which creates low morale, destroys assurance, undermines the legitimacy of governments everywhere, erodes personal and group commitment to constructive activities and encourages obstructiveness to reasonable policies and hopes. Thus, the effects of this position increase enormously the costs of creating the resources needed for expansion, make more likely misleading debate and misformulation of the issues, and make less likely constructive and creative lives. Ultimately, the position even increases the potential for the kinds of disasters which most of its advocates are trying to avoid.

Clearly, the first task is to gain acceptance of a more reasonable view of the future, one that opens possibilities rather than forecloses them. We believe that current prophets of peril are making forecasts that could indeed be self-fulfilling, if only in the short run. For if enough people were really convinced that growth should be halted, and if they acted on that conviction, then billions of others might be deprived of any realistic hope of gaining the opportunities now enjoyed by the more fortunate. Indeed, lacking the incentives that have guided them and their forebears, they too might soon despair, bereft of both ambition and goals, and irresponsible activist leaders might assume power. We believe that eventually—when the postindustrial economy has arrived—much of the industrial imperative and its appurtenances will erode or expire; but to weaken it prematurely, before it has run its natural course, would be to impose unnecessary trauma and suffering and make even more difficult the full exploitation of the many opportunities now available.

OVERCOMING THE KNOWN PROBLEMS OF THE NEAR TERM

Next among the tasks ahead is to find the appropriate means for dealing with the problems of the present and the immediate future. While our scenario for America and the world is generally optimistic for the long term, we do recognize the real possibilities of serious anomalies, dislocations and crises in the short term, any one of which could greatly complicate the process of getting from here to there. Among these potential difficulties are regional overpopulation, retarded economic growth, energy shortfalls, raw materials shortages, local famines, short-run but intense pollution, environmental surprises, and (most fearful of all) large-scale thermonuclear war. While we offer no solutions that will guarantee the avoidance of these problems, we do believe that acceptance of our position presents the best hope of both reducing the possibility of their occurrence and mitigating the consequences if any do occur.

COPING WITH THE UNKNOWN
PROBLEMS OF THE LONG TERM

Man's intellectual and physical resources must also be devoted to the task of monitoring and overcoming potentially catastrophic long-term environmental problems. Our first focus is here on earth, where we need to map the full terrain of possibilities, extrapolating from the known to the unknown—and still leaving room for possibilities beyond our extrapolations. To help in this effort, we would recommend the worldwide creation of a number of public and private institutions with various specific purposes, but all with an overall mission of the systematic and intense study of far-fetched and improbable phenomena, but phenomena which would be extremely important were they to occur. In effect, these institutions would together constitute an articulate lobby and an "early warning system" for long-term environmental problems. It is only fair to warn the public that anyone who studies such phenomena full time is almost certain to exaggerate their likelihood, impact and dangers. To do so is simply human nature. We do want the people making these studies to conduct them with an almost fanatic intensity, since such fanaticism can be very useful in sustaining interest, drive, and even creativity. But we do not want this fanaticism to be carried over into judgments on public policy. Our "fanatics" can alert us to the problems and perhaps eventually to their solutions, and they can put enormous effort into the study of both, but we also recognize that this kind of fanaticism, while useful in research and study, can be a disservice if it dominates public discourse.

The first purpose of this early warning system should be to alert the technological and scientific community, governments, and other relevant elites. We are not suggesting, of course, that these scientists be restricted from public communication, but we do believe that the general public is usually not in a good position to make early judgments on technical matters. If the experts do not soon reach a consensus, then the public must make its own judgment; and sometimes even if the experts and elites do reach a near-consensus, the public may choose to differ from them.

Our view is that such a system could evolve into a quite effective one. People are now beginning to understand these issues better, including the need for both "whistle-blowing" and concerned but responsible opposition. Often the problem is that there are well-developed biases which can lead to an almost automatic "cover-up" and a protection of vested interests and the status quo. But just as frequently—and this seems to be especially the case today—there is a kind of mindless "opposition for the sake of opposition," nurtured by institutions whose prestige gives them an aura of authority in the public mind. Yet even this kind of opposition is not intolerable and is probably worth the insurance it gives us—since its spokesmen are likely to be right at least as often as they are wrong. (Because these institutions are prestigious, people will listen longer and give more credence to their periodic cries of "wolf," but still be attentive when the wolf really is there.) Thus, society can afford to have cyclamates needlessly banned, without great tragedy, even though such an action should be avoided if the evidence does not justify it. Yet it is also important to understand that overreacting can eventually cause a serious loss of credibility.

On balance, we are confident that the task of monitoring and early warning—if sufficiently supported—could give us the very high probability of acquiring an assessment of long-term environmental problems that is credible and timely enough to permit effective remedial action. But we also believe that it is important to look beyond the earth, to outer space. [. . .] It could even turn out that a capability for self-supporting existence in space would make possible the continuation of earth's civilization and the resuscitation of human life on the planet following an irreversible tragedy [. . .]. We estimate the probability of such a calamity as too small, by itself, to justify such an effort. Nonetheless, its potential disutility is so enormous that a concerted international effort to create extraterrestrial self-sustaining communities, in concert with other space objectives, would probably be well warranted. In short, what we are proposing is a dual-purpose lifeboat for spaceship earth.

THINKING ABOUT THE POSTINDUSTRIAL ERA

We cannot forecast here what the nature, development and organization of life and society in the postindustrial era will be, even though we do believe that these are the real issues of the future, far surpassing in their significance—and in their difficulty—the more tractable issues we have dealt with earlier. People often talk about consciously choosing their future, but historically it is clear that only rarely has such choice actually been available—and then usually under an authoritarian political leader such as Augustus, Tokugawa, Napoleon, or Lenin. All of these leaders did make deliberate choices which set the courses of nations for a century or more. But the main concern of the future is negotiating the trip from here to there, and for this reason it is the short- and medium-term issues which tend to attract the most attention. One might like to be able to choose the future, but probably the best we can do is to influence the path by which we reach it.

Yet it is interesting—and in some ways useful—to set down the likely changes that our descendants will both create and confront. They do give us an outline of the possible shape of things to come, and in this way prepare and forewarn us as we contemplate the journey. It seems very likely that many subtle and sophisticated questions will arise as mankind—increasingly relieved of the burdens of simple sustenance and richer in technological capabilities and economic resources—continues its inexorable march across new frontiers. Indeed, some such questions are already arising.

The fundamental physiological and psychological aspects of human life are being altered today, and will be changed further tomorrow. Most of the great diseases of the past have been all but eliminated and death increasingly will be mainly the result of either accident or the simple wearing out of vital organs (here, too, new opportunities for life extension are arising through the rapidly growing science of organ replacement and soon of organ regeneration). As man progresses further in genetic research, he will move closer to the time when he will be able to influence the design of his offspring, perhaps even produce them ectogenetically. Man can now alter his mental state with drugs, and over time even influence his personality. Will man, within two hundred years, be able to condition his mind to increase his ability to learn, to communicate, to create, and will he have the power to affect others similarly, perhaps without their knowing it?

How will all of these potential changes, many of which are quite likely, affect human beings for whom work—in the postindustrial era—will be an activity of relatively short duration, and of a primarily self-serving nature? It is almost impossible to imagine such an existence. But already there are available electromechanical devices that effect enormous savings of labor, and the next generation of such devices—spurred by the computer revolution—will probably free man from the need to manage them, except for the preselection of appropriate computer programs. What kind of a life will a genetically engineered, vital-organ-replaceable, mental-state-adjustable, computer-robot-assisted human being want to live? Will he find satisfaction in the postindustrial era? Will he seek even more to test himself in the combat of sport, the risk of adventure or the challenge of exploration? Or will he be able and prefer to experience all of this—and more—through artificial stimulation? And what of social organization in this postindustrial era? Will people group as child-rearing families, in service-providing communities, under national banners? Or will these human beings of dramatically different makeup seek greatly altered institutions? It seems clear that there will be many more people and that most will have the means to obtain more in terms of goods and possessions than they can today. But will these goods be distributed as they are now, acquired with finite resources through billions of interacting calculations of marginal utility? Politics, in a famous definition, is "competition for scarce values." In a world of great abundance for almost all, but greater abundance for some than others, will the same competition still obtain? And in that world of greatly advanced communication and transportation, will we still see each other as being so different?

The postindustrial world we foresee will be one of increased abundance, and thus hopefully of reduced competition; it will be one of greater travel and contact, and thus possibly one of diminished differences among its peoples. But it will also be one of enormous power to direct and manipulate both man and nature; and thus its great issues will still be the very questions that confront us now, though enlarged in range and magnitude: Who will direct and manipulate, and to what ends?

Appendix

Herman Kahn:
A Bio-Bibliographical Note

Paul Dragos Aligica and Kenneth R. Weinstein

B orn in Bayonne, New Jersey, on February 15, 1922, Herman Kahn was the middle child of working-class Jewish immigrants from Poland. After the divorce of his parents, his mother relocated her three young boys, first to the Bronx, New York, and later to Los Angeles. During the Great Depression, young Herman worked menial jobs after school and on weekends to help support his family. After high school, he started college at the University of Southern California, but then put his education on hold after the United States entered World War II. It was during the early days of the U.S. Army's boot camp that Kahn's genius first received genuine recognition: having scored the highest-ever result on the military service's mental aptitude test, Kahn truly was smartest man in the Army.

From 1943 to 1945, Kahn served in Burma with the U.S. Army Signal Corps. After the war, he took advantage of the G.I. Bill and finished college as a physics major at the University of California at Los Angeles. He then enrolled at the California Institute of Technology, where he earned an M.S. in applied mathematics. He was forced to suspend his doctoral studies when a financial crisis struck his family. But just as he was about to embark on a career in real estate, he was recruited by his friend, the brilliant physicist Samuel Cohen (who would later invent the neutron bomb), to join the newly formed RAND Corporation in Santa Monica, California. Created in October 1945 by the U.S. Army Air Force (USAAF) and the Douglas Aircraft Company, RAND eventually emerged as a nonprofit corporation that conducted research to help the USAAF's successor, the newly formed U.S. Air Force, think through issues of war and peace in the nuclear age.

Kahn thrived in RAND's intellectually stimulating, generally collegial, sometimes competitive, and often eccentric atmosphere. After Cal Tech rejected his doctoral dissertation on the grounds that it was commercially sponsored research, he decided to abandon academia, and instead threw himself fully into his work at RAND. At RAND he would meet his future wife, Rosalie Jane Heilner, whom he would marry in March 1953.

Kahn's initial work was in RAND's physics department, the heads of which quickly recognized his powerful, intensely creative and sometimes quite unorthodox intellect. However, his deep curiosity, interdisciplinary outlook, and wide-ranging interests, especially in politics and economics, soon led him outside the physics department. In the mid-1950s, a new post—the "roving consultant"—was created specifically for his unique profile, allowing him to take part in in-house projects that interested him. He jovially made the rounds, popping into whatever studies or activities he found intellectually compelling. As he once remarked of the research by his RAND colleagues, "They were doing what I always wanted—making integrated studies of important questions and pontificating on a range of issues."

Working at RAND as the Cold War was intensifying, Kahn soon began to gravitate toward the emerging discipline of nuclear strategy. By the late 1950s, he had become a regular participant in high-level RAND research on the basing and operation of the nuclear-armed bomber aircraft of the Strategic Air Command (SAC); the development of what came to be known as the intercontinental ballistic missile (ICBM); selection of wartime targets; and strategies to deter or, if necessary, to fight nuclear and nonnuclear war. He and his RAND colleagues were horrified to find that the actual SAC war plan included only one option: a single, massive retaliatory nuclear strike to which SAC generals referred as the "Sunday Punch." Seeing the need to consider alternatives, Kahn and company examined potential strategic options in case deterrence failed.

Based on his work in this respect, Kahn was invited to give a series of lectures at the Center of International Studies at Princeton University. These lectures went on to form the basis for *On Thermonuclear War*, the book that would make Kahn famous—and infamous. Published in 1960 by Princeton University Press, the book was an aggregation of Kahn's various strategies for thinking about nuclear conflict, teeming with insights amid prose that was sprawling and sometimes undisciplined. But its core (and controversial) idea was that with proper and realistic planning, the serious consequences of nuclear war could be managed. Kahn argued that the prevailing wisdom of the time, that any nuclear war would annihilate both superpowers, was false; the existence of scenarios in which one or both sides survived necessitated thoughtful debate on the possibilities and consequences of nuclear strategy. *OTW*, as it came to be called, sold an amazing 30,000 copies and sparked fierce debates. While some critics praised Kahn for clear-sighted analysis, others roundly condemned the book for making nuclear war (in their view) more likely simply by discussing it as an actual possibility. As the mathematician James Newman wrote, Kahn was, "a monster who had written an insane, pornographic book, a moral tract on mass murder: how to plan it, how to commit it, how to get away with it, how to justify it."

Kahn's ideas were highly controversial and *OTW* launched a major national debate. Kahn cultivated a reputation for controversial ideas and provocative statements. His lecture series was carried out in a style designed to shock listeners into thinking about the perils and possibilities of the subjects at hand. Already an imposing figure at over six feet and three hundred pounds, he loved to stir up audiences with challenging remarks and paradoxical insights. He increasingly became a public figure of vast salience.

In 1961, after becoming dissatisfied with what he perceived as the increasingly bureaucratic working environment at RAND, Kahn went on to found Hudson Institute, a nonprofit think tank devoted to interdisciplinary research on what he termed "important issues, not just urgent ones." Kahn founded Hudson to be a more open and creative operation that would avoid the academic hierarchy and bureaucracy he saw as endemic to RAND.

At Hudson, Kahn responded to his critics by publishing two other books on nuclear strategy called *Thinking about the Unthinkable* and *On Escalation*. After his third book on nuclear strategy, Kahn shifted his interests into other fields, mainly in economics, politics, and the influence of new and as yet undeveloped technologies. In 1967 he coauthored *The Year 2000: A Framework for Speculation on the Next Thirty-Three Years*, which attempted to lay out what the world would be like by the end of the millennium. Kahn's writings such as *Things to Come: Thinking about the Seventies and Eighties, The Next 200 Years: A Scenario for America and the World,* and *The Resourceful Earth: A Response to Global 2000* were an answer to many of the doomsday scenarios and grim predictions of the late 1960s and 1970s. In 1970, he wrote *The Emerging Japanese Superstate: Challenge and Response*, a book that predicted the unprecedented economic boom and the rise of Japan as an important world actor more than a decade before it would became reality in the 1980s. Then in 1979, when Japan was emerging as a model for economic development and American anxiety over competition with Japan was rising, Kahn surprised his readers, and the Japanese, with *The Japanese Challenge*. The book presciently argued that without serious reform, the Japanese system would be unable to sustain the growth it had enjoyed for years. Even when the U.S. hit a recession in 1981–1982, Kahn optimistically responded with his final book, *The Coming Boom*. In this and other books, Kahn expressed his firm belief that unless poor management or sheer bad luck prevented it, technological advancements would lead to an increase in worldwide prosperity. As Kahn wrote, "One of the reasons we expect relatively high and sustained growth rates through the 1980s and 1990s is that a whole host of new technologies and technological improvements are now ripe for large-scale exploitation."

In person, Kahn was described as supremely confident and possessing a quick-witted sense of humor. His IQ was said to be "stratospheric" and for most of his life he possessed a photographic memory, able to recall anything he had heard or read. Despite his amazing intelligence, he had no air of superiority and instead, provoked by curiosity, sought out conversations with people in all walks of life. Kahn had scant concern for physical appearance; his clothes were often rumpled and disheveled and he was unable to maintain a kind of diet regimen for long. He was no cultural conservative and often found offbeat individuals more fascinating than their buttoned-up peers. His intellectual generosity was legendary.

On July 7, 1983, when Herman Kahn died suddenly of a massive stroke at age sixty-one, both friends and intellectual adversaries recognized that "the world lost one of its most creative and best minds." The next day, a statement issued by President Ronald Reagan honored Kahn as

> a futurist who welcomed the future. He brought the lessons of science, history, and humanity to the study of the future and remained confident of mankind's potential for good. All who value independent thinking will mourn the loss of a man whose intellect and enthusiasm embraced so much.

Kahn's work was bounded by a spectacular series of paradoxes and though many of his insights proved accurate, his legacy is not in the specific studies of events which came to pass. Kahn's most important contribution was the mindset and methods with which he approached problems and challenges. Though he could no more read the future than anyone else, he popularized and drew attention to a method of bold critical thinking challenging the prejudices, conventional wisdom, taboos, and traditions that tended to cloud people's vision. During his lifetime he was considered: "one of the world's great intellects," "a mental mutation" possessing "an incredibly high, stratospheric IQ," a "mesmerizing presence," "spectacular," "a provocateur in the sedate world of ideas," "a reformer," "a technological optimist," or "a futurist who attempted to cope with history before it happens." Kahn described himself as a "free-thinking intellectual [. . .] largely determined by a desire to do policy-oriented studies with practical applications [. . .] pragmatic, eclectic, and synthetic in thinking." "I'm against ignorance," Kahn once said, "I'm against sloppy, emotional thinking. I'm against fashionable thinking. I am against the whole cliché of the moment."

Selected Bibliography

Kahn, Herman. *Applications of Monte Carlo*. Santa Monica, Calif.: RAND Corporation, 1954.

———. *On Thermonuclear War*. Princeton, N.J.: Princeton University Press, 1962. Westport, Conn.: Greenwood, 1978.

———. *Thinking about the Unthinkable*. New York: Horizon Press, 1962.

Kahn, Herman, and Anthony Wiener, eds. *Crises and Arms Control*. Croton-on-Hudson, N.Y.: Hudson Institute, 1962.

Kahn, Herman. *On Escalation: Metaphors and Scenarios*. New York: Praeger, 1965. Westport, Conn.: Greenwood, 1986.

———. *The Alternative World Futures Approach*. Croton-on-Hudson, N.Y.: Hudson Institute, 1966.

Kahn, Herman, and Carl Dibble. *Notes on the Choice of a Basic National Security Policy*. Croton-on-Hudson, N.Y.: Hudson Institute, 1967.

Kahn, Herman, and Anthony Wiener. *The Year 2000: A Framework for Speculation on the Next Thirty-three Years*. New York: Macmillan, 1967.

Kahn, Herman. *Can We Win in Vietnam?* New York: Praeger, 1968.

———. *On Thermonuclear War: Three Lectures and Some Suggestions*. New York: Free Press, 1969.

———. *The Emerging Japanese Superstate: Challenge and Response*. Englewood Cliffs, N.J.: Prentice-Hall, 1970.

———. *Why ABM?* Englewood Cliffs, N.J.: Prentice-Hall, 1970.

Kahn, Herman, and Garrett Scalera. *Basic Issues and Potential Lessons of Vietnam*. Croton-on-Hudson, N.Y.: Hudson Institute, 1970.

This bibliography is arranged chronologically.

Kahn, Herman, and B. Bruce-Briggs. *Things to Come: Thinking about the Seventies and Eighties.* New York: Macmillan, 1972.

Kahn, Herman, and Chris Morgan. *Some World Economic and Population Scenarios for the Twenty-first Century.* Croton-on-Hudson, N.Y.: Hudson Institute, 1972.

Kahn, Herman, ed. *The Future of the Corporation.* New York: Mason & Lipscombe, 1974.

Kahn, Herman, and William M. Brown. *A World Turning Point, and a Better Prospect for the Future.* Croton-on-Hudson, N.Y.: Hudson Institute, 1975.

Kahn, Herman, and Lewis A. Dunn. *Trends in Nuclear Proliferation: 1975–1995.* Croton-on-Hudson, N.Y.: Hudson Institute, 1976.

Kahn, Herman, Leon Martel, and William M. Brown. *The Next 200 Years: A Scenario for America and the World.* New York: Morrow, 1976.

Kahn, Herman, and William M. Brown. *Long-term Prospects for Developments in Space.* Croton-on-Hudson, N.Y.: Hudson Institute, 1977.

Kahn, Herman, and Jane Newitt. *The Schools' Community Roles in the Next Ten Years: An Outsider Perspective.* Washington, D.C.: U.S. Department of Health, Education and Welfare, 1977.

Kahn, Herman. *World Economic Development: 1979 and Beyond.* Boulder, Colo.: Westview Press, 1979.

Kahn, Herman, and Thomas Pepper. *The Japanese Challenge: The Success and Failure of Economic Success.* New York: Crowell, 1979.

———. *Will She Be Right?: The Future of Australia.* St. Lucia, Australia: University of Queensland Press, 1980.

Kahn, Herman. *The Coming Boom: Economic, Political, and Social.* New York: Simon & Schuster, 1982.

Kahn, Herman, and Julian L. Simon, eds. *The Resourceful Earth: A Response to Global 2000.* New York: Blackwell, 1984.

Kahn, Herman. *Thinking about the Unthinkable in the 1980s.* New York: Simon & Schuster, 1984.

Index

About the Editors

Paul Dragos Aligica is a senior fellow at the Mercatus Center; faculty fellow at the James Buchanan Center for Political Economy, George Mason University; and adjunct fellow at Hudson Institute.

Kenneth R. Weinstein is the chief executive officer of Hudson Institute.

Lightning Source UK Ltd.
Milton Keynes UK
UKHW041848081020
371265UK00001B/10